NEO–MARXIST THEORIES OF DEVELOPMENT

Neo-Marxist Theories of Development

Edited by

PETER LIMQUECO and BRUCE McFARLANE

CROOM HELM
London & Canberra
ST. MARTIN'S PRESS
New York

Croom Helm Ltd, Provident House, Burrell Row,
Beckenham, Kent. BR3 1AT

British Library Cataloguing in Publication Data

Neo-Marxist theories of development
1. Underveloped areas–Economic conditions
2. Economic development
I. Limqueco, Peter II. Mcfarlane, Bruce
330.9172'4 HC59.7

ISBN 0–7099–1641–8

St. Martin's Press, Inc., 175 Fifth Avenue, New York, N.Y. 10010
First Published in the United States of Americain 1983

Library of Congress Cataloging in Publication Data
Main entry under title:

Neo–Marxist theories of development.

Includes bibliographical references.
Contents: Introduction / Bruce McFarlane and
P. Limqueco –– Sociologies of development / Frank T.
Fitzgerald –– Underdevelopment and dependency / Colin
Leys –– [etc.]
1. Economic development––Addresses, essays, lectures.
2. Marxian economics––Addresses, essays, lectures.
3. Underdeveloped areas––Addresses, essays, lectures.
I. Limqueco, Peter, 1939– II. McFarlane, Bruce J.
HD82.N45 1983 338'.09172'4 82–25078

ISBN 0–312–56409–0

Printed and bound in Great Britain
by Billing and Sons Ltd, Worcester.

CONTENTS

NOTES ON CONTRIBUTORS

Jairus Banaji, well known Indian theoretician and activist.

John Browett, Lecturer in Sociology, Flinders University of South Australia.

Frank T. Fitzgerald, Associate Professor of Sociology, The College of Saint Rose, New York.

Haldun Gulalp, Department of Political Science and Public Administration, Middle East Technical University, Ankara, Turkey.

Clive Hamilton, Institute of Development Studies, University of South Australia.

Colin Leys, Professor of Economics, Queen's University, Kingston, Ontario, Canada.

Peter Limqueco, Research Fellow, Arbetslivscentrum, Stockholm Co-editor, The Journal of Contemporary Asia.

Bruce McFarlane, Professor of Politics, University of Adelaide, South Australia. Co-editor, The Journal of Contemporary Asia.

P. Thandika Mkandawire, Deputy Executive Secretary, The Council for the Development, Economics and Social Research in Africa (CODESRIA), Dakar, Senegal

James Petras, Professor of Sociology, State University of New York at Binghamton.

Sheila Smith, Lecturer in Economics, School of African and Asian Studies, University of Sussex.

Chapter 1

INTRODUCTION

Peter Limqueco and Bruce McFarlane

Over the decade 1972-1982, Journal of Contemporary Asia promoted a number of research projects, discussions and debates about ways of analysing "underdevelopment" in Asia, Africa and Latin America. Not being convinced (in the light of the Cambridge critique of the methods and capital theory of orthodox economists) that the "investment-choice" theories of U.N.I.D.O., A.K. Sen and Little-Mirlees explained problems of underdevelopment, we gave space to other schools of thought. These included followers of Sraffa and the Cambridge school and "neo-Marxists", - followers of Paul A. Baran's theses about the development of underdevelopment. Unlike other journals (e.g. Monthly Review), J.C.A. subjected the latter school to serious and heavy criticism - notably the ideas promoted by Samir Amin, A Gunder Frank and I. Wallerstein.

In the following collection of essays we have brought together pieces which have criticized the major works of these authors, a series of critiques which are sceptical of the claims of the neo-Marxist writers to have established new and useful paradigms and important policy conclusions. I suggest that the reader who goes carefully into the critiques will not find them to be wholly negative and destructive, but to be full of suggestions for a better alternative in the study of underdevelopment.

The collection includes major survey articles by Fitzgerald, Leys and Browett which the reader should peruse for himself, instead of getting a "survey of a survey" here. They are followed by detailed criticism of individual writers of the school constituting "dependency theorists".

It is only proper in this introduction to bring out more sharply some of the ideological issues involved. Samir Amin himself has produced a number of key ideological texts. His Monthly Review article of February, 1980 condemns western workers and trade unions as accomplices of monopoly capital and enemies of the "true" working class on a global scale - the peasants. His book ,"The Law of Value and Historical

Materialism is not too strong on the facts.[1] What it includes as major items are an attack on the Piero Sraffa School at Cambridge (who have done more than anyone, Amin included, to bring tumbling down the hitherto imposing edifice of neo-classical economics) and a rejection of all Marxist research carried out within Eastern Europe - the Hungarian Academy of Science Publication by Tokei, on the Asiatic Mode of Production, being described as a ploy, a Trojan Horse, with which to batter neo-Maoist groups in Europe.

This casual treatment of alternative schools of economic thought comes out clearly in Amin's books and, quite properly it is something touched on by three authors in this volume: Mkandawire, Smith, and Leaver. It also underlines the need to treat with care the claims of the dependency school to be more "Marxist" than European alternative approaches.

Perhaps chapter four by Mkandawire is best described as a direct confrontation with the political economy of S. Amin. He draws attention to Amin's habit of citing himself and other "world systems" supporters, ignoring insights from non-Third World writers. Italian, Polish and British writers are dismissed as inherently unable to analyse economic relations between European and Asian states. In the case of M. Kalecki, an author who did much theoretical and practical work on problems of underdevelopment[2], the evaluation is one that simply could not have been carried out by anyone with the slightest knowledge of what the Cambridge School has done in integrating the work of Sraffa and Kalecki[3]. Mkandawire points out that at the practical level, the process of capital accumulation in Eastern Europe cannot be treated in the same way as that in Asian and Latin American countries, nor can it be seen as the same as that in Western Europe. It is difficult to see, then, how Amin and Frank can treat Eastern Europe as part of the "metropolis" area of the world as they do in their "geographical" approach to defining the world's "workers" and "proto-capitalists". It would seem to follow that S. Amin's dismissal of Eastern Europe as no more than bureaucratized capitalism, misses all the real issues, as does Frank's dismissal of China and Vietnam as Countries moving towards Capitalism [4]

The criticism of Amin by Mkandawire and Smith also gets to the heart of the method used by Amin in a series of works Instead of using the Marxian, Sraffian or Emmanuel theories of "unequal change" to explain how trade exploitation between two economies arises because of unequal labour productivities (as done by V.V. Dandekar)[5], Amin prefers to chatter about Sraffa and copy out the latter's equations without ever using them (as in his <u>The Law of Value and Historical Materialism</u>. Sometimes he vulgarizes Emmanuel's idea that unequal exchange arises between countries because of unequal compositions of capitals between different industries and departments by assuming subsistence-wages in the periphery countries. Amin's chosen example is a special case in which "unequal exchange" arises because the labour in the high productivity country receives a share of the surplus value, so that not only the capitalists, but also the labourers of the high productivity country participate and profit by the process of "exploitation" implied in the transfer of surplus value from the low productivity country. That is, to prove his own version of a "labour aristocracy" thesis, Amin seizes on a part of a Sraffa model where workers share in surplus. More elaborate use of the Sraffian "schemes", however, also provides other cases in which only the capitalists in the higher productivity country can participate in surplus, in any such exploitation, depending on initial assumptions.[6].

This is by no means to deny that Third World countries face serious problems posed by the policies and production fluctuations of the West. But a decline in western output would not be taken up by the Third World under today's conditions of international division of labour. Rather the foreign exchange earnings of Third World countries would fall sharply via a reverse-multiplier effect.

The actual problem now is the fall in the volume of world trade and the rize of a new protectionism since 1970, a process threatening future markets for the output of Third World countries. Quantitative restrictions on imports cluster in particular areas and are now tailored to the needs of particular industries as communicated to governments by industry lobbies. Textiles, clothing, steel, synthetic fibres and transport equipment each have a trade policy of their own. Export subsidies in relation to gross domestic product were, in 1979, higher everywhere except in the U.S.A., than they were in 1970 [7] .Such trends will be most difficult to reverse - until they are, western markets will be partly closed to Third Worlders for a long time.

This point has, of course, been raised at UNCTAD, and lies behind the demand for a New International Economic Order. But it is not necessary to be a Third World economist or embrace a "world systems" analysis to support such demands. Keynes supported[8] international action to stabilize the trade of Third World countries; Balogh has for many years exposed the devastating impact on Third World countries of the development of synthetics in the West and the braindrain which followed on political independence.[9] Rather as Sheila Smith has pointed out in chapter six, and elsewhere[10], the political attitudes which stem from the Amin-Frank-Wallerstein style of world-systems analysis can only hinder progress because it precludes, by assertion, theoretically and politically important work at the level of national economies. As Leaver puts it in chapter five, Amin reaches the limit of any entente cordiale, between Marxian theory and dependency theory when forced to draw political conclusions about Kampuchea, Iran and Angola. Support for rigid autarchic policies is shown by Leaver to be deeply embedded in Amin's discussion of centre - periphery relations, redistribution of world economic surplus, and international trade.

Andre Gunder Frank has been writing about the chain of control from metropolis countries to cities in colonial countries to rural areas. He has been politically active in favour of autarchic political movement and appears often at conferences dealing with the broad issues raised by a "new international economic order".

The distinguishing feature of Frank's analysis, as Leaver points out, was the claim that some areas of the globe (particularly Latin America) were capitalist from the16th Century, a claim based on his conception of capitalism as that social system which produces surplus product and appropriates it to owners as a result of commodity production for the market. This one-sided use of "economic surplus", potentially a most useful way of establishing the specifica differentiae of social systems, vitiates Frank's results. It also raises doubts as to the tendency of his followers to discuss his work as a product of a Marxian box of tools - as Leaver points out in chapter seven.

Does Frank know his economic history? Those brought up on Werner Sombart's account of the development of World Capitalism or even on a popular work like Leo Huberman's Man's Worldly Goods will find it hard to recognise the development of capitalism on a global scale from Frank and Wallerstein's version. A detailed case against Frank is presented in this volume by Jairus Banaji's article, especially in a criticism of Frank's later works (notably World Accumulation 1978) . Frank at least here goes back into the early development of capitalism, some 300 years ago. Banaji is not impressed by the use to which this economic history is put. Like other contributors Leaver and Mkandawire, Banaji highlights the political results of Frank's whole project which is to shift the focus from the struggle of all workers against all types of capital to one in which the initiative is taken by groups outside the Asian and Latin American working class.

The study of four Asian states by Clive Hamilton takes up the point made earlier by Leys concerning the desirability of using class-formation and class-struggle to investigate such countries - a prism which dependency theory precludes. Petras follows on with the same emphasis as Leys, if in a wider context. This leads Hamilton to the kind of argument many would like to see as a positive alternative to the dependency perspective. It implies that the internationalization of capital investment causing a transition from merchant-dominated capitalism to industrial capitalism is the process that is occurring in A.S.E.A.N. and some other Asian, Latin American and African countries. It implies that the development of the productive forces is the main force of change. It involves drawing attention not to "de-development" but to the rapid growth of the share of industry in national income and fall in the share of agriculture. Economic development is precisely about this structural change in the first phase of accelerated economic growth.

Moreover, the degree of "foreign control" requires empirical investigation and not an assumption of complete dominance. Foreign ownership of industrial assets has been declining in A.S.E.A.N. since the days of classical colonialism. In 1980 the level of this ownership in total industrial assets within A.S.E.A.N. amounted to 30-35% of the total. This is well below estimates for foreign control over Australian industry, and few claim that Australia is de-developing. It is also increasingly clear that foreign capitalists prefer joint-venture projects, a technique pioneered by the Japanese for their investments in Asian industries.

In relation to agriculture, there is occurring a change in, the form of capitalist domination now that we have full blooded capitalist penetration of agriculture, monetization of the rural economy and control of marketing by agribusiness (who often prefer to work with local ownership of plantations). Such a development within agriculture has not been handled well by dependency theory,

Industrialization and the growth of productive forces in A.S.E.A.N. is bringing different forms of control over labour power in different spheres of the economy. The result of this, as Hamilton indicates, is that the share of the working class in national income may be held down and even decline. Side by side with the growth of productive forces can go "immizerisation" in the sphere of income distribution.

Control over the labour force is exercised by force, by the setting up of company unions or by state control over workers' organizations. It also involves the techniques needed by capitalist industry at a higher level of its development: piece work, bonuses, quotas, which reduce the social costs (health, family bills) to the employer.

A clear implication from Hamilton's work is the need to look closely at what has been happening to the Asian working class: new work-control methods, work discipline, and management systems need as much study as "cheap labour". Such a study should be directed to firms in three categories: light industry (textiles, electronics, plastics, rubber); intermediate (assembly work) and heavy industry (machinery, construction etc.) Each group should be studied according to whether there is worker organization at the work place. Agricultural social relations still need close study - a minor test that could then be done, is to look at the complaint of Amin that Western socialists press only the interests of the industrial workers at the expense of the great majority of the labouring poor.

An additional point, brought out in reading Hamilton on industrialization after researching dependency theory on autarchy, is the need to use structural models of production to work out a strategy for more mature countries which is less dependent on imported materials and more productive of backward and forward linkages with other domestic industries. Such a model has been sketched by A. Lowe[11] and developed in a practical way by Sachs and Laski,[12] while Clive Thomas worked out a strategy which does not imply autarchy, but enables small economies to escape the immiserizing pattern of specialization in primary products for exports.[13] The core of the strategy that Thomas proposed was the development of a "basic materials" sector, one that is capable of producing goods such as textiles, iron and steel, paper, leather, fuel, plastics and industrial chemicals which enter into the means of producing all other goods. This underlines a point made by Sheila Smith in another context: national control is not the same thing as autarchy; the development of the productive forces might develop under relatively autarchic conditions, depending on the situation; national self-sufficiency can also turn into national self-insufficiency.

The historical periodisation and discussion of a world capitalist system in chapter 12, by James Petras, is very different from Gunder-Frank's dash into economic history in World Accumulation. Petras is closer to Resnick and Hymer. He looks at various stages in the growing web of power between countries based on capital investment and divides this aspect of the economic history of such countries into primitive accumulation (1500-1800), early monopoly capitalism (1800-1945) and late capitalism.[14] While there is exploitation of the "periphery" countries of the Third World, this is not linked (as in Amin) to the idea of a giant sucking machine taking out surplus from neo-colony to western metropolis. Rather the process of "exploitation" has its own different phases with different processes at work. The phases as seen by Petras include pirate colonialism, "extractive" kinds of colonialism and "dependent neo-colonisalism".

But this is quite different from the implication of the analysis of Frank, Wallerstein and Amin that the world economy has been capitalist for centuries.[15] Petras' point is that the problem of the "external impact" on Third World countries in this century is not one of absolute stagnation but of the conditions under which the process of capital accumulation takes place and its impact on the class structure - problems of the process of surplus extraction, the economic role of the State, the allocation of the work force. The further impact on class structure would appear to involve issues of the changeover from small proprietors to wage labourers or from rural workers to urban workers, or landlords to merchants or merchants to industrialists.

Surely this is the right focus of attention of political economy rather than a Frank-Amin emphasis on "blocking" of the growth of productive forces as a result of external ties. This does not preclude a discussion (as Petras demonstrates) of capital accumulation as an uneven, contradictory and exploitative process. Nor does it mean that shifts in economic activity in "peripheral" ex-colonial countries and relations with the metropolis country are not linked to changes in class alignments and class power. But the causation is likely to be the opposite to that proclaimed by dependency theory: the displacement of the metropolis from agro-mineral sectors is the result of the rise to influence of national social forces and represents a significant increase in national control over the process of capital accumulation as compared with the classical colonialist period.

The issue of changing internal class relations as a result of changes in the pace and structure of capital accumulation surely must be at the centre of attention in discussing Third World development. Kautsky in The Agrarian Question (English summary in Economy and Society, Vol. 5, No. 1) underlined changing class relations in the agrarian sector and the diverse ways in which capital and the State have used rural producers as a way of securing subsistence and surplus. Monopsony, regulations and force have been used to get trading profits and foreign exchange. A wage relation exists side-by-side with various forms of household and cottage production. Accordingly, it is essential to analyse relationships between crop producers and capital (as well as the State) in varying concrete conditions. Banaji in particular, takes up the issue of Frank's conceptual confusion concerning difference forms of the capital-labour relationship.

The parcellization of land is an issue to be incorporated into this kind of emphasis, in view of the claims by A.K. Sen and M. Lipton that, given a negative correlation between size of land holding and real agricultural product per man hour, the majority of Third World countries can benefit from going over to peasant-family agriculture. Although such conclusions are in doubt (if chemical rather than organic fertilizer is applied, small farms lose their productivity advantage), the process of parcellization is very important - Marx (in the 18th Brumaire of Louis Bonaparte) had assumed a trend towards concentration of land which has not occurred in peripheral countries, as Kautsky noted. H. Bernstein ("Notes on Capital and Peasantry") suggested in Review of African Polital Economy, No. 10, that "there is no single and essential "peasantry" nor any such homogenization of peasants at the level of politics and ideology."

Whether merchant capital became a central fact in the "development of underdevelopment" as argued in Geoffrey Kay's Development and Underdevelopment is also an important issue.

This suggestion implies that accumulation has largely been carried on by merchant capital on the basis of petty commodity production. Resnick has described this as one of "two roads to capitalism" but it seems closer to India than to (say) modern-day Singapore where wage labourers and capitalists meet in the process of capitalist production and accumulation. Merchant capital, by contrast, is a situation where "the circuits of the independent producer and merchant capitalist intersect only in the market" (Kay, p.70).

But did industrial capital, when it made its strong appearance in the post 1945 phase of the development of the world market, use merchant capital as its agent? Does not industrial capital inhibit the accumulation of merchant capital? Does it not demand a new pattern of trade away from a trade in luxury items, textiles and crafts to a constant supply of imported raw materials? The method of extracting surplus also changes with the rise of industrial capital - from unequal exchange, price manipulation and market rigging to industrial profits from the use of wage-labour in the labour process.

Such changes in class relations as a result of changes in the accumulation process seem to require close analysis. Petras suggests fruitful ways of providing this.

CONCLUSIONS

The first conclusion to draw from the above collection is that the "dependency" paradigm must now be transcended. Its development required little knowledge of economics, political economy or quantitative research methods. Worse, it led, as Sheila Smith shows, to an assertion that "periphery economies" have no room for manoeuvre, an assertion which was based on no analysis of capital accumulation or internal movements in income distribution and the structure of production. It led to the idea of a radical and complete break with the world system by individual Countries, without the qualifications, noted by economist Clive Thomas in his Dependence and Transformation. It led to the loose methodology of treating the "centre" and "periphery" as undifferentiated blocs, although the chapter on mining rent in Amin's Law of Value and Historical Materialism sees some rent accruing to the peripheral states and middle classes (and hence allows the possibility of some local accumulation of capital). This is a modification of the thesis of Accumulation on a World Scale which shows Amin can accommodate somewhat to new realities.

A second conclusion that we draw from a survey of the debate is the need to look closely at the origin and role of economic surplus within each of (a) poor and (b) rich countries, while recognising that such a concept cannot by itself provide a basis for satisfactorily probing the specificity of the structure of the capitalist mode of production in each case. Different forms of penetration by overseas corporations of the social system occurred, and these have to be traced out, incorporating also the mediating role of the post-coplonial state. We need, as well, a way of showing how and why a country moves from one "mode of production" to another. Here it is necessary that analysis avoids the twin errors of (a) concentrating only on external influences (like the demands of the world capitalist market or (b) operating with a closed system. Most important, we need to explain why one mode of production is dominant in a country at a particular time rather than another.

Another key weakness of dependency theory and of Frank and Amin's copnstant targetting of the "centre" as the cause of all exploitation is their inability to explain "South-South" contradictions, as Sheila Smith points out. Asian multinationals exploiting Asian workers do not appear in the centre-periphery or "North versus South" models. So when it became clear that the Sri Lanka Free Trade Zone was rapidly becoming an appendage of Asian multinationals, this kind of exploitation went unanalyzed, underlining the importance of looking at capital qua capital, and at worker-capital relationships in every country, instead of the "broad sweep" so favoured by the style of Ecole Normale Supérieure, in which "money smells" and some capitals are wickeder than others.

Perhaps this is another way of saying that the new Trans-Atlantic alliances of Wallerstein's "Binghamton School" (Fernand Braudel Centre for the Study of Economies, Historical Systems, and Civilizations) with Gunder Frank and Amin in Europe, or of elements in Monthly Review (U.S.A.) with the University of Bielefeld (Germany)[16] have become sects - groups of people who demonstrate that they are unusually remote from reality and have developed the language and methodology of the claque. Rejecting trade unions, the western labour movement, western socialist and communist parties, the good and bad experiences of the bloc of socialist countries, it is no wonder that Amin ends up defining the peasantry as workers, and the workers as capitalists.[17]

All of this surely is rooted in the way their analysis has run, as exposed in this book.

It could, I suppose, be argued that there is no real debate between "dependency theory" and "Marxism" because the former is not a coherent theory and the latter is open to widely different interpretations. This is a view that has been taken by Aidan Foster Carter and E. Mavros in the U.K., and would contradict the views expressed here by Fitzgerald, Leys and Gulalp. It seems to me to be sociological hairsplitting. Amin, Frank and Wallerstein made it quite clear at the U.N.I.T.A.R. Conference in New Delhi in 1980 that they do see their work as a theory, and that they make predictions from it: that capitalism will continue to exploit the Third World until capitalist imperialism is abolished; that revolution will end the centre-periphery spiderweb of centuries (a view disputed in this book by John Browett).

While it is true that "Marxism" is a diffuse body of ideas, sush critics of dependency as H. Bernstein, and John Taylor (as well as the authors in this book like Sheila Smith and T. Mkandawire) have used rigorous techniques of analysis clearly linked to Marx's political theory and political economy. At least there should be agreement now that neither a separate "mode of production" analysis for every individual country or part of a country, nor a view that "the whole system must be studied as a system" seem adequate in the light of experience.

There is more to the story of economic development of particular nations than that of participation in the re-distribution of world economic surplus. On the other hand, no country is untouched by international trade and investment. Perhaps what the sum of the contributions to this volume suggests to us is the need to approach the problem in this way: that the same social system because of "innumerable different empirical circumstances, natural environment, racial relations, external historical circumstances [will show] infinite variations and gradations in appearance, which can be ascertained only by analysis of the empirically given circumstances".[18]

Third World ex-colonies like Indonesia, India and Argentina have shown themselves just as capable of territorial expansionism and exploitation of peoples as the U.K., Germany and the former imperialist powers of Europe. Unfortunately, this seems likely to be lost on the guilt-ridden western scholars and the mindless anti-westernism of some Third Worlders who continue to uphold a "dependency perspective"

A debate among concerned Political economists about the perspectives of Baran, Frank, Amin and Wallerstein can be useful. The dependency school has had a large volume of work on the market for some years, and it is time to take stock of it. One thing though, needs to be avoided: the reduction of all the experiences of wars of liberation and socialist economic development to zero, as if Capitalist success were the only reality. On this crucial point surely Amin and Frank would be in agreement with their left critics.

NOTES

1. On Australia a country which pioneered the 8 hour day and women's suffrage as well as having a most militant trade union movement, all Amin could say was: "Why is Australia a world of absolute silence?" S. Amin "In praise of socialism" Monthly Review, Sept. 1974, p. 14.

2. M. Kalecki, Essays on Developing Economies, London, 1975.

3. Joan Robinson, "Who is a Marxist?", in Joan Robinson; Collected Economic Papers, Vol.5, pp. 252-3; G.C. Harcourt, "The Sraffian Contribution", in Bradley and Howard (eds), Classical and Marxian Political Economy.

4. A. Gunder-Frank, "Long Live Transideological Enterprise", Review, Vol.1, No.1, Summer 1977, pp. 91-140.

5. V.M. Dandekar, "Unequal Exchange: Imperialism of Trade", Economic and Political Weekly, Bombay, 5th January, 1980, pp. 27-32.

6. Dandekar, oc.Cit., pp32-33.

7. Jan Tumlir, "International Economic Order: Can the Trend Be Reversed?" The World Economy, March, 1982, p. 30.

8. J.M. Keynes, "The International Control of Raw Materials" republished in the Journal of International Economics, Vol. 4.

9. His more recent effort is T. Balogh, The Economics of Poverty, 1974.

10. Sheila Smith, "The Ideas of Samir Amin: Theory or Tautology", Journal of Development Studies, Vol. 17, October, 1980, p. 19.

11. Adolph Lowe, The Path of Economic Growth, Cambridge, 1976.

12. I. Sachs and K. Laski, "Industrial Development Strategy", in U.N. Industrialisation and Productivity Bulletin, 1971.

13. Clive Thomas, Dependence and Transformation, N.Y., 1974.

14. See S. Resnick and S. Hymer, "The Crisis and Drama of the Global Partnership" International Journal (Canada) Vol. XXV, 1970, pp. 186-189.

15. S. Amin, The Law of Value and Historical Materialism.

16. Both produced more Pol Pot and pro-autarchy pieces than contemporaries regarded as reasonable on the evidence.

17. S. Amin, "The Class Structure of the Contemporary Imperialist System", Monthly Review ,January 1980.

18. K. Marx, Capital, Vol.3, Moscow, 1962, ed. p.772.

Chapter 2

SOCIOLOGIES OF DEVELOPMENT

Frank T. Fitzgerald

Since the post-World War II years when "development" became a focus of concern within Western social science, the concept iself and the perspectives in which it has been couched have undergone a series of dramatic changes. As post-war imperialism faced movements for national independence or socialist transformation in the so-called Third World, modernization theory[1] was formulated to serve as an ideological cover and framework of policy orientation for continued capitalist expansion, geared to keeping and further incorporating Third World areas within the capitalist orbit. Dependency theory[2] arose in the late fifties and the sixties as an extensive critique of the modernization paradigm, which turned many of the latter's central concepts on their heads: development became the development of underdevelopment. Diffusion became the mechanism of dependency or imperialism. Recently, dependency theory has attained a new intellectual stature and perhaps its theoretical apogee in the form of world systems analysis.[3] At the same time, the critics of the dependency/world systems school have become more vocal and more incisive. World systems analysis has been attacked for allegedly confusing the capitalist world system with the capitalist mode of production[4] and, from a very different angle, for ignoring or mystifying classical Marxist class analysis.[5]

Development sociology, as should be clear from the above, has been rich in political debate, empirical disagreement, and theoretical innovation. There is no one sociology of development, but several competing sociologies. To wind through this labyrinth of controversy and clarify the major issues in dispute is the purpose of this paper.

I

Modernization theory conceptualizes development as movement along a continuum of historical change upon which all national societies can be placed according to indices such as

GNP, per capita income, acceptance of "modern" values, social differentiation, political integration, etc. This continuum is meant to describe a universal path of societal evolution, supposedly already followed by the modern, developed nations, and eventually to be travelled by the traditional, underdeveloped ones.

The end points of this continuum have the methodological status of ideal types. The concept of modernity or developed is fashioned by abstracting attributes from the social structures of the advanced capitalist countries, especially those attributes which supposedly typify the social structure of the "lead nation",[6] the United States. As Gabriel Almond baldly put it: "The model of the modern...can only be derived from the most careful empirical and formal analysis...of modern Western politics."[7] Modernization theory thus takes quite seriously and, by ripping it from its textual and historical context, reduces to absurdity Marx's famous statement that "The country that is more developed industrially only shows to the less developed, the image of its own future".[8]

At the other end of the modernization continuum sits the ideal type of traditionality or underdevelopment. Unlike the concept of modernity, the ideal type of traditionality is not comprised of attributes abstracted from a single "social system" or area of the globe. The reason for this is simple. While there is an identifiable lead nation which shows to all others what modernity means, traditionality is supposedly a state that has been shared by all societies. As Bert Hoselitz formulated it: "If there are 'developed' and 'advanced' countries in the present, they must have at some time been 'underdeveloped'."[9]

Many questions and criticisms have been directed at the adequacy of these ideal typical end points of the modernization continuum. First, it has been asked whether the ideal types of modernity and traditionality truly capture the essential features of the social structures from which they have been abstracted. Those, for example, who frame their analysis in terms of the Parsonian pattern variables[10] open themselves to the question of whether achievement or universalism are so all-pervasive and ascription or particularism so entirely absent in the most modern nations, and vice versa in the most traditional areas.[11] One can also question the methodological sense of constructing a concept of traditionality out of the wide diversity of social formations which preceded Western capitalism: the Inca and Chinese and Mogul Empires, the trading states of Africa, Feudal Europe, innumerable isolated subsistence economies, etc.[12] The fact, however, that these types of questions could have been raised, at least in part, by a leading proponent of the modernization approach[13] attests to the fact that, while telling, such criticisms stay well within the modernization paradigm. For such criticisms question the empirical adequacy of the particular ideal type concepts constructed by particular modernization theorists, but they do not, as stated, question the notion of universal end points and a universal path of social evolution along a continuum. Conceivably, with better empirical investigation and formal analysis, more empirically adequate ideal types could be formulated; that is, if we were to stay within the modernization perspective.

When it diagnoses the condition of the contemporary Third World, modernization theory sees underdevelopment, which it conceptualizes as development manqué. Contemporary Third World countries are "backward", "late-starters" which lack the attributes of developed modernity. Development will result from the "diffusion" of these attributes from the developed West. "Diffusion" in this schema serves as a code word for capitalist expansion in its economic, political, cultural guises. The modernization theorists have identified several levels at which diffusion can and should take place:

1) The individual/psychological level where "modern" values and skills - achievement orientation, "empathy", democratic values and political participation, political obedience - are seen as necessary for development.

2) The institutional and organizational levels where markets, division of labour, bureaucratic rationality, modern state structures, political parties, etc. are seen as prerequisites or necessary concomitants of development.

3) The technological and financial levels where know-how, advanced technology, capital, etc. are brought to the Third World.

This multi-level notion of diffusion has constituted another entry point for the critics of modernization. Petras and LaPorte,[14] for example, have convincingly shown that "political bargaining systems" such as are characteristic of the advanced capitalist nations are singularly unsuited for instituting the massive structural changes necessary for "development" in the Third World. Andre Gunder Frank,[15] Baran and Sweezy,[16] et.al., have demonstrated that capitalist aid and investment serve to siphon out rather than pump surplus into the Third World.

When modernization theorists examine Third World nations at close hand, they see societies split asunder in traditional and modern sectors commanded by corresponding elites. Traditional subsistence economies and political systems and modern commercial economies and political systems coexist in relative isolation within the same society. Modernization theorists locate the major obstacles to development within the traditional sector and postulate that the major political conflicts within Third World societies take place between sectors.[17]

It has been pointed out[18] that such an analysis ignores the myriad of ways in which the so-called traditional and modern sectors interrelate:

1) The extent to which "modern" urban commercial and "traditional" agro-mineral interests are integrated within the same social circles, families, or even the same person.

2) The extent to which the "modern" sector benefits from the low wage structure determined, at least in part, by "traditional" agriculture.

3) The extent to which "moderns" utilize "traditional" methods to ensure labour discipline, political quiescence, etc.

4) The extent to which "modern" import-substitution industrialization relies on the earnings of the "traditional" agro-mineral export sector.

This systematic interrelatedness of the so-called sectors helps to explain why no decisive conflicts in the Third World have developed between landed and urban propertied groups.[19] Contrary to the claims of modernization theory, the key conflicts in the Third World have been between the exploited classes and integrated dominant classes with the wherewithal to consume "modern" values and goods and with an interest in maintaining "traditional" social relations to ensure their social position.

Modernization theory's reliance on ideal types which fail to grasp the essence of the situations from which they are abstracted, its obfuscation of the actual relationships between Third World and developed capitalist countries by means of the deceptive concept of diffusion, its penchant for sectoral rather than class analysis, all derive, in the final analysis, from its master conception of a universal path of societal evolution. This master conception focuses on the nation as its primary unit of analysis and thereby ignores the international context which is so crucial to any understanding of historical development and current realities in the Third World. For several centuries now, the Third World has been part of a structured whole, a world political-economy. As a consequence, it has experienced different patterns of class formation, economic development, and much else that distinguish its path of evolution from that followed by the now developed capitalist countries. There is no universal path of evolution at the national level. Modernization theory falls with the fall of this, its master conception. It is to the dependency theorists that we must look for a clear conception of differential patterns of national evolution and their structured interrelatedness at the world level.

II

Dependency theory, while having its roots in the structuralism of the ECLA economists,[20] arose most directly and forcefully as an extended critique of the modernization perspective. In the first instance, the dependency theorists undertook a series of empirical investigations and theoretical reformulations which attacked the notion of "diffusion". The strategy here was to turn the concept of diffusion on its head by renaming it "mechanisms of dependency or imperialism" and by showing that its effects upon the Third World were essentially the opposite of what modernization theory supposed. Instead, these mechanisms resulted in:

1) Metropolitan appropriation of economic surplus from Third World producers through (a) super-exploitation of Third World labour, (b) unequal terms of trade imposed by monopolistic market structures, (c) transfer pricing by multinational corporations, (d) domination of metropolitan financial institutions which dictate the terms of borrowing and repayment, (e) metropolitan expansion financed by Third World savings, etc.

2) Metropolitan preemption of the requisites of production by means of (a) the take-over and control of Third World raw materials, (b) the plunder of Third World labour-power as in the slave trade, etc.

3) Metropolitan destruction of Third World industries such as (a) Indian textiles, (b) Mexican oil, (c) Vietnamese rice etc.

4) Metropolitan preemption of Third World markets through (a) tied loans, (b) MNC take-over of local markets, etc.

5) Metropolitan subordination of Third World production structures by means of (a) the imposition of an international division of labour within which Third World economies became outward-directed and dependent on metropolitan demand for their dynamism, (b) MNC take-over of Third World industries created by local efforts at import-substitution, etc.

6) Creation of social situations and class formations which do not replicate those of the metropole (even in its historical past) and which do not project a path of social evolution similar to that described by metropolitan countries; e.g. (a) the maintenance of landholding and mercantile classes, military regimes, etc. which mediate imperial domination, (b) the marginalization or at least limitation of a Third World national bourgeoisie through "participation" and mechanisms 1 through 5 above, (c) the metropolitan "bias" toward capital-intensive technology which limits the size of and stratifies the proletariat and which creates the conditions for an increasingly large urban sub-proletariat, etc.

The role of explicating and formalizing the implicit model behind the above inversion of the "diffusion" concept was taken up most influentially by Andre Gunder Frank,[21] who argued that it is false to suppose that development proceeds through the same stages in each country. Contemporary developed capitalist countries were never <u>under</u>developed as is the Third World today, but rather were <u>un</u>developed. Underdevelopment, instead of being caused by the peculiar socio-economic structures of Third World countries, is the historical product of the relations which have obtained between underdeveloped satellites and developed metropoles. In short, development and underdevelopment are two sides of the same coin, two poles of the same process - metropolitan capitalist development on a world scale creates the "development of underdevelopment" in the Third World. The major mechanism of this "development of underdevelopment" is the drainage of economic surplus from the satellites.

When Frank examined Third World countries at close hand, he envisioned the Chain of metropolitan/satellite relations, existing on the international level, replicated within each country. Rejecting the dualist thesis of modernization theory - and, by the way, of the dogmatic Marxists who see a stagnant fuedal sector in the Third World as holding back a dynamic capitalist one, and who await and support bourgeois classes and revolution against these feudal elements[22] - Frank argues that all of Latin America is capitalist because it is involved in the world-wide chain of metropolitan/satellite surplus appropriation. In fact, according to Frank, Latin America's most backward areas (e.g., Northeastern Brazil) were precisely those areas which had once been most strongly linked to the metropole. Institutions such as plantations and haciendas, regardless of their internal appearance, have since the Conquest been capitalist forms of production linked to the metropolitan market.

The result of this incorporation of all Latin America into the world capitalist system with its chain of metropolitan/satellite surplus drain was underdevelopment, economic stagnation. Economic development, acording to Frank, was experienced in Latin America only in those times when the metropolitan linkages were weakened - the Spanish depression of the 17th century, the Napoleonic Wars, the Depression of the 1930's and the two World Wars of the 20th century - and it came to an end precisely as the metropoles recovered from these disruptions and recemented their links to the Third World.

Frank's model was indeed a powerful advance over modernization theory, but it suffered from peculiar weaknesses of its own. First of all, dependency theory has usually suffered from a certain ahistorical character. Change within the Third World tends to be viewed as an outcome of its undifferentiated dependent status. As Colin Leys put it, dependency theory "... concentrates on what happens to the underdeveloped countries at hand of imperialism and colonialism, rather than on the total historical process involved, including the various forms of struggle against imperialism and colonialism which grow out of the conditions of underdevelopment."[23] Social classes, states, politics appear in the perspective as derivatives of economic forces and mechanisms. Classes, class projects, class struggles appear neither as the prime movers of historical change nor the prime movers of historical change nor the prime foci of analytic attention in most versions of dependency theory.

Secondly, in much of the dependency literature, the meaning of "development" and, therefore, of "underdevelopment" is unclear. Given that it is frequently argued that "development" occurs in the Third World when metropolitan/satellite linkages are weakened, does "development" imply autarchy? Since 'development' is an attribute of capitalist development in the metropoles, is the debate about the Third World's ability to replicate this path? If so, what kind of 'socialism'? Finally, on the assumptions of dependency theory, how can the various so-called 'economic miracles' of the Third World be explained?

This failure of dependency theory to clarify the many issues surrounding the question of 'development' pinpoints a key weakness of the perspective. Dependency theory advanced beyond the myths of modernization; yet, we can see in retrospect, it did not fully escape the imprint of these myths. In the work of Baran and in that of Frank, 'diffusion leading to modernization' was inverted to read 'dependency leading to underdevelopment', but the underlying problematic put forth by modernization theory escaped unscathed. The focus of analysis was economic growth as measured by GNP, per capita income, etc., all of which measurements disguised the underlying class basis of the phenomena. Modernization theorists argued that 'diffusion' brought growth, dependency theorists argued that dependence brought stagnation.

Within the dependency paradigm a reaction eventually came in the form of Fernando Cardoso's argument that 'in specific situations it is possible to expect development and dependency'.[24] From another angle, Bill Warren argued that imperialism itself was creating the conditions for rapid, sustained development in the Third World.[25] While these newer formulations severed the facile unity of dependence and stagnation, they unfortunately replaced it, especially in Warren's hands, with an equally facile unity of dependence and growth.

Both the stagnationist and growth versions of dependency theory ignore the necessarily contradictory nature of capitalist development at the national and international levels. Growth and stagnation would be better conceptualized as phases of the capitalist cycle, which embody class struggles and class projects. With growth or stagnation, the critical question should be "What class project or alliance of class projects stands at its base?" In short, "Who benefits?" But to ask this requires a focus on classes, which, as we have already seen, has largely been lacking from the dependency literature.

Dependency theory received its second wind with the theoretical boost given it by Arghiri Emmanuel's theory of unequal exchange.[26] In essence, Emmanuel argued that capital mobility on the world level creates world values, while labour immobility creates national wage rates. Differential wage rates, low in the Third World, high in the "First", render higher rates of exploitation in the Third World. The surplus from this finds its way through international trade at world prices into the pockets of the "First World" proletariat, which since the labour struggles which began in the 1870's has been able to capture a greater portion of world surplus in the form of wages.

Emmanuel's economic reasoning and his political conclusions have been well-disputed both from without the unequal exchange perspective[27] and from within that perspective,[28] so we need not dwell on them here. What is important to note for what follows is the extent to which this schema displaces relations of exploitation between classes in a national arena and inserts at the center of its analysis the problematic of the distribution of world surplus as between national units. "Class struggle" is transmogrified into struggle over the distribution of world surplus among national units, into an effort to capture a greater, or at least not a diminishing, proportion of world surplus within one's national boundaries.

This problematic has been taken up by Immanuel Wallerstein who has combined it with many of the standard arguments of dependency theory to form a new synthesis, world systems analysis.

Following Frank, Wallerstein has argued that the expansion of Europe starting in the 16th century signalled the end of pre-capitalist modes of production in those areas of the Third World incorporated within the world capitalist market. Talk of dualism or feudalism in the Third World is consequently mystifying. We cannot speak of stages of national development, but only of stages of the world system. The modern world system is unitary in that it is synonymous with the capitalist mode of production, yet disparate in that it is divided into tiers - core, semi-periphery, and periphery - which play functionally specific roles within the system as a whole.[29]

The primary advance made by world systems analysis over earlier versions of the dependency perspective is in its breadth of analysis. World systems analysis places a new emphasis on the multilateral relations of the system as a whole (analogous to Emmanuel's "world values"), rather than on the unilateral relations of metropole and satellite characteristic of dependency theory. Thus core-core and periphery-periphery relations become as central to the analysis as do core-periphery ones.[30]

Unfortunately, this new breadth moves us no closer to historically concrete class analysis than did earlier formulations of dependency theory. In the world system perspective all events, processes, group-identities, class and state projects are explained by reference to the system as a whole. As Petras put it, the key to understanding world systems analysis is its direction of generalization:

> Specific events within the world system are to be explained in terms of the demands of the system as a whole. Actors are acting not for their immediate concrete interests but because the system dictates that they act.[31]

Actions become reflexes of system imperatives, especially of the need for equilibrium in the distribution of world surplus amongst the states of the system. At the same time, class cleavages and political struggles and alliances within states become in Wallerstein's words "efforts to alter or preserve a position within the world economy",[32] that is, to capture an undiminished or increased portion of the world surplus within state boundaries.

As a result, the world systems perspective is riddled with "explanations" such as this: Welfare state ideology came about in the core states at the end of the 19th century as a result of the need of the world system (i.e., of the core bourgeoisie) to redistribute surplus to the core proletariat to enable it to buy more agricultural and light manufactured goods, which were then glutting the world market.[33] In such a view, class struggle becomes secondary, if truly important at all, while the core bourgeoisie takes on the attributes of an omniscient and omnipotent planning apparatus.

Most critiques of the world systems perspective have focussed on its understanding of the transition from feudalism to capitalism in Western Europe.[34] Here, since as Wallerstein has many times stated, his purpose in delving into the historical past is to illuminate the shape of the present, I would like to focus on a critical current issue: the question of the transition from capitalism to socialism. I will try to show that this question cannot be clarified by an analysis that focuses solely on the distribution of world surplus.

We saw above that for Wallerstein the modern world system is characterized by a single mode of production. This militant monism not only extends backwards to the demise of feudalism but also forward to the rise of socialism. According to Wallerstein:

> There are today no socialist systems in the world economy any more than there are feudal systems because there is only <u>one</u> world-system. It is a world-economy and it is by definition capitalist in form. Socialism involves the creation of a new kind of world system.[35]

Whether or not this implies a "big-bang" theory of the transition[36], it certainly makes it difficult to situate socialist states within the contemporary world.

Looking at the transition to socialism solely from the perspective of the distribution of world surplus, Wallerstein argues that socialist revolutions have been attempts to rise or maintain a position within the world system. Once in power socialist governments, even if they nationalize all domestic enterprise, must act in conformity with the "mode of operation of the capitalist market system".[37] Involvement in the world capitalist market, at whatever level and in whatever fashion, constrains socialist governments to behave as collective capitalists. Without using the terminology, Wallerstein is a consistent advocate of the state capitalism thesis.[38]

World systems analysis, again, focuses on the distribution of world surplus through state power. It correctly assumes that, because at any one time, say a particular year, the amount of surplus produced on the world scale is fixed, distribution of this surplus is a zero-sum game. But it moves from this true, but trivial, proposition to the notion that national "development", which here means upward mobility through the tiers of the world system, necessarily involves capturing greater amounts of the world surplus. And since the overall amount is fixed, "development", be it capitalist or socialist, involves upward mobility at the expense of other national units, particularly those of the periphery.

What is theoretically passed over here is that, while world surplus is at any one time a fixed amount, over time it expands because of increased labour productivity. A concrete examination of socialist "development" shows that it has taken place primarily through increasing labour productivity and greater use of internal resources, both of which have required internal class transformations. Once this is realized, the concept of a "world surplus" becomes a misleading abstraction. For the single concept amalgamates two very different quantities: 1) a capitalist world surplus, the lion's share of which is siphoned into the coffers of the core bourgeoisie, and 2) a socialist surplus which originates from increased labour productivity within particular socialist states and is largely retained for domestic utilization in those states by means of collectivist control over the national economy.

The class project of socialist revolution has been creation of bonds of social solidarity, increase of internally generated surplus and retention of that surplus for domestic use or for aiding other socialist states (international social solidarity), not "development" at the expense of the periphery.[39] By ignoring the peculiarities of the class project at the base of socialist revolutions and transitions and the fact that these conflicts are not over the distribution of world surplus but over the conditions under which this surplus is produced and for whom, world systems theory becomes a variant of bourgeois convergence theory. The technological level of states within the world economy determine the operating principles of the regimes: The Soviet Union and China become increasingly like the U.S., Cuba like Puerto Rico, and so on. The class basis of a regime's ability to control its economy and to replace individual competitiveness with collective mobility through social solidarity is ignored by world systems analysis, as is the class basis of a regime's mode of insertion into the world market. In short, classes appear in world systems analysis as the objects, not the subjects, of history.

III

The tendency of the dependency/world systems school to stray from widely acknowledged standards of Marxist analysis - its focus on distribution at the expense of production, its tendency to ignore or mystify class struggle - has understandably led to efforts to "return to Marx". These have taken at least two very different forms, which need to be carefully distinguished.

One such effort has taken the form of what we might call "modes of production" analysis. Deriving its inspiration and conceptual tools from Althusserian structuralism and its attendant school of Marxist anthropology,[40] it has found its way into English-language studies largely through the work of Ernesto Laclau.[41] While the literature of this approach is diverse and one sometimes feels that its advocates share a common terminology rather than a common theory, the terms themselves and the definitions typically given to them do tend to imply certain theoretical directions rather than others.

Against the monism of dependency/world systems theory, the modes of production approach argues that Third World social formations encompass several modes of production. This claim is partially based on definitional criteria: a mode of production is, according to this approach, defined by its "relations of production", i.e., the direct relation between the immediate producer of the surplus and its immediate appropriator. Involvement in market relations is irrelevant to the definition of a mode of production. And each couplet, serf-lord, slave-slavemaster, free labourer-capitalist defines a separate mode. Thus while the modes of production approach acknowledges the existence of a capitalist world _system_ knit together by market relations, it recognizes a capitalist _mode of production_ only where labour is "free".

Prima facie, this perspective appears to constitute at least a partial return to the sectoral analysis of modernization theory. The crucial difference, however, is that, unlike dualist interpretations, the emphasis here is on the interrelatedness of modes of production. It is argued that the capitalist, or in some versions feudal, expansion of the West in the 16th century, encountered pre-capitalist modes of production in the Third World which it did not or could not totally transform or obliterate, but rather which it simultaneously conserved and destroyed. It destroyed by draining these pre-capitalist modes of labour-power and raw materials. At the same time, it conserved these modes as arenas for the production of means of agricultural subsistence in order to keep the labour-power and raw materials so extracted cheap. In the jargon of this school, capitalism both dominates and "articulates" with pre-capitalist modes of production in the Third World.

A major difference between this school and world systems analysis is in its focus of analysis and direction of generalization. As we have seen the world systems approach would explain everything by reference to the system-imperatives of the whole. Compared to this the modes of production approach, at least in some of its variants (and with important exceptions, e.g., Samir Amin who attempts to conjoin both approaches in a single framework) signals a considerable narrowing of analytic focus. For in this scheme: "The character and development of all social formations must be understood in terms of the basic contradictions 'internal' to these formations."[42] Thus to the primacy of the "external" relations focussed on by world systems analysis, the modes of production approach counterposes the primacy of "internal" relations.

What frequently underlies this change of focus is the implicit notion (explicit in the work of Rey) that capitalist development in the core countries is homologous to that in the peripheral countries. In other worlds, it postulates that the sequences of the transition from feudalism to capitalism in the West will be replicated in the Third World. Thus Marx's analysis in volumes I and III of Capital become immediately applicable to the Third World, and are frequently so quoted and applied in the literature of this school.

This implicit denial of combined and uneven development sometimes comes perilously close to the universal stages of national development postulated by modernization theory. How are we to explain with this approach the fact that capitalist expansion into the Third World occasionally engendered its own "historical antecedents"? As Foster-Carter put it:

> ...the problematic of articulation must envisage a capitalism which not only conserves...[pre-capitalist modes of production]...but even or on occasion - in defiance of diachrony - actively creates them.[43]

In other words, how are we to explain West Indian slavery, reserve systems in settler regimes, etc. These, it seems, are only explicable as capitalist institutions, created by expansive capital for its own purposes.

The modes of production approach narrows the focus of its analysis in another regard. By identifying a mode of production solely on the basis of, again narrowly defined, "relations of production", it strips the concept of mode of production down to its barest bones and displaces from the centre of attention the much wider complex of relations of class, state, inter-state which define the dynamic of Third World social formations.

The outlines of a very different "return to Marx" can be seen in the recent work of Colin Leys and James Petras.[44] The focus of analysis here is not world system imperatives or articulated modes of production, but classes as the prime movers of history. Petras has done the most to systematize this approach, so we will focus on his perspective here.

Petras argues along with the world systems approach and against the modes of production theorists that capitalism, defined by the creation of surplus value, can have different relations of production. Typical of the Third World, in this view, has been labour scarcity and the availability of alternative economic activity, which has required coercive relations of production for capital expansion.

But Petras dissents from the "external" relations of world systems analysis and the "internal" relations of modes of production analysis. The salient feature of Third World societies is precisely the manner in which external and internal "class structures cross one another and the various combinations of class symbiosis and interlock".[45] Capitalist expansion on the world scale has engendered the existence of collaborative strata in the Third World which both orient production outwardly and exploit internally. Decolonization gave these strata access to the instrumentality of the indigenous state and the choice of several development strategies based on different internal and external class alliances.

First, there is the "neocolonial" strategy wherein the national regime participates with the core bourgeoisie in exploiting the indigenous labour force. Secondly, the national regime may undertake a "national developmental" strategy based on exploitation of the indigenous labour force and the limitation or elimination of the share going to imperial firms. Third, the regime may ally with the indigenous labour force, nationalize foreign and even indigenous enterprise, redistribute income, and generally undertake a "national populist" strategy as against core capital. Although we cannot go into it here, Petras has much to say about the interrelations amongst these strategies and the role of the imperial state in shoring up neo-colonial regimes and undermining the others.

What is important to notice is the new emphasis that is put on classes as the agents of history. The focus is not on development, i.e., growth, versus stagnation. Accumulation occurs, but in a cyclical fashion and on the basis of concrete class projects. Nor is the focus on world system imperatives. The world market, afterall, is the result of class activity extended beyond national borders. The relations of the world economy are not the result of impersonal market forces, but of the economic and political interplay of class forces across national boundaries and within nations. Nor, finally, is the focus on internal modes of production and their articulation. The wider interplay of class and state at the national and international levels is brought into full view. In the work of Petras and Leys, the key question that has tended to get lost in all other sociologies of development clearly surfaces: development for whom?

NOTES

1. For typical examples of modernization theory, see Walt W. Rostow, The Stages of Economic Growth (Cambridge: Cambridge University Press, 1960); Gabriel Almond and James Coleman, eds., The Politics of Developing Areas (Princeton: Princeton University Press, 1960); David Apter, The Politics of Modernization (Chicago: University of Chicago Press, 1965); etc.

2. For typical examples of dependency theory, see Paul Baran, The Political Economy of Growth (New York: Monthly Review Press, 1957); Andre Gunder Frank, Capitalism and Underdevelopment in Latin American (New York: Monthly Review Press, 1967); Theotonio Dos Santos, "The Structure of Dependence", in Readings in US Imperialism, K.T. Fann and Donald C. Hodges, eds., (Boston: Porter Sargent, 1971); etc.

3. For typical examples of world systems theory, see Immanuel Wallerstein, The Modern World System (New York: Academic Press, 1974); and his "Rise and Demise of the World Capitalist System", Comparative Studies in Society and History, 16, 1974; etc.

4. This criticism has been made by adherents of modes of production theory. See Ernesto Laclau, "Feudalism and Capitalism in Latin America", New Left Review, No. 67; John G. Taylor, From Modernization to Modes of Production (London: Macmillan, 1979); etc.

5. For this criticism, see James Petras, Critical Perspectives on Imperialism and Social Class in the Third World (New York: Monthly Review Press, 1978); Colin Leys, Underdevelopment in Kenya (Berkeley: University of California Press, 1975); and his "Underdevelopment and Dependency: Critical Notes", Journal of Contemporary Asia, Vol. 7:1, 1977, etc.

6. Reinhard Bendix, Nation-building and Citizenship (New York: Wiley, 1964).

7. Cited by Donal Cruise O'Brien, "Modernization, Order, and the Erosion of a Democratic Ideal: American Political Science 1960-70", Journal of Development Studies, 8, 1972, p. 353.

8. Karl Marx, Capital (Chicago: Charles Kerr, 1905), Vol. I, p. 13.

9. Bert Hoselitz, ed., The Progress of Underdeveloped Areas (Chicago: University of Chicago Press, 1952), p. v.

10. See, e.g., Seymour Martin Lipset, "Values, Education, and Entrepreneurship", in Elites in Latin America, Lipset and Aldo Solari, eds. (New York: Oxford University Press, 1967).

11. For a good example of this type of criticism, see Andre Gunder Frank, "Sociology of Development and Underdevelopment of Sociology", in Dependence and Underdevelopment, James Cockcroft, A.G. Frank, and Dale Johnson, eds. (Garden City: Doublebay, 1972).

12. For other approaches to the understanding of "traditional" social formations, see Karl Marx, Precapitalist Economic Formations (New York: International Publishers, 1965); Samir Amin, Unequal Development (New York: Monthly Review Press, 1976), Chap. 1.

13. Reinhard Bendix, "Tradition and Modernity Reconsidered", in his Embattled Reason (New York: Oxford University Press, 1970).

14. James Petras and Robert LaPorte, Cultivating Revolution (New York: Random Press, 1971).

15. Andre Gunder Frank, Latin America: Development or Revolution (New York: Monthly Review Press, 1969).

16. Paul Baran and Paul Sweezy, Monopoly Capital (New York: Monthly Review Press, 1968).

17. The notion of "dual economy", taken up by the whole of the modernization school, was given consistency by W.A. Lewis, "Economic Development with Unlimited Supplies of Labour" in his Theory of Economic Growth (New York: Harper Torchbooks, 1970). The dualist thesis and the political line that flows from it has its analogue in the classical debate over imperialism. Joseph Schumpeter, "The Sociology of Imperialisms" in his Imperialism and Social Classes (New York: World Publishing, 1955), argued that German imperialism resulted from a complex of "atavistic" attitudes left over from the feudal past and carried into the present by feudal elements which retained political hegemony. Schumpeter's political thrust was to appeal to the German bourgeoisie (the "modernizers") to throw off their feudal rulers (the "traditionalists") and to develop a "pure", for him non-imperialist, capitalism.

18. James Petras, Politics and Social Structure in Latin America (New York: Monthly Review Press, 1970): Irving Leonard Markovitz, Power and Class in Africa (Englewood Cliffs: Prentice Hall, 1977).

19. For an interesting historical case study which illustrates this point, see Frederick Pike, "Aspects of Class Relations in Chile, 1850-1960", in Latin America: Reform or Revolution, James Petras and Maurice Zeitlin, eds. (Greenwich, Conn.: Fawcett Publications, 1968).

20. On this background, see Philip O'Brien, "A Critique of Latin American Theories of Dependency", and David Booth, "Andre Gunder Frank: An Introduction and an Appreciation", both in Beyond the Sociology of Development, Ivar Oxaal, Tony Barnett, and David Booth, eds. (London: Routledge and Kegan Paul, 1975).

21. See, esp., his Capitalism and Underdevelopment, op.cit.

22. For an informative account of this schema and its ups and downs in recent years, see Jacques Lévesque, L'URSS et la Revolution Cubaine (Montréal: Presses de L'Unversité de Montréal, n.d.).

23. Leys, Underdevelopment in Kenya, op.cit., p. 20.

24. Fernando Cardoso, "Dependency and Development in Latin America", New Left Review, No. 74.

25. Bill Warren, "Imperialism and Capitalist Industrialization", New Left Review, No. 73. Warren's theoretical ineptitude, deceptive use of statistics, etc. have been well criticized by Philip McMichael, James Petras, and Robert Rhodes, "Industrialization in the Third World", in Petras, Critical Perspectives, op.cit.

26. Arghiri Emmanuel, Unequal Exchange (New York: Monthly Review Press, 1972).

27. See Charles Bettleheim's remarks contained in Emmanuel's book; Ernest Mandel, Late Capitalism (London: New Left Books, 1975), Chap. 11; Michael Kidron, Capitalism and Theory (London: Pluto Press, 1974), Chap. 5.

28. Samir Amin, Imperialism and Unequal Development (New York: Monthly Review Press, 1977), Part IV.

29. Wallerstein, The Modern World System, op.cit.; and his "Rise and Future Demise", op.cit.

30. For this, see Samir Amin, Accumulation on a World Scale (New York: Monthly Review Press, 1974).

31. Petras, Critical Perspectives, op.cit., p. 33.

32. Immanuel Wallerstein, "The Present State of the Debate on World Inequality", in his edited volume World Inequality (Montreal: Black Rose Books, 1975), p. 16.

33. Wallerstein, "Rise and Demise", op.cit., pp. 410-11.

34. See, e.g., Verl F. Hunt, "The Rise of Feudalism in Eastern Europe", Science and Society, Spring 1978; Robert Brenner, "The Origins of Capitalist Development", New Left Review, No. 104; Alex Dupuy and Paul Fitzgerald, "A

Contribution to the Critique of the World System Perspective", The Insurgent Sociologist, Spring 1977.

35. Wallerstein, "Rise and Demise", op.cit., p. 415.

36. For this view, see Ira Gerstein, "Theories of the World Economy and Imperialism" and Wallerstein's denial, "How Do We Know Class Struggle When We See It?", both in The Insurgent Sociologist, Spring 1977.

37. Wallerstein, "Rise and Demise", op.cit., p. 413.

38. For the state capitalist thesis, see Tony Cliff, State Capitalism in Russia (London: Pluto Press, 1974); for cogent criticisms of this thesis, see Ernest Mandel, The Mystifications of State Capitalism (London: Prinkipo Press, 1970) and his The Inconsistencies of State Capitalism (London: Pioneer Press, 1969).

39. On the nature of this class project, see James Petras, "Aspects of Class Formation in the Periphery", in his Critical Perspectives, op.cit.,; John Gurley, "Maoist Economic Development", in his China's Economy and the Maoist Strategy (New York: Monthly Review Press, 1976); Clive Y. Thomas, Dependence and Transformation (New York: Monthly Review Press, 1974); for a case study which begins to analyze some of the obstacles to the easy implementation of this project, see Frank T. Fitzgerald, "A Critique of the 'Sovietization of Cuba', Thesis", Science and Society, Spring 1978.

40. Esp. the work of Georges Dupre, Pierre-Philippe Rey, and Claude Meillassoux, for a discussion of which, see John Clammer, "Economic Anthropology and the Sociology of Development", in Beyond, Oxaal, et.al., op.cit.; Aidan Foster-Carter, "The Modes of Production Controversy", New Left Review, No. 107.

41. Laclau, "Feudalism and Capitalism", op.cit.

42. Richard Harris, "Marxism and the Agrarian Question in Latin America", Latin American Perspectives, Fall 1978, p. 16.

43. Foster-Carter, "Modes", op.cit., p. 67.

44. Leys, Underdevelopment in Kenya, op.cit.; Petras, Critical Perspectives, op.cit.

45. Ibid., p. 64.

Chapter 3

UNDERDEVELOPMENT AND DEPENDENCY: CRITICAL NOTES

Colin Leys

> ...this concept [dependence] fails to grasp the real nature of the process of underdevelopment. The immediate explanation for this is the theoretical framework employed...eclectic combination of orthodox economic theory and revolutionary phraseology... (Geoffrey Kay, Development and Underdevelopment: A Marxist Analysis, p. 103).

It is becoming clear that "underdevelopment" and "dependency" theory is no longer serviceable and must now be transcended. The evidence for this is (a) theoretical repetition and stagnation in the literature on underdevelopment and dependency theory (UDT): (b) the existence of fundamental problems of analysis which UDT cannot solve, or even formulate, and central problems of development strategy which are linked with these, and about which UDT is either silent - or ambiguous; (c) an evident lack of practical impact in favour of the popular forces in the struggles in third world countries, but on the contrary, a marked tendency for the underdevelopment/dependency "perspective" to be co-opted by developmentalists allied to international capital. The present article is an attempt to clarify all this, with the help of several recent sympathetic studies of the genesis of UDT and its variants, and to suggest what needs to be done about it.

UDT AND ITS PROBLEMS

By "underdevelopment and dependency theory" I mean the following general theses:

a. The social, economic and political conditions prevailing throughout today's "third world" ("less developed countries" in UN usuage) are not due to the persistence of an "original" (undeveloped or "untouched") state of affairs, but are the results of the same world-historical process in which the "first world" ("developed market economies") became "developed"; the development of the latter involved a closely associated course of development for the former, a process of subordinate development or underdevelopment.

b. The prime mover in this combined process was capital seeking profits, i.e. seeking opportunities to accumulate capital; specifically, capitalist merchants, capitalist bankers, capitalist insurers, etc., and finally capitalist manufacturers.

c. Their activities involved accumulating capital where this could be done cheaply, and investing it where the return to investment was highest, and this gave rise to a process of surplus removal from some parts of the world to others, perpetuating and rigidifying in new ways the low levels of productivity in the areas from which the surplus was taken; and also a structuring of these economies so as to subordinate them systematically to the structures of the economies where capital was being accumulated. This expressed itself in the "external orientation" of the subordinate economies (export of primary commodities, import of all manufactures); in monoculture; in dependent industrialisation (dependent on external forces - demand, strategic division of labour, technology, etc. - for its dynamics and structuration).

d. Secondary structural consequences of this served to reproduce the process and constantly block local initiatives to pursue an autonomous development path: e.g. the low incomes of the majority due to the creation of surplus labour and marginalisation imply a generally small domestic market; highly unequal income distribution implies a narrow import-oriented consumer demand; etc.

e. The corresponding emergence and formation of social classes at the capitalist periphery with interests in common with the bourgeoisie of the metropoles made possible the development of colonial neo-colonial and semi-colonial states representing successive types of such alliances.

f. The term "underdevelopment" refers to these self-perpetuating processes, these self-reproducing structures, and to their results. The term "dependency" is sometimes used to refer to exactly the same things, and sometimes more specifically to refer to the non-autonomous nature of the laws or tendencies governing change in the social formations of the periphery. In spite of disagreements between the users of the two terms their differences seem less important than their extensive points of general agreement.[1]

Of course this sort of outline misses part of the strength of UDT, which is to have stimulated the empirical study of institutional and structural mechanisms of underdevelopment such as multinational corporations, income distribution, fiscal and taxation policies, capital expenditure and aid programmes, etc. But I think its main thrust is roughly as sketched above. And in the context of the early 1960s when UDT emerged as a militant critique of the ruling ideas of developmentalism, its thrust was unquestionably a progressive one. O'Brien's comment that "the international economy is likely to prove a more seminal starting point for understanding development and underdevelopment than, e.g., traditional and modern society, stages of growth, achievement motivation, or even Myrdal's "causally inter-related conditions of a social system" is an understatement which reminds us of some of the intellectual deserts from which UDT rescued us, along with "integration", "nation-building", "political development", "modernisation" and much else. These were arid formulations because they started out from the premise (more or less inarticulate) that underdevelopment was a "primal" or "original" condition and proceeded to ignore the historical and "transitive" relationships between development and underdevelopment, and hence the whole phenomenon of imperialism. They nearly all ignored the existence of social classes, and treated the state as an instrument of popular will, or at least of the public interest as interpreted by a minority on behalf of the public. They had in fact a highly ideological character, as we can now easily see in the light cast by UDT. And some of them embodied this in the particularly stultifying forms of abstracted empiricism and "grand theory". In fact all these features of bourgeois development theory have been made apparent by UDT. The question is, however, whether UDT is free from all of them itself.

As for UDT, then, it is true that the charge that it has tended towards theoretical repetition and stagnation is necessarily subjective; and it is probably more accurate to say that UDT was characterised from the first by a proliferation of attempts to formulate characterisations, models and analyses of underdevelopment or dependency <u>in general</u>,[2] it is significant that the few attempts at systematic theorisation - for instance by Amin or Szentes - have been by economists and have not really systematised the kind of total perspective - social, political, ideological and economic - implied in the more general formulations through which UDT is chiefly known. As I will indicate below, this reflects the genesis of UDT <u>as a criticism of bourgeois development theory</u> which, while radical in intention, really remains within its problematic, so that the systematisation of UDT could only produce a revision of bourgeois development theory, and an ultimately non radical one at that. The sense of theoretical repetition and stagnation which the UDT literature eventually conveys (as O'Brien says, "was it really necessary to write so many millions of words to establish just this perspective?") seems to me then, to be due to the necessity of staying at the level of a general "perspective" if the fundamental difficulties inherent in that perspective are not to be immediately apparent.[3]

The sort of difficulties involved include the following (the list is not in any order, let alone comprehensive):

a. The meaning of "development" in UDT is obscure. Insofar as it implies a concept of development it is evidently that of the capitalist development experienced by the capitalist "metropoles". But if the study of underdevelopment suggests that the underdeveloped countries now cannot follow a development path at all similar to that of the "metropoles", it is a matter of great consequence if the analysis of how they become and are kept underdeveloped does not itself disclose what "development" can or should mean for them, or how it is to be accomplished. The fact is that this does not seem to be so, and this is shown by the great variety of practical-political positions arrived at (often somewhat independently of their theoretical formulations) by different UD theories, though UD theorists actually often adopt very vague practical-political positions, if any, and largely confine themselves to interpreting and explaining what has happened in the past.

b. Exploitation. Much UDT is unclear whether the masses in the underdeveloped countries suffer from exploitation or not, and if so, to what extent. Most of the theorists imply, at least, that the masses of the third world are exploited as well as oppressed, but do not make it clear how. The issue was posed in the debate between Charles Bettelheim and Arghiri Emmanuel over Emmanuel's Unequal Exchange and is raised again in a sharp way by Kay even though his formulation is not perhaps as clear as one would like ("capitalism has created underdevelopment not simply because it has exploited the underdeveloped countries but because it has not exploited them enough").[4]

c. Primitive concepts. It is hard to deny that UDT is to say the least very broad-gauged. The centre-periphery metaphor is seldom if ever replaced by a concrete typology of centres and peripheries. The same is true of "dependence". It is sometimes said (e.g. by Cardoso) that there are "different forms" of dependence but unless these are identified and the differences theoretically explained, the question arises whether this perspective is not a fairly arbitrary way of sensitising us to one set of relationships at the cost of anaesthetising us to others - i.e. sensitising us to only one dimension of a more complex interdependency.[5] And it is not really an accident that these simplistic pairings, developed/under-developed, centre/periphery, dominant/dependent resemble those of bourgeois development theory (traditional/modern, rich/poor, advanced/backward, etc.); they are basically polemical inversions of them. But the result is a very serious weakness: the empirical meaning of "underdeveloped" has to be pretty slight if it must embrace India and Brazil as well as Haiti and Tanzania. It is also clear that Portugal, Britain, the USA and Japan (not to mention the USSR) are "developed" in different ways that are seldom if ever clarified in UDT, important though this is. (Before 1974, for example, it was conventional wisdom for some UD theorists that a neo-colonial solution in Africa was "impossible" for Portugal because of her own underdevelopment; it is clear that the concepts these words denote are far too weak for making the theoretical distinctions needed to analyse the important political questions involved here).

d. "Economism" and "mechanicism". UDT tends to be economistic in the sense that social classes, the state, politics, ideology figure in it very noticeably as derivatives of economic forces, and often get very little attention at all. Classes, for instance, tend to appear as categories resulting from the structural evolution of underdevelopment or dependent development; thus landlords are technically backward, domestic bourgeoisies are weak and comprador in outlook, wage-labour forces are small and highly differentiated, etc. Classes do not appear as the prime movers of history in this perspective, and a corresponding theoretical eclecticism is apparent ("elite" is often used alongside "class", for instance). And UDT tends to be mechanical in the sense that processes tend to be presented as resulting from a "logic" of mechanism, a system of vicious circles reinforcing each other (e.g. low productivity means low real incomes which mean narrow markets which mean high levels of protection for manufacturing which mean high cost production which means lower real incomes - etc. etc.). This results in accounts which appear curiously static; "underdevelopment" can appear as inescapable (something countries are "locked into" - as the "breakdown" of capitalism appeared in the marxism of the Second International. Little attention is paid to the struggle against imperialism and the social and political consequences of underdevelopment; still less do most UD theorists concentrate on this struggle as the key to overcoming underdevelopment. A good example of the confusion and vulnerability of UDT on something obviously central is the debate stimulated by Warren, as to whether "underdevelopment" precludes rapid and "independent" capitalist industrialisation at the periphery, and if not, whether (as Cardoso implies) the "dependent capitalist industrialisation" through MNC branch plants is ultimately different from other kinds of capitalist industrialisation; if not, are we not back with "late development" and "catching up"?

e. Imperialism. On the whole this concept appears in UDT

only as an "extra", often with a qualifier (such as "economic imperialism", "cultural imperialism", etc.) and often meaning no more than the mechanisms and institutions of penetration and control employed by international capital in the third world. There is a certain ambivalence, to say the least, towards the Leninist conception of imperialism as a historical stage of capitalism, an ambivalence which is I think primarily political and only secondarily theoretical; i.e., in the third world context the adoption of such a concept implies a break with the perspective of reform which much UDT has not really made. But avoiding the concept means, frequently, avoiding realities which are central to the situations with which UDT is meant to deal.

f. Units of analysis. Another area where the conceptual imprecision of UDT is unacceptable concerns the units of analysis which should be central to it - social formations, modes of production, world economy, etc. The positive merits of UDT turn on its insistence on the importance of trans-national or trans-state relationships in explaining the course of events in underdevelopment in third world countries. Yet concepts used to analyse these are often far from clear. For instance Frank's well-known characterisation of the whole Latin American economy as "capitalist" from the 16th century seems to preclude a systematic analysis of the class forces there (over that time they can't all have been either capitalists, compradors or proletarians - and are they yet?); yet the problematic of the "articulation" of different modes of production, which is implied by Laclau's equally well-known critique of Frank, presents its own difficulties.

g. What causes underdevelopment? Curiously enough, it is not clear that UDT provides any explanation of why more capital did not get invested and accumulated in the third world in the past, or of why it should not now take advantage of cheap labour and soak up the vast pools of unemployed people in the third world today. This is connected, of course, with the failure to be clear about the question of exploitation; it shows again how UDT offers only a general interpretation of a current situation, a system of mechanisms broadly taken as "given", rather than putting forward a theory of the "laws" governing the historical appearance and subsequent evolution of those mechanisms.

The list could be extended. Booth's remark that Frank's formulations "sensitise us to certain features of economic change and at the same time anaesthetise us to other features" can fairly be applied, it seems, to UDT generally. But the comment does not go far enough. The trouble with UDT is not that it is a theory still at an early stage of development, a theory with various gaps needing to be filled up and ambiguities to be resolved (as I myself used to suppose). The real trouble is that concepts which primarily "sensitise" do not belong to a coherent theoretical system, based on a consistent political standpoint and a consistent method of analysis; they are ideological rather than scientific. This is why UDT is "stalled", and why its real gains - the detailed analyses of the institutions and structures of underdevelopment - are being appropriated more by the ideologists of international capital than the workers and peasants of the third world.

UDT AS "MARXIFIED STRUCTURALISM"

In order to understand this better we must look again at the origins of UDT, taking advantage of the excellent recent studies by Foster-Carter, Girvan, O'Brien and Booth.[6] What these all confirm is that the main line of descent of UDT, almost wholly a New World Phenomenon, was a series of revisions of orthodox (bourgeois) economic analysis, beginning with the critique of international trade theory which was the starting-point of the ECLA "school". This initial revision explained the failure of Latin American and Caribbean economies to develop by identifying structural obstacles which would have to be overcome by appropriate policies to change the structures - policies summed up in the phrase "inward-oriented development", and meaning particularly, industrialisation through import substitution. This was followed by a further revision which explained the failure of _this_ strategy in terms of a new set of structural barriers, often structures which were introduced in the very process of inward-oriented industrialisation and tended to defeat the object of the original restructuring policy (e.g. the high import-content of MNC branch plant industrialisation); or structural obstacles at another _level_, which were revealed in the course of the initial restructuring effort (e.g. highly unequal income structures, urban-rural imbalances, etc.), structures which in turn often seemed to be aggravated by the new strategies. "Underdevelopment" and "dependency" then emerged as concepts embracing all these newly apparent structures and mechanisms. At the same time, as the fresh "layers" of structural obstacles were identified they came more and more to be seen as part of a long-term process involving successive _stages_, each with its distinctive institutional mechanisms reinforcing or modifying economic and social structures, but always reproducing their fundamentally subordinate character, serving development elsewhere, minimising its benefits and maximising its costs locally. The main stream of UDT can thus be seen as eventuating in _radical structuralism_ - i.e. as a structuralist analysis of the obstacles to capitalist development in the third world in which progressively more and more of what were originally seen as means to structural change - international manufacturing companies, third world governments and the interests they mostly represent, etc. - come to be seen as yet further structures which themselves need to be changed.

The central weakness of radical structuralism is obvious. Inverting Cleaver's dictum that "if you're part of the solution you're part of the problem", radical structuralism cannot escape the difficulty that the solution always turns out to be part of the problem. This is particularly clear in the case of Gunnar Myrdal, who is not a dependency or underdevelopment theorist but who certainly is a structuralist and a social-democrat, and whose _Challenge of World Poverty_ identifies as main causes of poverty the very governments and international agencies to whom he also appeals for solutions. In the case of the earlier writings of Best, Girvan and their collaborators in the West Indies, it appears in the shape of a reform programme for an anti-imperialist government based on an alliance of progressive local capitalists with the popular masses - which was, in fact, just what the existing governments of the West Indies generally claimed to be.[7] Neither Myrdal nor the New World Economists appear to suggest how the problem is to become the solution; their utopianism is quite clear.

But in the case of UDT the central weakness is partly concealed, thanks to the convergence of its main stream with another stream - Marxism, and especially neo-Marxism of various kinds. In the case of Frank there was the influence of Paul Baran, whose _Political Economy of Growth_ appeared in 1957, and as Frank himself says, the influences of the Cuban revolution. More generally there was the impact of de-Stalinisation and polycentrism on the Latin American communist parties, and the subsequent influence of Maoism added to the already complex pattern of Latin American Marxism, with its strong Trotskyist currents. But whatever the diversity of channels, the Marxist stream certainly mingled with that of structuralism in the 1960s, to the point where O'Brien, for instance, could refer to them as "different _traditions within_ the theory of dependency",[8]

The immediate effect of "marxifying" radical structuralism was to shift the implied solution to the problem of underdevelopment from economic nationalism to _socialism_, and to shift the means from utopian recommendations of radical structural reforms to _revolutionary struggle_. But this was an illusion. It is no less utopian to appeal to "revolution" and "socialism" to solve the problem _as radical structuralism formulates it_, than to the existing third world governments or the USAID, since a structuralist analysis doesn't disclose the potential class forces on which a revolutionary struggle can be based, or the contradictions which condition and are developed by the struggle, or a strategy or organisational forms of struggle, or - _a fortiori_ - a "socialist" solution, since a socialist solution must itself be disclosed by the interests and capacities of the revolutionary forces and their strategy, which have not been identified at all. In short the "marxification" of radical structuralism, or "left" UDT, does not rescue radical structuralism from its dilemma, for the basic reason that it has been built up through successive revisions of bourgeois economics, and like a Russian doll, the final outer layer has essentially the same shape as the innermost one. It is an analysis whose central concepts and problematic are ultimately still those of bourgeois social science, especially bourgeois economics, in spite of the fact that it uses words which denote the concepts of historical materialism; i.e. it understands the relations of production and exploitation in the third world in a way which still idealises and mystifies them.

The converse of this, of course, is that the "marxism" of the most marxist of UD theorists becomes utopian. This seems to me the main difficulty with Frank's political position, at least as it emerges from his writings. Emphasising revolutionary class struggle for socialism as the only solution to underdevelopment, he rejects dogmatic formulae for this struggle and recognises the great variety of patterns and stages of underdevelopment in the different countries of Latin America. But he does not himself offer much in the way of analysis which would make the reality and meaning of this "solution" more apparent and concrete. The main thrust of his work is a historical-structural analysis of surplus extraction and transfer, and structural subordination of periphery economies through the mediation of subordinate (or "lumpen") bourgeoisies; not of the structures of oppression and exploitation, i.e. the modes and relations of production, and the class struggles and class organisations developing within these. Kay's polemical comment cited at the beginning of this paper would be unjust if applied to Frank without qualification, but there would still be an element of truth in it.

What is more, "marxist" or "left" UDT is not merely utopian in its own way, but ultimately cannot escape being ideological. An example of this is my own idea that some of the limitations of UDT of which I had become somewhat aware in my work on Kenya were "gaps" which could be "plugged" by grafting on a treatment of what was missing, e.g. an analysis of classes. The result was distinctly lifeless, uninspired by any real concept of class struggle.[9] In order to arrive at an analysis of classes for the purpose of relating class struggle to the problem of development, I needed to break away from the problematic of structuralism itself. So long as I remained within it, I remained a prisoner of its ideological effects, including a concept of social class which is ultimately residual and passive. More significantly, I would now say that I think UDT itself is really ahistorical, in the same way that bourgeois development theory is, and for the same reason (i.e. its problematic is the same). It does have a time dimension, of course, which some versions of bourgeois development theory conspicuously lacked. But this is not the same thing as history. The mere extension of the model to allow for change, or to see the present as the end of a chain of events extending back into the past, is not to make it historical; i.e. does not explain underdevelopment by reference to social forces which have been identified as a result of a coherent and consistent method for sifting out from the complex flow of events the patterns that allow us to make sense of it, now and in the past. The stages familiar from UDT (such as mercantilism, liberalism, neo-mercantilism, etc.) are rather empirical periodisations with at most a good deal of descriptive and heuristic value, not the product of a systematic analysis of the interplay of political and social as well as economic forces which resulted in the geographical extension of the sway of capital, or of the new struggles generated by this process.

Most of the points made above are made, implicitly where not explicitly, in Frank's "reply to critics", where he also makes the illuminating observation that the concept of "dependence" can best be understood as the product of a very specific historical period, viz. the long post-war "boom", or phase of rapid capital accumulation;[10] it refers, in fact, to that boom, seen from Latin America. The end of that phase of the accumulation cycle, he remarks, shifts attention to its cyclical nature, and the concept of "dependence" necessarily gives way to the concepts needed in order to understand not just one phase, but "the process of capital accumulation in the world - with special reference to the participation of Asia, the Middle East, Africa and Latin America - from 1500 to the present", a task he has set for himself and which he says is also being undertaken in different ways by others such as Laclau, Hinkelammert, Marini and Torres (and we should presumably add Amin, Wallerstein and Anderson). (I have reservations about this programme, to be mentioned in a moment.)

Meantime the ideological character of UDT is best demonstrated by its vulnerability to what Kay calls "conservative re-absorption" of the kind represented by the World Bank's recent adoption of a "poverty-oriented" aid philosophy under MacNamara's Presidency, and the corresponding "reorientation" of bilateral aid doctrines by the USA and other countries. What this comes down to is the adoption of non-radical structuralism. This says, in effect, that not all solutions are part of the problem: the World Bank isn't, nor are MNCs (if third world governments pool their bargaining knowhow and co-ordinate their collective leverage), nor are all third world governments, at least not monolithically. On the other hand, radical structural change is (a) unlikely, and (b) usually turns out to be very unpleasant (to whom is not usually made clear) and unpredictable in its outcomes, and (c) who are we (in the bourgeois democracies) to advocate such radical changes for others (etc. etc.), so let us pursue structural reform instead.[11] This position is in my view simply the expression of a political programme of large-scale international capital and the states and international agencies which represent it. The assimilation of structuralism is at best partial in such perspectives, but even if it were more complete, it would still be what it is, i.e. a form of bourgeois ideology, whose character has been very adequately revealed by the critiques of Baran and Amin and the polemics of Frank.[12]

We must therefore go forward, not backward; not merely "beyond the sociology of development" (the title of Oxaal, Barnett and Booth's book) but beyond the sociology of underdevelopment in two ways: not merely into a different kind of theory, but into a more clearly defined relation between theory and practice. A genuinely historical theory will allow us to analyse the process of combined and uneven development of capitalism on a world scale, as it has been experienced (or "participated in" as Frank rightly puts it) in particular countries, and hence as it presents itself to any one of them now, in the form of a class struggle conducted in the framework of a particular inherited structure of productive relations, forms of exploitation and exchange relationships, and a particular structure of relations of political and ideological domination, internal and external, etc. A serious and systematic application of historical materialism does not mean the application of a ready-made formula taken from the texts of Marx and Engels, or Lenin or Trotsky or Mao Tse-tung, but the application of the method and conclusions to be drawn from such texts plus the practice out of which they emerged, and by which they have since been continually revised.

And this is why it is not merely a question of a different kind of theory (i.e. different from UDT or disguised radical structuralism) but also of a more clearly defined relation between theory and practice. The reason I am not too happy about Frank's conclusion that UDT should give way to the analysis of the process of capital accumulation from 1500AD to the present is that it seems even more liable than UDT to be an academic exercise in the literal sense of the term, and hence liable to be still more vaguely related to political practice, and hence, finally, liable to take on an ideological character all over again. It is not that such an analysis is unnecessary; it is very necessary. But what is involved is hardly less than a history of the modern world; and any such product conceived of primarily as a product of scholarship (let alone individual scholarship) or "social science" (to use Frank's term) rather than as a work of synthesising the experience of the political practice of particular classes on a world scale, and hence proceeding by a process of provisional formulations based on the experience of specific struggles, and so necessarily consisting of a protracted and collective endeavour, seems to me likely to prove essentially ideological. Perhaps Frank himself should not be interpreted too literally when he seems to propose the task in these terms, but without going into detail over the examples we already have (such as Wallerstein's and Anderson's work). I think it will be important to envisage the development of an historical context for future theory by way of successive approximations, arising out of studies of historical situations specific enough for the study to be related in a very explicit way to the contemporary class struggles within them.[13]

SOME THEORETICAL QUESTIONS

In conclusion, and in the context of what I have just argued, I wish to raise three theoretical issues from among the many which have to be confronted: the question of exploitation, the question of modes of production and their "articulation", and the question of the reasons for underdevelopment.

a. Exploitation. UDT generally holds or implies that the condition of the people in underdeveloped countries is the result of exploitation, and this certainly appeals to "common sense" as one contemplates generally the record of colonialism in, say, Peru or the Congo. But Marxist economists such as Bettelheim and Kay rightly question "common sense". While there may be "super-exploitation" in the periphery, i.e. extraction of surplus value from workers through coercive sanctions in pre-capitalist modes of production, or in the course of primitive capital accumulation (forced labour, etc.), the direct exploitation by capital of wage workers at the periphery is typically less than in the capitalist metropoles if the level of exploitation is the proportion of the value of what the workers produce that is not paid to them in wages. In the metropoles wage levels are much higher but productivity is higher still, thanks to the higher organic composition of capital. The problem of the underdeveloped countries is then, Kay argues, that the workers are exploited without being exploited enough - in the sense that they are subject to severe downward pressure on wages, to extract the maximum absolute surplus value, but do not benefit from the higher real wages that they could be paid if capitalists were forced to try to increase relative surplus value by more investment leading to higher productivity. In fact, Kay argues, the value of wages may be lower in the metropoles than at the periphery, even though wages are much higher there in terms of purchasing power; meaning that the labour time necessary to produce the goods their wages buy is probably smaller than the time taken to produce the relatively few goods the third world workers can buy with their wages.[14]

Against this Emmanuel argues that it is artificial to treat the metropoles and the periphery countries in isolation from each other in this wage.[15] If a pair of shoes can be produced anywhere in the world in ten minutes of labour-time, that is the (world) value of a pair of shoes and the proper measure of the value of real wages everywhere; the tendency of this interpretation is to make the real wages of third world workers seem much lower as a proportion of what they produce, and hence to make their level of exploitation higher. By adopting this general standpoint one can also argue that merely because sufficient capital has not been invested to make workers as productive as workers employed in similar work elsewhere, it does not follow that they are less exploited. If capitalists choose in certain areas not to extract the maximum surplus value from the workers that is possible using the best available equipment and organisation, that is because in those areas political, social and economic conditions permit them to pay such low wages as to make the additional investment unnecessary. This line of argument has, it seems to me, considerable force, and corresponds to our "common-sense" feeling that low-paid workers in under-capitalised operations are more exploited than higher paid workers in more efficient plants in the same line of business.

At all events, it is not hard to see that these arguments all have a rather abstract quality and that what is at issue is not so much a "correct" theorisation of the locus and relative levels of exploitation as between first and third world countries and workers, as certain practical-political implications that have been supposed to follow from one position rather than another. Thus Bettelheim, for instance, was really anxious to show that the exploitation of workers in France or the USA was the source of the economic power behind imperialism and hence of the oppression (and hence "superexploitation") of workers in the third world; and to discourage the idea that third world workers had a common cause with the bourgeoisies and petty-bourgeoisies of their own countries against both foreign capital and foreign workers (who were considered by Emmanuel to be sharing in the exploitation of third world workers through the operation of the terms of trade).

Perhaps by now we are free to dislodge the discussion from such an abstract and universal plane. Is it really necessary to hold that all workers in all underdeveloped countries are more or less exploited than all workers in all the metropolitan countries? Is it not clear that the technical concept of exploitation, formulated by Marx in the context of the competitive capitalism of a single social formation, cannot be stretched to cover unambiguously all the complex relationships between workers and capitalists and workers and workers throughout a world capitalist economy? So, for instance, when a multinational corporation moves its television manufacturing operation from the USA to Taiwan it does so precisely to reduce the overall level of real wages it pays and so increase absolute surplus value. The Taiwanese workers are evidently more exploited than the US workers whom they replace, using identical equipment. They are also likely to have higher real incomes than Taiwanese workers in plants with much lower organic composition of capital and who as a result produce less per hour of labour. Which of these two groups of workers is considered more exploited depends both on relative real wages and relative productivity, but also on the position one takes on the general theoretical issue discussed above. Furthermore, both are directly exploited in a way that the Taiwanese peasant producer selling his crop to realise a still lower real income, is not. All three groups of workers are in differing ways victims of an international and national structure of social relations and political domination which condemns them to (among other things) a level of real incomes which the development of the forces of production on a world-wide basis has long since rendered unnecessary. The practical political implications of these theoretical distinctions are not unimportant, affecting workers' and peasants' solidarity, and the possibilities of international class co-operation too; but they are only part of the ensemble of relations which also affect solidarity, consciousness, organisation, etc. In short the general question about exploitation in the third world needs to be dissolved into a series of more particular questions about the forms, degrees and effects of different kinds of exploitation in different national and international contexts, and the way these relate to forms, degrees and effects of domination and oppression and the struggles waged against both.

b. Units of analysis: modes of production and their "articulation". As soon as we move beyond the broad perspective of UDT according to which the condition of the "periphery" is accepted as simply being, as a matter of fact, complementary to the process of capital accumulation at the centre, two questions arise: (i) how; and (ii) why. Frank did not really propose an answer to the second question (nor did Baran). Frank's answer to the first question was that in Latin America, it was done by means of changing forms of monopoly through a hierarchy of centres of surplus expropriation/appropriation (extraction and transfer), the top of which lay in the capitalist metropoles; and that the bottom of the hierarchy consisted of institutions established for this purpose, hence capitalist institutions, not feudal institutions (the latifundium was "born as a commercial enterprise").[16] The conditions of servitude on the latifundium were only "fuedal -seeming", for the latifundium was not an institution "beyond the reach of capitalist development". The practical implication of this view seemed to be that the task of the revolution was not one of first overthrowing feudalism in Latin America, and only then going on to overthrow capitalism; and hence it was not a question of the proletariat and peasantry allying with the national bourgeoisie against feudal landlords; on the contrary, the feudal-seeming landowners were really capitalist and both they and the so-called "national" bourgeoisie were playing and had always played a subordinate role in alliance with imperialism, so that the struggle of the workers and peasants must be waged against all of them, and must be a struggle to move from capitalism to socialism.

Laclau in his well known critique points out that (a) this conceptualisation includes in "capitalism" all productive processes, and the social formations dominated by them, which are in a significant exchange relationship with capitalist social formations (so that e.g. Russia in 1850 would presumably have to be described as "capitalist"); (b) capital, in the form of merchant capital, was being accumulated long before capitalism - i.e. social formations dominated by the capitalist mode of production - was established; in particular, long distance trade and commodity markets existed long before capitalism.[17] The colonisation of Latin America was in fact a feudal colonisation, the response of Iberian feudalism to a general feudal economic crisis which could be relieved (though not resolved) by extending the area of land under servile cultivation through overseas expansion. The latifundium was not a "feudal-seeming" but really a feudal institution. Subsequently, with the establishment of capitalism as a dominant mode of production in parts of Western Europe, there arose a world capitalist system, i.e. primarily a system of (unequal) exchange linking social formations dominated by pre-capitalist modes of production, including those of Latin America, to those dominated by the capitalist mode of production. The effect was to consolidate the pre-capitalist modes of production, not to destroy them (for reasons touched on below). This means that the first revolutionary task in such situations is to overthrow the pre-capitalist relations of production, and the corresponding superstructures. Specifically, it means that in some parts of the world the revolution has to accomplish some of the tasks historically undertaken by the bourgeois-democratic revolution in Europe before the task of building socialism can be tackled - liberating servile labour, democratising national and local institutions, abolishing all kinds of privileges, taboos, destroying archaic forms of ideological domination, etc. It follows that any call for "socialist revolution" which ignores this, and the strategy, organisation, programme, alliances, etc. which it implies, will be utopian. At any rate, Laclau argues, such vital issues cannot even be posed in terms of the formulations used by Frank.

This has been endorsed in various forms by writers such as Bettelheim and Rey who can be lumped together as theorists of the problematic of the "articulation" of different modes of production.[18] According to this view, the way in which the capitalist mode of production is "articulated" with precapitalist modes of production which continue to exist in the era of capitalism constitutes, in Rey's terms, the "field of contradictions" of the class struggles in the social formations where this articulation occurs (above all, in underdeveloped areas). This field is determined by capitalism's need to "conserve" the precapitalist modes of production at the same time as it "dissolves" them (i.e. it transforms them from modes of production subject to their own "laws of motion" to modes of production whose motion is primarily determined by the laws operating in the capitalist mode of production, and hence also progressively transforms the content, and eventually the form, of their relations of production).

Reacting against this in turn Banaji has recently argued that writers of this school, including Laclau, reduce the meaning of "mode of production" to that of "mode of exploitation", or "form of the labour process", a "simple category" of analysis, like an ideal type, formed by abstracting a few empirical features from a given situation.[19] On this basis a "feudal mode of production" is held to exist whenever labour is serf-like, i.e. one slave plantation does not make a slave mode of production, nor yet to quite a number. What constitutes a slave mode of production in the historical sense is a much wider ensemble of relations, including class, state and ideological relations, which together are governed by determinate "laws of motion" which at the level of any given <u>enterprise</u> (in this case, a plantation) is revealed in the logic of its operations, the economic motivation of its owners and managers (production for social consumption not for profit), the specific rationality of its production, consumption, savings and investment decisions, the degree of exploitation of its labour force, etc. On this basis the plantations of the West Indies were capitalist notwithstanding the reality of the slavery on which they rested,[20] the twentieth century plantations established in Peru by large US and British firms using forms of servile labour are capitalist, not feudal; and the peasants of Kenya who produce leaf for capitalist tea companies at a closely controlled price are a kind of wage labourers, not participants in a "peasant mode of production". In other words, Banaji agrees with Laclau that the Latin American latifundium was a feudal institution but disagrees with him in thinking that the persistence of its feudal form necessarily implies the continuance of its feudal <u>content</u> once the "laws of motion" of feudalism, to which it was once subject, have been displaced by the "laws of motion" of the capitalist mode of production, as increasingly occurred from the seventeenth century to the nineteenth. The political implication of this seems to be that the nature of the revolutionary task is different in cases where a pre-capitalist mode of production has really survived, from those where its forms may have survived, and even become more "highly developed" (as Banaji considers happened in Europe to feudal production precisely when it began to be subordinated to capitalism), but where its laws of motion have ceased to be at all autonomous.

These general formulations sometimes have a rather abstract and even scholastic quality, but it seems to me they must be taken seriously. The alternative is only new forms of utopianism. At the same time I think both Laclau and Banaji's presentation of the matter suffers from a neglect of its political aspect, i.e. of class struggle and class domination (including state power). This does not mean that this aspect is "given" and can be known independently of the determination of the mode(s) of production, forms of labour process, etc.; but just as Banaji thinks that modes of production cannot be determined merely be reference to the mode of exploitation, but must be "living" ensembles of relationships with a definite "logic" and historical tendencies, so I do not think they can be determined independently of the determination of the classes, forms of state, etc., which are based on them and which also determine their development. (The same point was made in another context by Bettelheim in his debate with Sweezy.)[21] I suspect in fact that the apparent abstractness (and some of the difficulty) of the problem of deciding whether a pre-capitalist mode of production still "exists" in a particular situation or just how far and in what ways it is being transformed into a mere subordinate form of the capitalist mode, disappears when it is firmly linked to the problem of exploring the past and present course of class formation and class struggles.

c. Why does capitalism "underdevelop" some countries? Laclau pointed out that UDT really sidesteps this issue; Frank, in particular, sees a single contradiction between the bourgeoisie in the metropole and the masses in the periphery from the sixteenth century till today. But if the initial dependency was one within feudalism, the reasons for it cannot be identical with those which explain capitalist dependency. Laclau holds that the initial feudal dependence turned on unequal exchange between Latin America and Europe, made possible by holding down price levels in Latin America by an extremely ruthless use of servile forms of labour, thereby "reducing the economic surplus of the peripheral countries and fixing their relations of production in an archaic mould of extra-economic coercion, which retarded any process of social differentiation and diminished the size of their internal markets".[22] Subsequent <u>capitalist</u> underdevelopment (i.e. once the capitalist mode of production had become dominant in Europe in the nineteenth century) was due to a different central cause, the decline in the rate of profit caused by the increasing organic composition of capital. The maintenance of pre-capitalist modes of production in the colonies and semi-colonies, he hypothesises, maintained the average rate of profit by offering opportunities for high rates of return due to the low organic composition of capital and the use of extra-economic coercion of labour in those modes. This hypothesis refers to the competitive phase of capitalism and explains capitalist underdevelopment in that stage only.

Kay, as I understand him, takes a different view. Labour at the periphery may have been (and may still be) subject to extra-economic coercion and also may be paid a much lower real wage than the "free labour" of the metropoles but it does not follow from this that profit rates are higher; this depends on the relative rates of surplus value and ratios of constant to variable capital at the centre and at the periphery. Part of what seems to be at issue here is an empirical question, which Laclau poses: during the nineteenth century was the growth in the organic composition of capital in fact more rapid than the growth in the productivity of labour in the metropoles? If it was, the profit rate would have tended to fall and the maintenance of pre-capitalist modes of production at the periphery would have tended to offset this for the reasons Laclau suggests. If it was not, the rate of profit would have tended to rise, not fall, and the only reason for capital to be invested in the periphery at all would be to secure particular commodities needed for production in the metropole (cotton, minerals, etc.) and cheap foodstuffs (reducing the value of the real wages paid in the metropole). Working on the latter assumption, Kay suggests that the explanation of capitalist underdevelopment is really historical and structural, and is to be sought in the special characteristics of merchant capital. Merchant capital, he argues, deriving its profits entirely from unequal exchange and from maximising the flow of transactions, destroyed the pre-existing social frameworks in the periphery (Kay evidently has Africa particularly in mind); and actually created conditions inimical to the investment of industrial capital which, once it gained supremacy over merchant capital in the metropoles, sought quite limited ends in the periphery (cheap raw materials and food supplies) using merchant capital as its agent. Playing this role of agent, merchant capital was forced to maintain the forms of pre-capitalist modes of production, and social relations of production, in order to maximise the production of commodities for metropolitan markets, and maintain conditions for regular and reliable trading.[23]

Although there seems to be some difficulty with both these views, they have the great merit of being genuine theories, and I suspect that if they are understood as theories applicable to more limited places - i.e. Latin America and Africa respectively - and to specific phases of metropolitan development - they will prove capable of contributing to the sort of general theory that is needed.

CONCLUDING REMARKS: THEORY AND PRACTICE

Consideration of these theoretical questions serves to suggest once more that a large part of the difficulty of resolving many of them is due to the same cause that is ultimately responsible for the ideological nature of UDT itself - a particular form of political practice. In the case of UDT that practice, it is safe to say, was primarily that of planners in the state apparatuses (planning offices) of third world countries, of their advisers and mediators (with international capital) in regional economic policy bureaux, such as ECLA, and of the personnel of the "aid and trade" network, from UNCTAD to the IBRD/IMF. The underdevelopment and dependency "perspective" really expressed the "unhappy consciousness" of progressive intellectuals (including academics) within or close to this set of institutions, on or just over the dividing line between reluctant acceptance and impatient rejection of the structure, but not starting out from or conditioned by involvement in the entirely different practice of a radical working class or peasant party. The ambiguities of UDT reflect the ambiguities of their position.

The work of the critics of UDT, on the other hand, while it may be much less ambiguous, does show a tendency to theoreticism, abstractness and generality, reflecting perhaps the primarily academic practice of most of those concerned. There is, certainly, no uniquely certified connection between theory and the political practice of the exploited and oppressed classes, and the problem of making any such connection is aggravated by the difficulty, in many parts of the third world, of identifying effective current forms of popular politics, and establishing links with them. Nonetheless it looks as if it will be very important to resolve this question as a condition of useful theoretical advance.

NOTES

1. Cf. F.H. Cardoso, "Imperialism and Dependency in Latin America" in Bonilla and Girling (eds.), Structures of Dependency, 1973, pp. 15-16.

2. See for instance, "A Dependency Bibliography" by William C. Smith Jr., in Bonilla and Girling, op.cit.

3. Philip J. O'Brien, "A Critique of Latin American Theories of Dependency" in L. Oxaal, T. Barnett and D. Booth (eds.), Beyond the Sociology of Development, 1975, p. 25.

4. Cf. C. Bettelheim in Appendices I and III to A. Emmanuel, Unequal Exchange, 1972, pp. 300-07 and 352-55, and A. Emmanuel, ibid., Appendix IV, pp. 380-83; and G. Kay, Development and Underdevelopment: A Marxist Analysis, 1975, p. 55.

5. D. Booth, "Andre Gunder Frank: An Introduction and an Appreciation", in Oxaal et.al., op.cit., pp. 75-76.

6. See notes 3 and 5 above; and A. Foster Carter, "Neo-Marxist Approaches to Underdevelopment" in E. De Kadt and G. Williams (eds.), Sociology and Development, 1973, and N. Girvan, "The Development of Dependency Economics in the Caribbean and Latin America", Social and Economic Studies 22/1, 1973.

7. Cf. Girvan, op.cit., and L. Best, "A Model of Pure Plantation Economy", Social and Economic Studies 17/3, 1968.

8. Loc.cit., p. 11; italics added.

9. Cf. Leys, Underdevelopment in Kenya, 1975, esp. Ch. 6

10. "Dependence is Dead, Long Live Dependence and the Class Struggle: An Answer to Critics", Latin American Perspectives 1/1, 1974.

11. A study of MacNamara's speeches in the past five years shows that a remarkably large proportion of the main theses of UDT have been incorporated in them, though naturally in skilfully deradicalised versions. For an official systematisation see the IBRD/IDS study, Redistribution with Growth, 1975, which is criticised, with replies by some of the authors, in Leys, "The Politics of Redistribution With Growth", IDS Bulletin 7/2, 1975.

12. Cf. S. Amin, Unequal Development, 1976; and Frank, "Sociology of Underdevelopment and Underdevelopment of Sociology", in Latin America: Reform or Revolution.

13. I. Wallerstein, The Modern World System, 1974; P. Anderson, Passages from Antiquity to Feudalism, 1975, and Lineages of the Absolutist State, 1975.

14. Kay, op.cit., pp. 50-54 and 115-16.

15. Emmanuel, loc.cit., pp. 382-83.

16. A.G. Frank, Capitalism and Underdevelopment in Latin America, 1967.

17. E. Laclau, "Feudalism and Capitalism in Latin America", New Left Review, 67, 1971.

18. Cf. C. Bettelheim in Appendix I to Emmanuel, op.cit., pp. 293-99; and P-P. Rey, Les Alliances des Classes, 1973.

19. J. Banaji, "Modes of Production in a Materialist Conception of History", Economy and Society, forthcoming.

20. An interpretation which seems to have the explicit endorsement of Marx: "The fact that we now not only

call the plantation owners in America capitalists, but that they _are_ capitalists, is based on their existence as anomalies within a world market based on free labour" (_Grundrisse_, p. 513).

21. Cf. P. Sweezy and C. Bettelheim, _On the Transition to Socialism_, 1971, pp. 15-17.

22. Laclau, _op.cit._, p. 35.

23. Kay, _op.cit._, pp. 105-7.

Chapter 4

ACCUMULATION ON A WORLD SCALE

P. Thandika Mkandawire

The publication by Monthly Review Press of Samir Amin's major work opens to the Anglo-Saxon world a very important school in the study of the problems of underdevelopment. Sometimes referred to as the "Dependency School", it has had great impact on students of underdevelopment in French and Spanish-speaking countries. This "school" is, of course, far from homogeneous since it includes such diverse schools as "structuralists", radical liberals and Marxists. What all the members of this school have in common is an acute awareness of the problems arising from the bifurcation of the capitalist world into "centre" and "periphery" economies and the impact of the relationship between these economies on the development and under-development of the latter.

Samir Amin, Director of the United Nations African Institute for Development and Economic Planning in Dakar, Senegal, is a Marxist. As a Marxist, he is seriously pre-occupied with the historical character of underdevelopment of backward countries. Of course, this pre-occupation with the historical nature of underdevelopment is not the monopoly of Marxists. Bourgeois historians such as Rostow and Kuznets, to name only a few, have spent much effort to study the process of development in today's developed nations with the hope of discovering the laws of development, or a set of conditions which, if properly reproduced in the underdeveloped countries, can bring about those processes which characterized the growth of the materially advanced nations. From these historical studies, certain "paradigms" have been constructed to depict the possible course of transition of the underdeveloped countries. Generally missing in these historical studies is a history of underdevelopment itself. In fact, in the more dogmatic formulation of the bourgeois historical view, the underdeveloped countries are viewed as a "pre-historical" in the sense that they have as yet to enter the historically established path towards self-sustained growth. Even where some history is conceded to these countries the profound impact of their colonial experience and their domination by the metropolitan countries is treated as some unfortunate, albeit necessary, thing of the past with no lasting impact upon the present and future of these countries.

For Marxists, this perception of the historical process of development and underdevelopment is merely formal and ahistorical. In particular, it fails to take into consideration that historical time is not uni-linear and that future societies will not be able to replicate the paths traversed by other societies at a previous time. In the words of Dos Santos:

> " All societies move towards new forms of society. The historical experience of developed capitalist societies has been completely transcended; their basic source of private capital formation in foreign trade, the incorporation of vast masses of workers in industrial production, their indigenous technological development, constitute options no longer open to underdeveloped countries."

The historical origins and context of contemporary backwardness then suggests that new models of accumulation must be constructed to deal with the new phenomenon of "dependent accumulation". Attempts by bourgeois economists to construct models for the study of development have generally started with the elimination of this historical problem. Strange as it may seem in face of mounting historical evidence, the most elegant models of accumulation in underdeveloped countries (the Arthur Lewis and Fei-Ranis models, for example) have assumed "closed" underdeveloped economies in which accumulation is autocentric. Foreign trade and the exploitative relations with the metropolitan powers may later be introduced into the models as a further complication of an otherwise autonomous accumulation process.

Samir Amin takes the "openness" of these backward economies as the crucial impetus to their present experiences and problems. He starts his study with the observation that the process of underdevelopment has taken place within the global context of capitalist accumulation and dependence for the periphery economies. It is precisely the absence of autocentric expansion in the dependent economies that has characterized their accumulation process. An economy experiencing autocentric accumulation must at least have one sector to produce the means of production (the capital goods sector) and another one producing mass consumption goods to feed the workers employed in both sectors. Marx, basing his theoretical abstraction on the historical experience of England, developed the famous 'two department schema' for the study of capitalist accumulation in an essentially auto-centric structure. Unfortunately, this historically valid abstraction has been abused in forms of "two-sector" models that have been put forward as useful abstractions for the dependent economies of today. Amin demonstrates convincingly that the dependent economies lack the structural coherence that was implied earlier in the Marxian two department schema and later in the "two sector models" of growth. The dominant linkages in these economies are those between an export sector and a "luxury goods" sector. In most cases, the capital goods sector is totally lacking and where it exists, it is linked either to the export sector or "luxury goods" sector and not to the mass consumption goods sector which was historically the case in the advanced countries.

A recurring point in Amin's book is that the centre-periphery relationship implies dominance and, therefore, inequality and disharmony. Today most economists would concede that colonial rule implied economic exploitation, although some (like Rostow) would justify colonialism as the necesary "shock" to "traditional societies". Generally, however, bourgeois economists consider exploitation as basically a political problem in the sense that the removal of any extraeconomical means of domination by, say, granting political independence, allows for the operation of the "law of comparative advantage" in a way beneficial to all parties. Such a law guarantees equal exchange since all "factors of production" are rewarded according to their marginal productivities and there is a general tendency towards the equalization of factor prices that countervails any such disharmonious processes as uneven development. Amin challenges this dogma with the "Theory of Unequal Exchange" as developed by Emmanuel.[2] There are two versions of the "Theory of Unequal Exchange". one is the neo-Ricardian one based on the theoretical work of Sraffa and the so-called Cambridge School and the other is the Marxian one. In the Sraffian version, the main thrust of the theory is to challenge the neoclassical theory of production and distribution. More specifically the neo-Ricardian critique has destroyed the basis of the neoclassical claim that "rewards to the factors of production" (or income distribution) is purely a market phenomenon by showing that there is no such thing as "capital" which is quantifiable without a knowledge of prices (and, therefore, income distribution). We cannot, therefore, derive the structure of income distribution by knowing the 'marginal productivity' of factors whose quantity cannot be obtained without prior knowledge of income distribution. The implication of this thesis on international trade is only now beginning to be perceived but it does pose a serious problem to the believers of theorems of "comparative advantage" since it brings back the political element in the distribution of income between nations and classes.

The Marxian theory of "Unequal Exchange" used by Amin starts from the distinction between values and prices. Amin observes that a large number of the export commodities of the underdeveloped countries are produced with modern technology so that the productivity of labour in the periphery and the centre is equalized for these commodities. Although monopoly is rampant, the law of the equalization of profit rates does still operate under capitalism. But the wages of periphery economies are much lower than those of the centre, even for equal labour productivities. Under such conditions, the rate of exploitation of labour is much higher in the periphery economies. The transformation of values into prices on the assumption that the rates of profit are equalized, demands that values be transferred from economies with higher rates of surplus (exploitation) to those with lower rates of surplus. This is, of course, the old "transformation problem" of Marx except that while in Marx the transfer of values was necessitated by the differences in the organic composition of capital and, therefore, different rates of surplus given same wage rates, in the Amin version the differences in the rate of surplus are due to differences in the "organic composition of labour" or wage rates. The theories of unequal exchange are still in an embryonic stage but they promise to shed light on the current world division of labour and the resultant international specialization.

As a result of the dominance the non-equivalence of exchange and the asymmetric international specialization, there have emerged certain peculiar social formations in the periphery. While as in both the centre and periphery capitalism is dominant it has not achieved the exclusivity in the periphery that it immediately achieved in the centre by destroying pre-capitalist agriculture and industry and replacing these with purely capitalist forms of organization and production. Thus at the periphery, capitalism remains dominant without being exclusive. It has destroyed pre-capitalist handicraft and agriculture without replacing them with capitalist ones so that the social formations of the peripheries consist of modern capitalist structures and deformed pre-capitalist structures. This is not one more crude version of the structural asymmetry of the peripheries that goes under the term "dualism" since in Amin's version the deformed pre-capitalist structures were an intergral part of the process of the assimilation of the underdeveloped countries into the world capitalist order. The modern capitalist part and the deformed precapitalist are constituent parts of a whole - the dependent economy.

Another important characteristic of the social formations that emerge from this dependence is the predominance of agrarian and commercial capitalism in the national sector, industrial capitalism being in the foreign sector. Agricultural and commercial activities are about the only activities in which the national bourgeoisies has room to stretch its puny muscles without being gobbled up by the transnational giants. The weakness of the local bourgeoisie vis-a-vis foreign capital largely explains the tendency to a peculiar form of development towards bureaucratic structures. The ideological expression of this type of 'statism' takes the form of certain particularized "socialisms" (Islamic socialism, African socialism etc). The hopes by the local bourgeois to achieve autonomy by increased state participation in the economy never become more than just that - hopes. In the first place it is never quite clear whether it is the state that "nationalizes" foreign private capital or foreign private capital that "privatizes" the state. And in the second place as long as state ownership does not lead to disengagement from the world capitalist system, the dependent economy simply continues to play the same vicious subordinate role, only this time under the guise of "state ownership".

Given these structural and institutional developments, the periphery economy is faced with problems of transition that were never experienced by today's advanced nations in the early stages of their development. The onslaught from without, by means of trade, carried out by the capitalist mode of production upon the pre-capitalist modes of production, causes certain retrogression such as the ruin of crafts without their being replaced by local industrial production. This has contributed to extreme sectoral inequalities in productivity in the periphery and the system of prices transmitted to it from the centre has led to forms of income distribution not conducive to the development of a balanced industrial structure.

Furthermore, there is a disarticulation of the periphery economy due to the adjustment of the orientation of production to the needs of the centre which prevents the transmission of the benefits of economic progress from the dynamic poles of the economy to other sectors since large parts of economic activities are progressively "marginalised" in the course of dependent accumulation.

Clearly, in such economies structural paradigms developed for the study of centre economies have limited application. Amin discusses at length the truncated impact of the Keynesian multiplier and accelerator as a result of the structural incoherence of periphery economies. In these economies, it is not the traditional "leakages" such as hoarding and imports that account for the restricted impact. Rather it is (a) the absence of linkages in both consumption and production and (b)export of monopoly superprofits that have the effect of transferring the impact of the multiplier and accelerator to the centre economies.

Although Amin's discussion of the limits of Keynesian analysis is well-taken, I believe he unnecessarily belabours the point about the inadequacy or inappropriateness of the Keynesian policies in the study of periphery economies. Most conventional economists would agree.

The Keynesian aggregative model, in which multiplier

income effects of a single injection of purchasing power play so crucial a role, conceives the underemployment equilibrium in terms of idle capacity, involuntary unemployment and a generally elastic supply curve of output. It is now generally accepted that in underdeveloped countries there is no involuntary unemployment at least insofar as employment cannot be stimulated simply by an increase in effective demand. Nor does observed excess capacity in the periphery economies suggest an elastic supply curve of output since there are so many other bottlenecks other than inadequate demand that restrict full utilization of capacity in the industries of the periphery. Indeed, about the only concept borrowed from Keynesian analysis that has been extensively used (and abused) has been the Harrod-Domar capital-output ratio, a concept that Amin correctly observes is easily derivable from Marxian analysis.

Amin's unduly long criticism of Keynesian economics is extended to a critique of Kalecki which I found hard to swallow. Amin seems opposed to any theories that confine themselves to the realm of prices and do not introduce, analysis in terms of value but I believe this is a misunderstanding on the part of Amin of the relationship between values and prices in Marx. Price analysis is important in Marx. Indeed, the whole point of the "transformation of values and prices" was to show that the value system, the quantity system and the price system are an integral part of the capitalist system. The value analysis is an instrument to lay bare the social relationships between men which are hidden behind the veil of exchange. The quantity system shows the technolgoical properties of production while prices, because they are directly observed, are used as the basis for decision-making and, therefore, have a practical meaning. Where perfect competition prevails, the relationship between these three is quite straightforward. When monopoly arises, however, there are serious divergencies between these systems and a price analysis without any direct reference to values becomes necessary. The only fundamental relationship between value and prices that remains is that a positive rate of surplus in the value system is a necessary condition for a positive profit rate in the price system. The inequality in the rates of profits (due to monopoly) calls for an entirely different analysis of capitalist accumulation and it is in this sense that Kalecki's work and that of Baran and Sweezy are an important contribution to Marxist economics. It is strange that Amin who embraces Baran's and Sweezy's contribution fails to see the similarity between their contribution and that of Kalecki.

In any case, the most significant negative effect of the Keynesian system has not been so much the belief by economists in the applicability of its policy recommendations to the periphery economies as the adoption of its categories of analysis (national income accounting systems) used in the empirical studies of underdevelopment. The Keynesian preoccupation with final demand obscures the actual process of the production of commodities by means of commodities and labour that one derives from the Marxian and input-output systems. It is this empirical application of Keynesian categories that vitiates the works of such economic historians as Kuznets since in the Keynesian system the notion of the study of accumulation - simply vanishes.

Amin's views on the socialist countries of Eastern Europe raise some important questions. For Amin, these countries are no more than bureaucratized capitalism. This view prevents him from really integrating the economies of these countries in a study purported to be a study of "accumulation on a world scale" although these countries together account for more than 30% of world production. The laws of accumulation in these countries differ significantly enough from those of either the periphery or monopoly capitalism to warrant a separate treatment. It would also be interesting to know what Amin thinks is the role of these countries in attempts by the periphery countries to "disengage" from the world capitalist system. Surely, the presence of the socialist bloc has facilitated (militarily and economically) the disengagement of some of the periphery countries from the world capitalist system. One need only mention Vietnam, Cuba and North Korea in this respect and it would not be too farfetched to include China in this list.

It is sometimes said that economic assistance from the socialist countries has done nothing to alter the structures that reproduce dependence and underdevelopment but I believe this is more a reflection on the dependent economies than on the exploitative intentions of the socialist countries. No socialist country can force a dependent "sovereign" state to use a donated textile mill to produce clothing for the masses. In fact, what we see in practice is that cloth produced in "friendship" textile mills is just as likely to be exported as that produced in foreign capitalist mills. There are times when socialist economic assistance turns out to be no more than subsidy to capitalism particularly with the growing tolerance of the West towards socialist aid in infrastructure. Amin's dismissal of socialist accumulation leaves one with the impression that not only does he have an extremely elastic view of capitalist accumulation but that his call for "disengagement" is rather utopian since it tends to negate all attempts to disengage (except perhaps the Chinese one) that have so far been made.

NOTES

1. T. Dos Santos "The Crisis of Development Theory and the Problem of Dependence in Latin America", in H.

Berstein, Underdevelopment and Development (Penguin, 1973).

2. A Emmanuel, Unequal Exchange: A Study of the Imperialism of Trade, (Monthly Review Press, New York, 1972).

Chapter 5

SAMIR AMIN ON UNDERDEVELOPMENT

Richard Leaver

With the end of yet another development decade drawing near, a strange situation can be observed in the trends of inquiry into the dialectic of development and underdevelopment. A decade ago, this academic field was the near-exclusive preserve of left-liberal theorists, and the Marxist input was clearly a secondary current; today the reverse is more nearly true. As if this is not odd enough in itself, it is equally peculiar to witness the increasingly intense level of debate amongst Marxists, a debate which seems to have gathered momentum and fed off their increasing dominance of the field. The label of Marxist is no longer self-explanatory; everyone is liable to identify themselves as a Marxist, but of a different sort. Marxism has almost become the exemplar of pluralism.

This increasing schism amongst self-proclaimed Marxists is partially testified by the recent shift in the arguments of Aidan Foster-Carter, who has enjoyed the status of a disseminator of knowledge within Marxist circles. Over the last five years Foster-Carter was intent upon delimiting the parameters of what he perceived as a distinctive 'neo-marxist paradigm' that was invading development studies which stood apart from both classical Marxism and the liberal sub-discipline of economic development.[1] But more recently, even he has been forced by this pluralist tendency to throw up his hands in despair at the futility of his task of finding a common denominator for such a paradigm.[2] Other recent work by Marxists in related fields exhibits increasing concern over the possibility of a crisis in Marxist theory itself stemming from this division of interest and opinion.[3] Anyone familiar with the recent work of scholars such as Emmanuel, Kay, Warren and Frank cannot but be struck by the substantive points of disagreement between them. The issues are complicated enough without even considering the exponential growth of the secondary literature witnessed in the recent books of Nabudere, Saul, Arrighi and Caldwell.

It seems particularly inappropriate to describe this current situation in development studies as constituting a paradigm shift. This is not only because of the difficulty of identifying a 'neo-marxist paradigm', but also because there has been no major defection of liberals towards any alliance with Marxism. The dynamics of development studies is best depicted as the waxing and waning of two quite independent traditions,[4] each with its own debates and problems, and addressing each other in an eye-to-eye confrontation at only a few nodal points. The decline of liberal development studies has little to do with the embarrassing questions asked of it by radicals. Rather, this fall from grace is to be explained almost entirely in terms of the practical failures of the tradition. This has led to a certain amount of theoretical introspection and recantation - and even some inoffensive alliances with radical phraseology - but there has been little systematic attention paid to the foundations of liberal social sciences as genus, or the relationship between the discrete 'disciplines' constituted by that tradition.

The rejuvenation of Marxist thought in development studies draws primarily from a number of theoretical developments internal to the history of Marxism; its dynamism is not externally oriented. The most important of these begin from the critique of the theory and practice of Stalinism. This project, which has occupied a variety of theorists ranging from Mao to Althusser, has succeeded in eliminating, as the vector resultant of these different thrusts, the simple evolutionary teleology which was passed off as historical materialism by the Soviet state. The publication in 1964 of Marx's Pre-Capitalist Economic Formations was a significant milestone in removing the maker's seal of approval from this 'automatic Marxism', although it did little to direct the reconstruction of Marxism which remained as a problem.

The form in which Marxism has been remade has developed unevenly and out of quite different traditions. Even in 1964, continental Marxism was marked both by the debate on unequal exchange, and by the early work of Godelier concerned to turn historical materialism into a living method capable of bringing together the disparate liberal 'disciplines'. Apart from occasional glimpses, neither of these influences were felt in English-speaking circles for another decade. There the tendency of the times was well captured in the title of Oliver Cox's 1964 book, Capitalism as a System. This book is hardly a 'lost classic', but its title does show the persistent epistemology. The line of inheritance of this tendency can be traced back to the peculiar reading of Durkheim by Radcliffe-Brown that inspired British Social Anthropology and which was very influential in left circles at the time[5]. Contemporary 'neo-marxism' is one site of this incipient debate between structural and structuralist methods.[6]

In this context, the translation into English of the four major theoretical works of Samir Amin within the space of five years serves an important bridging function for English-speaking Marxists concerned to break out of the structural impasse. For quite apart from his stupendous rate of output, Amin has increasingly refined the structuralist contribution to contemporary 'neo-marxism'. He also possesses a comprehensive knowledge of conventional development economics, and it was the critique of that field which absorbed a disproportionately large share of his Accumulation on a World Scale.[7] His more recent Unequal Development,[8] although repetitive at times, is concerned particularly with the characteristics and dynamic properties of the social formations of peripheral capitalism. Imperialism and Unequal Development[9] is an uneven collection of essays intended to complement the latter as a companion volume; its quality is primarily redeemed by the final seventy page essay "The End of a Debate", first written in French in the early seventies and occasionally alluded to in the footnotes of the literature. This review will look at some of the themes that emerge from these works which seem particularly significant to the direction of "neo-marxism" in general, and forward a few tentative criticisms on the way forward.

MARX,"NEO-MARXISM" AND PERIODIZATION

One of the paradoxes of the "neo-marxist" revival has been the rather strained relationship it has established with Marx's own work. It is well known that Marx's writings on the non-European world, although slight and often journalistic in style, were hardly complimentary; in fact, he is best remembered on this question by the rather provocative throw-away lines and analogies which made such lively reading. We have, for instance, his rather open disgust for the stultifying effects of village life, his analogy between the political consciousness of peasants and a sack of potatoes, and the apparent determinism whereby colonialism was seen as a progressive force in destroying the stagnancy of the Asiatic mode of production by introducing an external dynamism into the growth of the forces of production.[10] In all of these arguments, Marx was quite demonstrably following in the footsteps of the established prejudices of European scholarship on the non-west.[11] Many "neo-marxists" have been forced to argue that Marx was eurocentric in his thought and that their own work breaks with this practice by providing an anlysis of imperialism from "the perspective of the periphery". Reconciliations with the spirit of marxism have hinged on the weak argument that Marx's oriental writings were not to be taken too seriously.

It is to Amin's credit that he disposes of this

ideological problem and restores the writings of Marx to their proper place. He argues, in essence, that the object of analysis of "neo-marxism" is substantially different from that of Marx. Marx was concerned to analyse the laws of tendency within the "pure" capitalist mode of production, while the "neo-marxist" revival has a different task - the investigation of the contemporary form of the capitalist world system and the manner in which this system constrains and involutes the development of the periphery. In other words, the world capitalist system cannot be reduced to the capitalist mode of production. The system deals with relations between social formations which are not reducible to the status of "economistic laws". The analysis of this system requires us to return to the "global plan of historical materialism", Marx's ultimate legacy, and to implement that plan in its "true worldwide context". For this task, Amin reaches out to Althusser and his followers for the appropriate concepts of modes of production, social formation, the articulation of instances, etc.[12]

He also argues that Marx's works on the non-west must be situated as products of their epoch. This means more than the simple but true observation that Marx's sources on the non-west were rudimentary; it involves a comprehension of the periodization of the capitalist system, of the different functions assigned to the periphery in each of those periods, and of the different consequences for the periphery which flowed out of each period. Amin reminds us that Marx lived in the period of competitive capitalism when colonialism referred either to the case of the "white dominions" or the trading monopolies of the mercantilist period. One characteristic of this period was the favourable movement of the terms of trade to the benefit of the periphery which reflected the rapidity of technological progress at the centre of the system. Wage levels at the centre were at near-subsistence levels, a consequence of the importation of consumption goods and cheap raw materials from the periphery. The distinctive specialization in world trade established in this period kept the rate of profit at the centre high by keeping wages at the centre low. All of these characteristics were to change with the growth of monopolies at the centre.

The importance of Lenin's theory of imperialism to Amin can hardly be overstressed. In an age where Lenin's theory is so many different things to different people - and in particular, where the dominant tendency is to stress Lenin's legacy from Hobson[13] - Amin is content to return to fundamentals. Lenin is praised for realizing that the growth of monopolies at the centre and their extension went hand-in-hand with the formation of revisionist social democracy as the ideology of the labour aristocracy. Equally important, monopolies made possible the rapid expansion of the export of capital. It was the export of capital which had the effect of reconstituting the world capitalist system on a higher basis; thus it marked off a new period in the history of the system as a whole. Capital exports had the consequence of making the costs of production in different social formations common knowledge. Earlier forms of expansionism and long-distance trade provided no benchmark for the comparison of prices of production across national boundaries, and exploitation was founded only on the differential subjective valuation of the worth of commodities. But once capital from the centre, partaking in the generalized equalization of profit rates, was located in the periphery, exploitation of the periphery took the form of unequal exchange because wage differentials between centre and periphery outstripped the respective productivity differentials. The exploitation of the periphery became more systematic in form.

The periodization makes good sense. But regardless of whether one agrees with it or not, Amin should be congratulated for encouraging "neo-marxists" to think about the different forms taken by the world capitalist system, and the different functions performed by the periphery at different points in time. The truth of the matter is that structural "neo-marxists" have tended to see the world capitalist system in a highly aggregative manner; Frank, for instance, invited us to stress the continuities of the system as a whole over the particularities of any given situation.[14] This exaggerated sense of permanence and constancy across time and space reflects the time-honoured problem that the structural method has had with systemic change - a luxury that can no longer be afforded in an age when the extent of differentiation within the periphery is proceeding at a rapid rate and the system is in the throes of reorganization. Phenomena such as OPEC, the de-domiciling of capital, the continuing political unity of the "Third World" and the onset of neo-mercantilist tendencies amongst OECD states can hardly begin to be understood using such undifferentiated concepts.

Amin's interpretation of Lenin will also prove provocative. He is strongly opposed to the underconsumptionist interpretation of Lenin and the rather Stalinist conception of "necessity" which accompanies it. The export of capital is not pre-ordained; it is as much a product of the class struggle and the rise of labour aristocracies as it is of economic "laws".[15] Amin always employs the idea of a "law" very flexibly. So, for instance, while he argues that there is an inherent contradiction between the capacity to produce and the capacity to consume within the capitalist mode of production, that contradiction never comes to fruition in a generalized crisis.[16] Luxemburg is reproached for failing to see the active role played by credit in expanded reproduction of the capitalist mode. The "solutions" are dictated by the structure of the class struggle, and each of them displaces this contradiction in specific ways. But the "lonely moment of the last instance" never comes. Such intepretations should be welcomed.

CHARACTERIZING THE SYSTEM: UNEQUAL EXCHANGE

For Amin, the whole of the liberal disicipline of development economics is "pre-Leninist" - that is, it is erected upon the assumption that the national economy takes precedence over the world economy, and that the latter is merely a "spillover" of the former. It might well be added that when liberal social science breaks with this image, as both political and economic analysis have tended to do in reaction to OPEC and the MNC's, it tends to the opposite extreme of stressing the homogeneity of the globe with "cobweb models" and talk of "interdependence". "Neo-marxism" has always carved out a distinctive niche for itself by accepting the primacy of the whole over the parts and by distinguishing between the centre and the periphery of that unity. But whereas structural "neo-marxists" merely asserted this organic analogy, Amin tries very hard to pin down the kernel which makes it a living reality. It is a clear indication of his structuralist proclivities that he turns to the concept of value to identify the basis of the system.

Amin's position on this matter finds its most mature expression in his above-mentioned essay "The End of a Debate", where it is elaborated in the context of his critique of Emmanuel and Bettelheim's contributions to the theory of unequal exhchange. The crucial problem here concerns the scope and function of the concept of value in Marxist theory, and the manner in which calculations of value can be harmonized with historical materialism as a method. Amin finds little sustenance in the discoveries of neo-classical economics; the idea of value present in classical economics becomes totally subjective and tautological under this influence, making comparisons across national boundaries meaningless and denying any systemic qualities to the international economy by adhering to the outdated Ricardian assumptions of mobile labour and immobile capital. Furthermore, neo-classicism begins from pre-given consumer preferences which necessarily exalt the use-value of commodities and posit a supra-human rationality of exchange which can in no way be reconciled with the prevailing conditions of production. The result is psychologism run wild; economics is transformed into "the ideology of universal harmonies".

The Emmanuel-Bettelheim debate[17] on the other hand, is erected upon Ricardian theory and therefore avoids some if not all of these neo-classical pitfalls. The theory of unequal exchange advanced by Emmanuel inverts Ricardo's assumptions on the grounds that the conditions of mobile capital and immobile labour are more realistic in the present age. It can then be shown that exchanges between centre and periphery necessarily involve the systematic transfer of value for the low-wage levels could be treated as an "independent variable" in the system, determined by historical and moral elements within each national economy. For this, he has been compared with the Keynesian position.[18] Bettelheim refused to accept that wages could depend on the productivity of labour; this situated his critique back within the inescapable circuit of interdependencies which enmesh marginalist formulations.

For Amin, there is a serious trade-off involved in this debate between historical materialism and an objective theory of value, with Marxist theory as the two-time loser. Emmanuel's; "methodological pluralism" in his treatment of wage determinations has the undesirable effect of driving a wedge between production and exchange to the detriment of historical materialism, while Bettelheim's linkage of wage levels to national productivities makes it difficult to conceive of the reality of imperialism through an objective theory of value. This is a trade-off he seeks to destroy. Emmanuel is praised for his inversion of Ricardian assumptions; Amin sees this as establishing the correct abstract characterization of the imperialist system in the pre-eminence of international (or world) values.[19] This accurately captures the reality that commodity production in the imperialist epoch is international rather than national, that the capitalist mode of production is dominant at both the centre and the periphery of the system. And, as we have already seen, he treats the question of wage levels in the process of expanded reproduction as a resultant of the specific form of the class struggle, with dynamic equilibrium always possible.

The implications of this very recent interpretation are quite fascinating. Firstly, the pre-eminence of world values re-establishes exchange-value as the dominant value form over use-value. From this it follows that the products entering into international trade do not do so on the basis of irreducible use-values. So, for instance, peripheral exports such as tea and coffee enter world trade not because they cannot be grown elsewhere. Even in cases like this, substitutes exist for these "specific products"; the fact that they are produced in the periphery and enter into world trade indicates that, under the dominant price structure of the age, these goods maximize the rate of surplus value at that point in time.[20] To argue that tea and coffee are traded because they can only be grown in the periphery is to admit that use-value predominates over exchange-value, which in turn is restatement of the theory of consumer sovereignty in a disguised form. Yet this is precisely what Amin does at times argue. In Unequal Development we are told that:

"... 75 per cent of exports from the periphery came from modern enterprises with a very high productivity, and the rest - mainly exotic agricultural products - simply cannot be produced in the advanced countries.[21]

This changed position requires clarification, for its effects would seem to be far-reaching.

An important distinction set up by Amin in the light of these early arguments is that between primitive accumulation and expanded reproduction. He contends that unequal exchange is a modern form of primitive accumulation practiced by the centre against the periphery. He attempts to show that assuming equal productivities and 5:1 wage differential between centre and periphery, the $26 billion of peripheral exports (in 1966) coming from modern industries would cost $34 billion if they were produced at the centre. The case is even more blatant when exports coming from "backward" sectors are investigated, for here wage differentials vastly outstrip productivity differentials. He calculates that the $9 billion currently expended on such exports would swell to $23 billion if they were produced at the centre. So the overall picture is that the centre "saves" $22 billion through the operation of unequal exchange - a saving which runs close to 20% of the value of the product in the periphery. The "gains" to the centre are only 1.5% of its product, but these accrue mainly to the MNC's who directly partake in unequal exchange.[22]

The magnitude of such figures is already the subject of a heated debate.[23] Yet what remains most important is the methodology used to derive them.[24] Some real problems arise when employing the equations of the transformation problem in this way. For these equations, in assuming the equalization of profit rates, are implicitly assuming a system of competitive capitalism. This assumption cannot be made under monopoly conditions, as Amin admits. Monopolies appropriate a disproportionately large share of the total part of surplus value through their political nexus with the state, so "draining" the surplus value distributed competitively amongst small producers. And this inflated share is in turn distributed amongst individual monopolies in proportion to their political power. Now it is totally unrealistic to see world trade as competitive; it more closely approximates trade between monopolies, for even the exports originating from the peasant sector where competitive assumptions might apply are channelled through state trading monopolies on their way to world markets. Unequal exchange, as calculated by Amin, would seem to be a rare case. The distribution of surplus value between DC's and UDC's in the act of international trade would seem to depend primarily on political power. Of course the DC's have had more of this, but as to how we might quantify the benefits derived from it eludes me.

Although these attempts at measuring the extent of exploitation are fraught with hazards, his conceptual distinction between primitive accumulation and expanded reproduction is useful. It suggests that although the functions of the periphery for the centre may be profitable, they are not 'necessary' to the sustenance of the centre because they do not directly enter into expanded reproduction. This seems to accord with our present age, when serious thought can be given to the possibilities of substituting for such fundamental products as Middle Eastern oil. His point - that new "solutions" to the contradictions of expanded reproduction can always be found - needs to be heeded, and the class consequences of these "solutions" thought out. And the sorts of debates which characterized radical circles in the Vietnam period[25] need to be reformulated in the light of these concepts.

PERIPHERAL CAPITALISM AND DECAY

In the social formations of the centre, the dominant capitalist mode of production is expressed in the articulation of the capital goods and consumer goods sector. This mechanism of expanded reproduction underwrites the autocentric characteristics of central capitalism. According to Amin, capitalism at the centre tends to become the exclusive as well as the dominant mode of production; it dissolves all lesser modes into their constituent parts and incorporates these elements into the process of expanded reproduction. Hence the social formations of central capitalism converge around the model of the pure capitalist mode. Class divisions are simplified to bourgeois and proletariat, despite the multiplication of secondary political and ideological stratifications.[26]

But although the capitalist mode of production is similarly dominant at the periphery, this dominance assumes a crucially different form. Although this dominant mode destroys the autonomy of precapitalist modes which it encounters there, Amin argues (following Bettelheim) that it does not disintegrate these modes into their basic components. Instead the contradictory effects of dissolution/conservation come into play, with the result that the tendency to exclusivity of the capitalist mode at the centre is never realized. The linkage between capital and consumer goods sectors which is at the heart of expanded reproduction in the central formations is never effected in the periphery. Instead it is the export sector which becomes tied to the tertiary sector and defines the basic tendencies of the peripheral social formations, expressed in the "disarticulation" of the economy.[27] So while the pre-eminence of world values expresses abstractly the unity of the system as a whole under the dominance of the capitalist mode of production, this unity does not imply the homogeneity of the parts. On the contrary, the stark contrast between centre and periphery is the final disproof of evolutionary theories of "economic" development and "nation-building".

The origins of these structural differences may generally be found in the manner in which the periphery was brought into the ambit of the world system. The most common method was through the mechanism of trade, accompanied by the application of force. Trade gave to the peripheral economies their external orientation, and created a local class structure compatible with this outlook. The prime element of this class structure is the absence of any genuine national bourgeoisie; even contemporary policies of import-substitution express in a new form the extraversion of the peripheral economy. This absence is due to the manner in which external trade broke up the natural articulation of petty producers and agriculturalists in the pre-colonial era; trade led to the decimation (either through technological or political superiority) of petty commodity production in order that markets for metropolitan products could be secured. In the social formations of central capitalism there was no directly comparable process to this. There, the "freeing of the serfs" led to their absorption into the young manufacturing sector. But in the periphery, former artisans were forced back on to the land or harnessed as a labour force for the extraction of minerals in which the periphery may have enjoyed a natural advantage. The extraversion of the economy was reinforcing the tendency towards agrarian crisis, and cementing the parameters of a dependent class structure at the same time.

As in the case of the social formations of central capitalism, peripheral social formations do converge around a general model which is nonetheless quite distinct from that of the centre. This model has four main characteristics; the dominance of agrarian capital in any truly national class formation, the complementary role fulfilled by local merchant capital to foreign interests, the pronounced growth of bureaucracy which dominates "civil society" up to the limit of state capitalism, and the rising levels of social inequality and active "proletarianization".[28] But there are neither economic laws nor bourgeois class formations which challenge the dependent status of the peripheral social formation or the rules of profitability which daily reconfirm that dependence. Growth is spasmodic and confined in its extent - a succession of "miracles" that lead nowhere in an economy that is never internally integrated. The foreign exchange constraint is ever-present as a bottleneck, while the state moves from one fiscal crisis to another as bureaucratic growth, state subsidies and personal emmoluments eat into its limited portion of the surplus. The forms of dependence do vary, but the fact of dependence is never challenged.

The last characteristic of peripheral social formations - the rising levels of "proletarianization" - is a contentious point, the site of one of the most heated debates in "neo-marxist" work. The debate here is an old one,[29] resurrected in the contemporary period by Laclau's critique of Frank.[30] Stripped to its essentials, the debate runs as follows. For Marx, the proletariat was defined by its "double freedom"; i.e. it is both freed from servile obligations and able to sell its labour power freely on the market, and it is free also in the sense of being unencumbered by possession of the means of production. A strict application of this definition to the conditions of peripheral social formations reveals that very little labour is free in both of these senses and that the proletariat, so defined, probably amounts to no more than 3-4% of the workforce. One also sees some strange counter-intuitive phenomena at work; for instance, an archetypal 'capitalist venture', such as the Green Revolution in India, generated an increase in the level of semi-feudal "bonded" labour rather than free labour. Hence the proletariat is defined by reference to the immediate relation of production into which it enters, the conclusion is inescapable - that the proletariat is politically insignificant in the periphery, and that the present political task for socialist strategy does not consist of the over-throw of capitalism so much as its development.

Frank's arguments on this point were that the apparently semi-feudal producer in the periphery nonetheless produces for a world market and that it is the loss of autonomy which constitutes the essence of the proletariat. More recently, authors such as Wallerstein have redecorated these structural arguments without reformulating the terms of reference of the debate.[31] Amin's contribution flows out of his abstract characterization of the system of world capitalism as a unity marked by the pre-eminence of world values, the dominance of the capitalist mode of production, and the all-pervasiveness of unequal exchange. In other words, under the process of the formation of the imperialist epoch, pre-capitalist modes of production have been

> "...reduced ....to a simple form, a "shell" whose content has become a relation of the sale of labour power...(producers at the periphery)...are mostly proletarianized and sellers (although indirectly) of their labour power".[32]

So it is "the separation of the producer from the means of production"[33] which is at the essence of the process of proletarianization. This may satisfy some as an improvement on the status quo insofar as Amin is clearly tring to retain the conclusions of Frank while basing his analysis at the level of productive relations, but my preference would still lie with a more disaggregated mode of class identification.

Amin proposed that we employ a "model of decadence" to explain the transition of the system as a whole in the direction of socialism. He argues that

> "...when a system is outgrown and superseded, this process takes place, not in the first place, starting from the centre, but from its periphery..."[34]

Such a model of "decay from the periphery" applies not only to the transition to socialism but also helps explain the birth of capitalism, as a peripheral, or marginal, case of the more general tributary mode of production, which this peripheral condition defined by the acute degradation of the community to the point where it loses dominium eminens of the land. This specific "backwardness" of feudal Europe in relation to the Chinese and Arabian centre of civilization found expression in the absence of a strong and centralized authority over the peasants. Commercial activity was more independent, the flight from localized tyranny was more likely to succeed, and hence the formation of the elements of the capitalist mode of production was more easily effected. By contrast, at the "centres" of the tributary mode feudalization was seen by the peasants as a regression, and peasant revolts led to the restoration of centralized state control.[35]

These are interesting and novel thoughts that should be well received. But in the present political climate, Amin's brief analysis of the strategy of the Cambodian revolution is sure to attract a disproportionate share of attention.[36] He argues that differentiation within the Cambodian peasantry was marginal, and that this degree of differentiation has been exaggerated by sociologists unable to distinguish the extraction of a surplus from the relations of social domination. This relative lack of class formation set Cambodia apart from the more typical and "central" tributary made as found in both China and Vietnam. Imperialist forces were faced with a dilemma in such situations, in that potential collaborators within the countryside are numerically and strategically weak. They could either expropriate peasant lands, turn them over to white settlers, and proceed to exploit the peasants as a pool of labour or as specialized producers by the use of taxes and monopolistic control of peasant output. But, Amin argues, the principal contradiction in such situations remains external to peasant society and symbolized in the opposition between the town and the whole of the peasantry. Consequently the correct revolutionary strategy does not follow the Chinese pattern of "the rich peasant line" but seeks to unite the peasants against the domination of the town and capital. The ideological leadership of the working class is essential to the success of this strategy because it converts the traditional peasant uprising into a stage in the socialist transformation of the world system. Such an alliance also weakens the enemy by dividing it, while preserving the real basis of unity amongst the peasantry. Amin concludes that this strategy and these conditions are rather typical of Africa, whereas the fully developed tributary mode of production is somewhat more confined to China and Egypt.

Larger questions remain, however, about the project which Amin is engaged in. He pushes the entente cordiale between Marxist concepts and dependency theory which is passed off as "neo-marxism" to its limit. The systematic basis of this synthesis ultimately tells against it when faced with political analysis of contemporary situations such as those in Cambodia and Iran. For there we need concepts which can inform revolutionary strategy with more precise information than the generalized signal that the periphery is ripe for revolt. This may be true - although the unexpected stability of the ASEAN states in the years after the Guam doctrine might lead to doubts - but it is clearly evident that we need better indicators of the quality of the revolutions which do not occur. And it may be questioned whether this "neo-marxist" approach can help in this task more satisfactorily than any well-informed political analysis. Amin does disaggregate the "lumpen-concepts" of early structural "neo-marxism" to a significant extent, and even attempts the introduction of some structuralist principles. But it might still be argued that the organicist radicalism which is built into the notion of the world capitalist system makes these attempts insufficient to handle the ultimate problem of structural thought - the analysis of the sources and directions of change.

NOTES

1. Aidan Foster-Carter, "Neo-Marxist Approaches to Development and Underdevelopment" in E. de Kadt and G. Williams (eds.) Sociology and Development (London: Tavistock, 1974), pp.67-105 (an earlier version appeared in JCA, Vol.3:1, 1973) and "From Rostow to Gunder Frank: Conflicting Paradigms in the Analysis of Underdevelopment", World Developmemt,4, 1976,pp.167-180.

2. See the introductory remarks to his recent article "The Modes of Production Controversy", New Left Review, 107,1978,pp.47-77.

3. For example the comments by Jean Copans and David Seddon in their "Marxism and Anthropology: A Preliminary Survey" in D. Seddon (ed.) Relations of Production (London: Cass,1978),pp.40-41

4. See, for instance, the recent paper by Richard Higgott which argues strongly that liberal theories of modernisation have not disappeared so much as undergone a change in form; "From Modernisation Theory to Public Policy: Continuity and Change in the Political Science of Political

Development", paper presented to the 49th ANZAAS Congress, Sociology section, Auckland, New Zealand, January 1979.

5. Some pertinent reflections upon this reading can be found in David Goddard, "Limits of British Anthropology" New Left Review, 58, 1969.

6. For a good attempt to distinguish these methods, see Chapter 2 of Miriam Glucksmann, Structural Analysis in Contemporary Social Thought (London: Routledge and Kegan Paul, 1974).

7. Samir Amin, Accumulation on a World Scale, tr. B. Pearce (New York: Monthly Review Press, 1974) two volumes.

8. Samir Amin, Unequal Development, tr. B. Pearce (Sussex: Harvester Press, 1976).

9. Samir Amin, Imperialism and Unequal Development (Sussex: Harvester Press, 1977).

10. These arguments are economically assembled and plausibly argued by Shlome Avineri in the Introduction to his edited book, Karl Marx on Colonialism and Modernization (New York: Doubleday and Co., 1969).

11. A clear demonstration of this is provided by Perry Anderson, Lineages of the Absolutist State (London: New Left Books, 1974), pp.462-472.

12. See Chapter 1 of Unequal Development.

13. Michael Barratt Brown has been the main propagator of this view; see his "A Critique of Marxist Theories of Imperialism" in R. Owen and B. Sutcliffe (eds.), Studies in the Theory of Imperialism" (London: Longman, 1972).

14. See Andre Gunder Frank, Capitalism and Underdevelopment in Latin America (Penguin, 1971), pp.36-38.

15. Imperialism and Unequal Development, p.106.

16. Ibid, pp.205-208, 239-252.

17. See Arghiri Emmanuel, Unequal Exchange, tr. B. Pearce (London: New Left Books, 1972).

18. Michael Barratt Brown, The Economics of Imperialism (Penguin, 1974), pp.72,230. Although this comparison is correct in political terms, it lis unfair insofar as Emmanuel does not accept the marginalist foundations upon which Keynesian theory is based.

19. Imperialism and Unequal Development, pp.186-191.

20. Imperialism and Unequal Development, pp.208-216.

21. Unequal Development, pp.147-148.

22. Accumulation on a World Scale, Vol.1, pp.57-58 and Unequal Development, pp.143-148.

24. Some of these problems are discussed in my earlier review of Amin, "Accumulation on a World Scale", Arena, 42, 1976, pp.100-116, especially p.114ff. There is the additional aproblem of deciding which terms remain constant in the transformation of values into prices. Is total price = total price of production? Or is the rate of surplus value = rate of profit?

25. E.g. the famous Magdoff-Miller debate. See Harry Magdoff, "The Logic of Imperialism" and S.M. Miller et.al.,

"Does the U.S. Economy Require Imperialism?" both in Social Policy, 1(3), 1970.

26. Unequal Development, pp.293-294.

27. For a clear statement of the centre-periphery contrast in this respect, see Samir Amin, "Accumulation and Development: A Theoretical Model", Review of African Political Economy, 1, 1974.

28. Unequal Development, pp.333-364.

29. See the classical debate between Sweezy and Dobb, updated and reprinted in R. Hilton (ed), The Transition from Feudalism to Capitalism (London: New Left Books, 1976).

30. Ernesto Laclau - "Feudalism and Capitalism in Latin America" in Politics and Ideology in Marxist Theory (London: New Left Books, 1977), pp.15-50.

31 Immanuel Wallerstein - "The Rise and Future Demise of the World Capitalist System: Concepts for Comparative Analysis" Comparative Studies and History, 1974, pp.387-415.

32. Imperialism and Unequal Exchange, p.191.

33. Unequal Development, pp.14,360-361.

34. ibid. p.10

35. ibid. pp.51-58.

36. Imperialism and Unequal Development, pp.147-152.

Chapter 6

CLASS ANALYSIS VERSUS WORLD SYSTEMS: CRITIQUE OF SAMIR AMIN'S TYPOLOGY OF UNDERDEVELOPMENT

Sheila Smith

INTRODUCTION

Despite the heterogeneity of analytical approaches which are included in the term "dependency theory" (see Palma, 1978), it is possible to distil some commonly held contentions, including the following:

(i) the world system is such that the development of part of the system occurs at the expense of other parts. The mechanisms by which this occurs include trade and unequal exchange, the transfer of surplus to central/metropolitan countries by multinational corporations, and the transfer of technology under restrictive conditions which prevent its diffusion in underdeveloped countries (LDCs) and benefit its owners in developed capitalist countries (DCCs);

(ii) underdevelopment is not simply non-development, but is a unique type of socio-economic structure brought about by the integration of LDCs into the world capitalist system;

(iii) dependent countries lack the capacity for autonomous, self-sustained growth, and can expand only as a result of the growth of DCCs.

These contentions can be summarized by the following quotation from Amin: "The accentuation of the features of under-development in proportion as (sic) the economic growth of the periphery - in other words, the development of under-development - necessarily results in the blocking of growth, in other words, the impossibility - whatever the level of production per capita that may be attained - of going over to autonomous and self-sustained growth, to development in the true sense" (Amin, 1974, p.393).

There are some excellent general critiques of dependency theory, including Warren (1980), Leys (1977, 1978) and Palma (1978). I will attempt to summarize these criticisms briefly, before presenting the main part of this paper, which is a more detailed critique of the views of Samir Amin.

Warren argues that dependency theory is static, in the sense that dependency is given, thus "the centre periphery paradigm on which the entire theoretical structure rests ... remains largely unexamined. The shifting geographical distribution of world economic power (in favour of the LDCs) is simply assumed to unfold under the control of the centre" (1980, p.163). This means that proponents of dependency ignore the considerable bargaining power of LDC national States vis-a-vis multinationals. Imperialism is assumed to be a "monolithic structure"; imperialism is generally equated with the world market, thus "the possibility of any non-dependent capitalist Third World progress" is excluded by definition (1980, p.164). Finally, "dependency theory assumes: (a) that there is a latent, suppressed historical alternative to the development that actually took place; (b) that the failure of this alternative to materialize was the result primarily of external imposition - even if mediated through internal social forces - and not of the choice of the internal directing groups; (c) that the latent (suppressed) alternative would have been more autonomous and therefore would have achieved more rapid development" (pp.166-7, emphasis in original). Warren goes on to illustrate his contention that all the normal indicators of 'dependency' point to increasingly non-subordinate economic relations between poor and rich countries, as regards trade diversification, control of foreign investment, structural change and balance of payments accounts.

In response to Warren's empirical evidence, proponents of dependency theory might counter with two arguments:

(a) Warren is equating growth and development, which is not legitimate. As shown in the Amin quotation above, economic growth at the periphery is compatible with the development of under-development.
(b) Many of the rapidly growing LDCs are exceptions and their experience is not generalizable for the periphery as a whole.

Neither of these arguments is sustainable. The first is sometimes based on a moralistic expectation that capitalism ought to be nice. The existence or otherwise of capitalist development needs to be grounded on something stronger than its niceness and nastiness. Alternatively the first argument is based on the view that capitalist growth at the periphery is 'distorted', which implies some 'correct', standard type of capitalist growth. (For more details, see Smith, 1980, pp.14-15). The second argument is an illustration of the circularity of dependency theory - all LDCs are dependent, except when they're not. Furthermore, as Leys argues, Britain was an exceptional case, and, summarising his views, he states that "The debate about dependency and under-development has not shown either that capitalist development cannot occur at the periphery or that it is eventually bound to. What it demonstrates is, rather, the need to study and theorise the conditions under which some peripheral countries have, and others have not, experienced significant measures of growth" (Leys, 1978,p.244).

This brief resume of some criticisms made of dependency theory in general is clearly inadequate to dispose of it. I shall therefore proceed by attempting a more detailed discussion of one theorist - Samir Amin. This discussion is an extension of a previous article (Smith, 1980), which was based on three works: Accumulation on a World Scale (1974), Unequal Development (1976) and Imperialism and Unequal Development (1977); the present discussion includes two later works: The Law of Value and Historical Materialism (1978), and Class and Nation, Historically and in the Current Crisis, (1980).

The rest of the paper is organised as follows. After a brief summary of Amin's analysis of world capitalism, the critique of Amin is in three parts: first, a discussion of the ways in which Amin attempts to immunize himself from criticisms; secondly, some general criticisms; thirdly, a discussion of the spurious nature of Amin's claims to 'scientific objectivity', and finally, a discussion of the political implications of Amin's ideas.

SUMMARY OF AMIN'S ANALYSIS OF WORLD CAPITALISM

According to Amin, it is necessary to analyse capitalism at a world level in terms of two categories, centre and periphery. The basic difference between centre and periphery is that capitalist relations in the centre developed as a result of internal processes, whereas capitalist relations in the periphery were introduced from the outside. Thus central economies are autocentric: autocentric capitalist growth is characterized by the balanced internal relationship between the sector producing mass consumer goods and the sector producing capital goods. In contrast, peripheral economies are "subject to the logic of accumulation in the centres that dominated them" (1980,p.133). The form of domination has changed with the political independence of peripheral nations, from direct colonial rule to technological dependence, domination by multinational companies, etc., but this has been associated with a deepening, not a lessening, of underdevelopment.

In peripheral economies, low wages, modern technology and hence high labour productivity provide the basis for unequal exchange and hence for super-exploitation: "all plans for a dependent development policy worked out in constant prices lead to a blocking by a double deficit, in the external balance and in the public finances; all plans for such a policy worked out ex post, at current prices (relative prices of imports and exports) lead to this same blocking occurring even sooner. There is only one explanation for this, namely, that the price structures are distorted (through the effect of combined class struggles on the world scale) so as to aggravate exploitation in the periphery" (1978, p.63). Unequal exploitation and unequal exchange dictate inequality in the international division of labour, and lead to a 'distorted' structure of demand at the periphery, since the domestic market for mass consumer goods is restricted by the low level of wages, and since demand is dominated by 'parasitic classes' demand for luxury goods. This 'distorted' structure of demand has effects, both on the structure of domestic production and on the composition of imports. Peripheral economies are subject to a 'vicious circle' of development: "in order to reproduce its own conditions of existence, the peripheral formation must still contain precapitalist modes of production or else produce non-capitalist modes which, being dominated, provide the capitalist mode with its cheap labour" (1977, p.218).

Amin rules out completely the possibility of 'proper' capitalist development at the periphery: "in the imperialist period...the door to the establishment of new capitalist centres is henceforth closed, while the era of the stages of the socialist revolution is opened (1980, p.114), and "complete, autonomous capitalism is impossible in the periphery. The socialist break is objectively necessary there" (1980, p.131). In order for the productive forces in the periphery to develop the imperialist system must be broken up, since "the contemporary imperialist system is a system of centralization of the surplus on the world scale...characterized by the acceleration of accumulation and by the development of the productive forces in the centre of the system, while in the periphery these latter are held back and deformed" (1980, p.252).

There are four important political conclusions to be drawn from Amin's analysis:

1. Peripheral economies have no freedom of manoeuvre in relation to world capitalism.
2. Only a radical and complete break with the world capitalist system will provide the conditions necessary for 'genuine' development.
3. The working class in countries of the centre benefits from the exploitation of the periphery: this provides the objective explanation for the pro-imperialist political and ideological characteristic of the workers' movement in the centre.
4. The principal contradiction in the world is between the peoples of the periphery and imperialist capital. Hence, "In the periphery, the socialist transition is not distinct from national liberation. It has become clear that the latter is impossible under local bourgeois leadership and thus becomes a democratic stage in the

process of the uninterrupted revolution by stages led by the peasant and worker masses" (1980, p.252).

CRITIQUE OF SAMIR AMIN

(A) Amin's Self-Immunisation from Criticism

Criticizing Amin is difficult, and potentially hazardous, for several reasons. First, Amin's analysis is concerned with 'essences', thus any critique based upon actual events can be countered by accusations of superficiality and of concern only with 'appearances'. Secondly, Amin proceeds by a mode of argument which I have described as "assertion plus threat" (Smith, 1980, p.13), i.e., an assertion is followed by a 'threat' or an insult applied to anyone who might disagree. This mode of argument is often combined in Amin's work by an attempt to proclaim himself the 'true' intellectual descendant of Marx, the 'Marxist of them all'. One example is the following: "It is worth noting that the concepts of centre and periphery, basic to my analysis, but rejected by all pro-imperialist currents within Marxism, were introduced by Lenin in direct relation to his analysis of the imperialist system" (Amin, 1980, p.132). A further example is: "West-centredness systematically distorts Marxism. Through dogmatic rigidity, it has virtually turned an instrument of revolutionary action into an academic discipline. The debate over unequal exchange has convinced me that insistence on the 'pre-eminence of production over circulation' is nothing but an ideological excuse" (Ibid, p.204). Finally, "in the periphery the absolute pauperization of the producers exploited by capital has revealed itself in all its brutal reality. But it is there, precisely, that the pro-imperalist tendency among Marxists pulls up short, for it is from that point onward that Marxism becomes subversive...The consequences that follow from this contradiction constitute the real problems - which are of no interest to dogmatic professional Marxism or, for that matter, to revisionist and crypto-revisionist labour movements" (Amin, 1978, pp.34-35). At the risk of being labelled a revisionist or a pro-imperalist Marxist, or even not a proper Marxist at all, I should like to argue that assertions plus threats or insults are not an adequate substitute for a serious critique of other persons' arguments.

The final, and most unacceptable, reason for the difficulty of criticizing Amin, is that the pro-imperalist degeneration of Marxism in the centre is objectively given. This is most clearly argued in Amin 1978, for example: "The objective basis of the pro-imperalist tendency among Marxists is constituted by the fact of imperialism itself and its implication: the hegemony of the social democratic and revisionist ideologies among the working classes at the centre of the system. On the theoretical plane, this tendency finds expression in the tirelessly renewed striving to eliminate the question of the collective, worldwide genesis of surplus value and its distribution" (Amin, 1978, p.116). "Of course the revolutionary credential of the intelligentsia, which at the centre is in the service of capital, is here, in the periphery, in the camp of revolution" (Ibid, p.124). This means that a correct analysis of the world, or any part of it, can only be generated at the periphery, and thus intellectual work in countries of the centre must be automatically dismissed: "As for the trends of that famous 'Western Marxism'...they are all linked with trends in bourgeois, and therefore pre-Marxist philosophy. Consequently, even when they ask the right questions, they are incapable of answering these questions because their society is not ready for the answers. Refusing to break with imperialism, they can be re-absorbed, especially through psychologism in one form or another (Freudo-Marxism, feminism, and so on)" (Ibid, p.125, my emphasis).

This form of argument is an extreme example of economic reductionism: by locating a person's class position, Amin is 'reading off' their political and ideological stance, without even considering the content. Amin's argument is also extremely dangerous, since it is teetering on the brink of racism, by claiming an intellectual privilege for his own ideas because they are generated within the periphery, and not because of their content, whilst dismissing any critique from the centre by labelling it 'pro-imperialist'. The status of arguments is therefore pre-determined, resulting from the location of their owners in centre or periphery.

Despite the predetermined status of my ideas, generated as they are in a Western ivory tower, I wish to argue that all ideas and arguments should be examined on their merits, and not according to the status of their originator; and furthermore, that the political orientation of struggles and ideas cannot be 'read off' from the geographical location of those struggles.

(B) Some General Criticisms

(i) Amin, along with many other proponents of the dependency or under underdevelopment school, regards the periphery on the one hand, and the centre on the other, as undifferentiated blocs. There are many purposes, however, for which this view is both unhelpful and misleading. Significant differences among less developed countries can take political or economic forms; examples of the latter are differences between oil exporting economies, newly-industrialising countries, countries with a significant industrial sector based upon the domestic market, exporters of non-oil primary commodities, etc. It cannot be seriously sustained that all these groups of economies face a single, monolithic structure of imperialism, and that none of them have any freedom of manoeuvre in relation to imperialism. Examples of political differences include differences between countries which are attempting to construct a socialist transition whilst remaining to some degree involved with the 'international capitalist system', either through trade or foreign investment, such as Angola, Zimbabwe, Nicaragua; and on the other hand, countries such as South Korea, Singapore, Nigeria, Hong Kong, Ivory Coast, which remain firmly within the capitalist political camp. To deny the significance of these latter differences involves denigrating the heroic struggles which took place, denying the important victories of political participation of the mass of the population as well as the economic changes resulting from liberation, and, further, involves an arrogant dismissal of the economic strategies formulated in those countries for a transition to socialism. The latter is indeed an arrogance stemming from a presumed intellectual omniscience, generated, not in the centre, but in the periphery.

Amin regards empirical evidence which runs counter to his view as superficial. Yet his methodology is suspect: how are his assertions to be disproved? Amin's methodology proceeds as follows: there are two categories of country, A and B; countries in A have characteristics X, Y and Z; countries in B have characteristics O, P and Q. Countries' membership of A and B determines all important features of those countries. If research uncovers the existence of X, Y and/or Z in countries in B or O, P and/or Q in countries in A, this research is either wrong, or superficial, or has failed to understand Marxism. This methodology is a recipe for tautology, rather than a procedure for analysing the world. Some examples of evidence which would be dismissed by Amin by means of this procedure are as follows: the development of multinational companies based in less developed countries such as Brazil, India and South Korea. By June 1979, the cumulative total of foreign investment by South Korean companies has reached US$134 million, involving 367 projects. Around one-third of this had occurred during the first 6 months of 1979 (Lueddel-Neurath, 1980, p.51); evidence of mass consumption of Brazilian produced manufactured goods in Brazil, rather than their consumption exclusively by 'parasitic classes' (Wells, 1977); and evidence of the increased production of capital goods in LDCs (Schiffer, 1981). The latter three examples are instances of attempts to inquire into the actual nature of capitalist development in LDCs, and to that extent are, however, dismissed by Amin as irrelevant before the answers have been discovered. This research into the specificity of particular economies is deemed unimportant by Amin.

(ii) In presenting a criterion of capitalism in the centre as a 'standard' and capitalism in the periphery as a 'distortion', Amin implies a strange assessment of the process of capitalist development in the centre. He argues that, because of domination by the centre, "the development of under-development is neither regular nor cumulative, in contrast to the development of capitalism at the centre. On the contrary, it is jerky and made up of phases of extremely rapid growth, followed by sudden blockages" (1976, p.289). If Amin's view of 'standard capitalism' is one of regular, steady, even progress, then all capitalisms of the centre are 'distorted', and the yardstick by which peripheral capitalism is judged is an abstract, utopian one.

(iii) Given Amin's confidence of the correctness of his view of the world, it is surprising to find major inconsistencies in it. In Accumulation on a World Scale, Amin argues that "so long as an under-developed country continues to be integrated in the world market, it remains helpless ... the possibilities of local accumulation are nil" (1974, p.13). However, in The Law of Value and Historical Materialism, in a remarkably sensible chapter on Mining Rent, Amin argues that the formation of mining rent is conditioned by the emergence of a bourgeosie in the periphery that mining rent is a result of attempts by peripheral states to impose a real royalty for access to their resources, and that " the transfer from centre to periphery which this rent constitutes should enable accelerated accumulation to take place in the periphery ... The necessary condition for this accelerated accumulation is access to the centre for the periphery's industrial exports" (1978, p.74). Thus, it seems, the periphery has room for manoeuvre, the possibility of local accumulation in the periphery is not nil. Yet Amin still wants it both ways: "The bourgeoisie of the periphery is (thus) a productive class, even though it is dependent and parasitic" (1978, p.78).

THE 'SCIENTIFIC OBJECTIVITY' OF AMIN'S ANALYSIS

One of the central features of Amin's analysis is the argument that the periphery is underdeveloped because of super-exploitation, and that the resulting super-surplus is transferred to the centre: "contrary to the bourgeois theory of under-development, the periphery is not poor but impoverished, because it is super-exploited" (1980, p.163). Several means are employed by Amin to establish that this super-exploitation is an objectively provable phenomenon: first, Amin's claim to be the true heir of Marx means that his application of historical materialism to the world capitalist system is the only correct use of Marx's method, and that anyone who disagrees has failed to understand Marx; secondly, to provide an acceptable scientific proof, Amin attempts to quantify this super-surplus. In order to illustrate the basis on which his claim rests, I shall discuss the quantification of the super-surplus in detail.

Table 1 is reproduced from Class and Nation (Amin, 1980, p.151). The first thing to note is that no source is given for the numbers. The second remarkable feature is that the 75 million unemployed persons, constituting 6 percent of the world's population, receive no income. The arbitrariness of the division of persons and income into classes hardly needs to be stated. However, after defining the class categories, Amin poses the following question: "Is it possible to use a table of the equivalents, expressed in incomes, of production within the capitalist system, to analyse the contradictions within this system ... and pinpoint the tendencies in the accumulation which they control?" (Ibid, p.156). The answer he provides is in three parts:

1. a 'vulgar economist' would regard the income of each class as a measure of its contribution to production, since 'vulgar economists' are concerned only with 'appearances', i.e. prices.

2. a 'vulgar Marxist' would proceed thus: for group A, total value produced is $2,220 billion, the value of labour power $1,040 billion, surplus value $1,080 billion, and hence the rate of surplus value approximately 100 percent. For group B, total value produced is $460 billion, surplus labour (income accruing to land proprietors) is $185 billion, thus the rate of surplus value is 185/275, or 67 per cent. So although workers in B are poorer than in A, they are less exploited.

   It should be noted that an extreme degree of vulgarity would be needed in order for a Marxist to equate prices and values in this way. Indeed, Amin rejects the reasoning of his imaginary vulgar Marxist, on the grounds that the reasoning "derives from a systematic obfuscation of the fact of imperialism, expressing a bourgeois point of view within distorted Marxism, whether social democratic or revisionist" (Ibid, p.157).

3. The only correct way of interpreting the table is by starting with "a comparative analysis of working conditions which define the comparative productives and the rates of extraction of surplus labour" (Ibid). Furthermore, the prices in the table are "distorted", due to "different conditions of the class struggle and the extraction of surplus labour" (Ibid, p.159). So to interpret the table correctly, one should reason as follows:

"Suppose that the direct producers in the centre ... are exploited under technical conditions which maximise the productivity of their labour in each of the branches of production concerned: and take 100 as an index of this productivity for each of these branches. The return to labour here is about $4,300 per worker and the value created about $8,700, the rate of surplus value being about 100 per cent" (Ibid). Note that Amin follows his imaginary vulgar Marxist here by directly equating prices and values in the centre. Not so in the periphery, however. In industry in the periphery Amin assumes that the index of comparative productivity is 50. Taking this productivity difference into account, "the value produced by ... 50 million workers (in industry in the periphery) at the average rate of

Table 1
World Income Distribution by Class (1975)

	(1) Millions of Persons	(2) Percentage of (1)	(3) Average Income Per Person ($)	(4) Total Income (Billion of $)	(5) Percentage of (4)
A. Centres					
Peasantry:	35	3	4,300	150	6
Working class					
"inferior" category	50	4	3,000	150	6
"superior category	60	4	4,500	270	10
Proletarianized petty bourgeoisie	110	8	5,200	570	21
Middle and bourgeois layers	90	7	12,000	1,080	40
Unemployed	25	2	—	—	—
TOTAL of A	370	27	6,000	2,220	83
B. Peripheries					
Peasantry:					
poor and exploited	600	44	200	120	4
middle	150	11	400	60	2
owners and capitalists	50	4	1,000	50	2
Working class	50	4	600	30	1
Proletarianized petty bourgeoisie	80	6	800	65	2
Middle and bourgeois layers	20	1	6,800	135	5
Urban employees	50	4	—	—	—
TOTAL of B	1,000	73	460	460	17
GRAND TOTAL	1,370	100	1,950	2,680	100

Discrepancies in percentages result from rounding.
Source: Amin, 1980, p.151

Amin's calculations for all sectors can be summarized in Table 2:

Table 2

Sector	A Productivity Index (Centre = 100)	B Number of Workers in Periphery	C Value Produced per Worker in Centre	D[1] Total Value in Periphery at "Effective Prices"	E[2] Total "Apparent" Value in Periphery
Industry Proletarianized	50	50mn	$8,700	$220bn	$165bn
Petty Bourgeois	30	80mn	$8,700	$210bn	$ 65bn
Agriculture	10	750mn	$4,300[3]	$320bn	$230bn
TOTAL				$750bn	$460bn

1. Col. D = 100 x B x C
   A
2. Col. E=total value of output per sector from Table 1.
3. This figure is less than average income per worker in the centre because Amin assumes that "the contribution of dead labour (capital)" is zero in the periphery. The figure of $4,300 is the actual earnings of the workers in agriculture in the centre.

Source: Deduced from Ibid, pp. 159-161.

exploitation of the centre (100 percent) would be 0.5 x 50 x $8,700 or $220 billion. If the value of the industrial production in the periphery given empirically, i.e., in going prices, is less than this, it is because the rate of exploitation of the workers is much higher than in the centre (their salaries are not even half of those in the centre, but are seven times less), and because the resulting extra surplus labour is not necessarily made up for the volume of profits that would presuppose a considerably higher rate than in the centre. As a result, effective prices differ from prices of production" (Ibid, p.160, my emphasis).

The purpose of this exercise can now be revealed: the difference between the "apparent" output of the periphery of $460 billion and the value of output at something called "effective" prices of $750 billion is almost $300 billion; this sum is transferred to the centre by means of a 'distorted' price structure, where it swells the income of both workers and capitalists. In case our credulity is being stretched at this point, Amin states that "This statistical illustration of the nature of the imperialist problem is not arbitrary. On the contrary, the basic statistics and hypotheses are conservative and tend to under-estimate the magnitude of the surplus labour extracted on the periphery of the system" (Ibid, p.161).

To establish the destination of this mysterious $300 billion, Amin states that: "The volume of surplus labour extracted from the workers, employees and peasants of the periphery is obviously much too great for me to believe that it is retained completely by the local exploiting classes in the form of rent and profit. The local income of these exploiting classes ($185 billion) is, in fact, less than the extra surplus labour extracted ($300 billion)" (p.162, my emphasis). There are two points to note here. First, Amin clearly regards himself and his 'beliefs' as adequate judges of his own assertions. Secondly, he establishes his assertion by comparing apples and pears: the $185 billion is in 'apparent' prices, the $300 billion in 'effective' prices, so it is difficult to tell which figure is the largest without using a long piece of elastic. However, Amin supports his assertion further by the following argument "if ... this surplus labour were retained by the local exploiting classes, we would see a prodigious development of capitalism, which could then resolve the problem of under-development" (p.162-3). This possibility has, however, already been ruled out completely, by the assertion quoted above.

The final conclusion Amin derives from this exercise is that, although the transfer of $300 billion from periphery to centre benefits mainly the monopoly capitalists, it also benefits workers in the centre by allowing them to carry on their economic struggles under more favourable conditions, "but at the same time these conditions create a fertile soil for the political illusions of reformism, which has thereby achieved hegemony among the workers of the centre" (p.164). Finally, a self-congratulatory peroration: "my analysis corresponds to the interests of 90 percent of the men and women of the capitalist world. It lays the basis for a worker-peasant alliance, an alliance of all exploited workers, on the basis of internationalism, that is the conditions necessary to change the world" (p.166).

A rough approximation to a sensitivity analysis will indicate that Amin's calculation of a 'supersurplus' depends crucially on the level of the productivity index selected. If the productivity index for the periphery were as in Table 3, then the 'supersurplus' would disappear:

Table 3 Productivity Indexes for the Periphery (Centre = 100)

	Amin's Productivity Index	Productivity Index at which supersurplus = zero
Industry	50	38
Petty Bourgeois	30	10
Agriculture	10	7

At productivity indexes below these, the transfer of the supersurplus is in the opposite direction. Since no justification is produced by Amin that peripheral industrial productivity is 5o per cent of central, rather than 38 per cent, the very existence of the 'supersurplus' becomes rather questionable.

One conclusion which might be derived from this exercise is a 'circulationist' one: that the problems of the periphery could be resolved by 'recycling' the super-surplus to the periphery as a basis for accumulation. Amin would, of course, deny the charge of circulationism in assertive terms. Then what, one may ask, was the purpose of the exercise?

Even if we were able to accept the procedure by which Amin has qualified the extent of the 'white man's burden', what exactly does that exercise tell us? Capitalist development has always been characterized by exploitation, yet the demonstration of the exploitation of the working class was not an adequate basis to show that capitalism is not historically progressive. To believe that economic conditions in LDCs would be better if imperialist super-exploitation did not occur is a very curious creed for a Marxist, particularly one who is cognizant of the dramatic changes which have occurred in LDCs in the last 35 years.

Amin's 'analysis' rests on a set of unverified assertions, added to a set of fabricated numbers which are manipulated by means of some arbitrary calculations to produce the conclusion that he first thought of. No credibility can be attached to any stage of the procedure.

No attempt is made to consider how actual prices come to be what they are, since actual prices are asserted to be meaningless. No dynamic analysis of changing conditions of production and distribution of particular commodities is deemed necessary. In fact the issue of changing conditions of production and distribution of commodities is an issue which only a 'reformist' would raise, but by ruling out a discussion of such specific questions, Amin is denying the validity of specific research, and all freedom of manoeuvre of all governments in all LDCs, in order to establish the dangerous political conclusion that only a complete break with the whole capitalist system can provide the basis for 'true' development. Isn't that what Pol Pot's regime did in Kampuchea?

SOME POLITICAL IMPLICATIONS OF AMIN'S IDEAS

Since little credibility can be attached to Amin's economic analysis, it is important to examine the political conclusions he derives with such confidence. In my earlier article (Smith, 1980), I discussed the dangerous implications of Amin's denial of national economies as units of analysis or as levels of political struggle and action. There are other, equally dangerous, implications however. His clear message is that imperialism is the main enemy, that all ills in LDCs are attributable to imperialism, and all LDC struggles are objectively anti-imperialist and hence pro-socialist. Without denying the evils of imperialism and exploitation in poor countries, Amin's argument is the crudest kind of Third Worldism, and rests on the notion that people who are poor, non-Western and super-exploited by imperialism will not exploit each other. Thus this view abstracts from class analysis within LDCs, from the dynamics of exploitation within LDCs and diverts attention from difficult and complex issues of countries' internal political and economic dynamics. For example, the Tamil tea estate workers in Sri Lanka are worse off since nationalisation; this issue cannot be analysed only by reference to imperialism, but requires an analysis of internal class structures. Furthermore, Amin's position provides a basis for the suppression of working class and socialist organizations in LDCs, under the guise of nationalistic anti-imperialism. As Bill Warren argued "The inter-relationship between anti-capitalist and anti-imperialist ideology ... became quite complex. On the one hand, anti-imperialist and anti-capitalist rhetoric and ideology ... became closely interwoven. On the other hand, the fact that the two never fused completely always left the foreign devil to be called out, to fortify the position of those who wished to strengthen themselves against imperialism without opting for a socialist path" (Warren, 1980, p. 117). Warren's argument seems particularly apt in considering, for example, recent events in Iran, though Amin would presumably applaud those events as objectively progressive. Definite prescriptions for political and economic transformation cannot be derived from generalized, abstract assertions without considering the specificity of countries.

Amin's prescription of withdrawal from the world capitalist system as the only basis for 'true' development makes little sense for large economies, let alone small ones, aside from ignoring the reality of increased economic strength and bargaining power of LDCs in relation to world capitalism, and aside from ignoring the lives of millions of persons in countries where a socialist revolution is not on the medium term agenda, let alone the short-term one. In fact, Amin's capacity to ignore the lives of millions has been amply demonstrated by his support for Pol Pot.

REFERENCES

Amin, Samir, (1974), Accumulation on a World Scale; (1976), Unequal Development; (1977), Imperialism and Unequal Development; (1978), The Law of Value and Historical Materialism; (1980), Class and Nation.

Leuddel-Neurath, Richard (1980). 'Export Orientation in South Korea: How Helpful is Dependence Thinking to its Analysis?', IDS Bulletin, Vol.12, No. 1 December.

Leys, Colin, (1977), 'Under-development and Dependency: Critican Notes', Journal of Contemporary Asia, Vol. 7, No.1; (1978), 'Capital Accumulation, Class Formation and Dependency', Socialist Register, 1978, (eds. R. Miliband and J. Saville).

Palma, G., (1978), 'Dependency: A Formal Theory of Under-development or a Methodology for the Concrete Situations of Under-development?' World Development, Vol.6

Schiffer, Jonathan, (1981).' The Changing Post-War Pattern of Development: The Accumulated Wisdom of Samir Amin, World Development,' Vol.9, No. 6 June.

Smith, Sheila, (1980), 'The Ideas of Samir Amin', Journal of Development Studies, Vol. 17, No. 1, October.

Warren, Bill, (1980), Imperialism: Pioneer of Capitalism.

Wells, John, (1977), 'The Diffusion of Durables in Brazil', Cambridge Journal of Economics, September.

Chapter Seven

THE DEBATE ON UNDERDEVELOPMENT: "ON SITUATING GUNDER FRANK"

Richard Leaver.

The critique of Gunder Frank by Ernesto Laclau[1] has provided much food for thought in radical circles during the past years. Generally, the dominant impression has been that Laclau etches out the weaknesses in Frank's theoretical apparatus, exposing the ideological underpinnings of that perspective and the extent to which Frank himself is trapped by the problem of dualism as posed by his immediate adversaries. Frank initially came out of this debate with Laclau as the loser, and his failure to make a public reply was widely interpreted as an admission of defeat.

It is my intention to re-trace the steps of that debate by paying particular attention to Laclau's seminal contribution. I will suggest that Laclau is to some extent conducting a version of a straw man argument against Frank. It is also my belief that Laclau fails to come to terms with a number of important points raised - in a somewhat indirect manner, admittedly - by Frank, and that those points are central to any radical theorist concerned with the problem of underdevelopment/development. They penetrate to the core of marxist theory, and challenge the utility of the concept of mode of production in the context of the colonial and neo-colonial situation. I will also argue that Frank, far from being the 'bumbling Marxist' that Laclau suggests, should be correctly situated outside of marxist theory. This, of course, does not mean that he has nothing to say to marxism.

Laclau asserts that Frank's works are conceptually confused, insofar as he shares with his immediate adversaries a propensity to define the concepts of capitalism and feudalism in terms of exchange relations. Hence, for Frank, capitalism = feudalism + the market, whereas for marxists, capitalism and feudalism are modes of production that must be defined in terms of productive relations. Frank's concept of capitalism is far too broad to be of any analytic value, as indeed it must be given the nature of the task which he has set i.e. arguing for the necessity and possiblity of socialist revolution in Latin America. This generality obscures the vital distinction between capital and capitalism in marxist thinking, and Frank helps the case in this regard by mis-quoting Marx on exactly this point.

As a preliminary defence of Frank, it is important to observe that:

1. the validity of Laclau's criticisms rests on the fundamental assumption that Frank is a marxist - without this assumption, "Frank is at liberty to abstract a mass

of historical features and build a model on this basis" as Laclau puts it. Hence Laclau argues incessantly that Frank is a marxist (pp.20,25,26,27,28). There is simply no evidence for this. Despite Laclau's desire, Frank at best claimed to "contribute to the building of a more adequate general theory of capitalist economic development and ... underdevelopment"[2] and has since bluntly stated his position: "I have never had the temerity myself to claim to be a Marxist; and nowhere in my published - or unpublished - writings can or will anyone find such a personal claim. Who then makes false or pseudo claims?"[3] This is quite correct - no claim exists.

2. Related to the above point, there is Laclau's desire to make a "conceptual clarification". But within what common framework? Laclau leans heavily here upon Frank's reply to Rodolfo Puiggros[4] where Frank tries to frame his theory in terms of the mode of production. But Laclau forgets that in this one instance the terms of the debate are dictated by Puiggros, and Frank's reply necessarily reflects this. For if left to his own devices, Frank never argues in terms of 'modes of production .[5] Wherever the terms appear in his works, Frank is referring scornfully to the theories of his C.P. adversaries. I would suggest, then, that there is no common ground upon which Laclau can construct his 'conceptual clarification', and that Laclau is largely talking past Frank in this regard.
3. Laclau also points out that Frank misquotes Marx at a vital point, and that this intellectual error blurs the distinction between capital and capitalism. Now I would not deny the absence of this distinction in Frank, but I would suggest that it is not simply due to an error in translation, and that its roots are far more systematic and purposive. Laclau does not see that Frank gives an accurate translation of that same passage at an earlier date.[6]

Taken separately, these points lack force, but collectively I feel that they do, in fact, add up to something quite significant. For essentially Laclau reads Frank not through Frank's own framework but through his own theoretical concepts. Frank is then criticized for the inadequate way in which he defines these concepts - concepts which are alien to him. The impression is left that Frank is a blunderer, and that all that is needed to transcend his efforts is to employ a modicum of conceptual rigor. This is far from the case, as I shall demonstrate.

Laclau moves from his analysis of Frank's 'theoretical mistakes' in an attempt to create a superior analytical framework. His keystone is the concept of mode of production, which he defines as "the logical and mutually co-ordinated articulation of:1) a determinate type of ownership of the means of production; 2) a determinate form of appropriation of the economic surplus; 3) a determinate degree of development of the division of labour; 4) a determinate level of development of the productive forces." Furthermore, he is of the opinion that "property in the means of production constitutes the decisive element" within this totality (p.33). And indeed, Laclau wields it decisively. The free labourer's sale of his labour power becomes the specific difference between capitalism and feudalism - it is "fundamental" (p.25), "decisive" (p.27). Immanuel Wallerstein has neatly encapsulated Laclau's argument - "if proletariat, then capitalism"? Laclau argues, therefore, that the mode of production can be identified by investigating the relationship between the direct producer and the surplus appropriating non-producer, and that this relationship is the logical starting point for marxist analysis. Having identified the existince of feudal productive relations within the periphery, Laclau sets about the task of explaining how the feudal mode of production serves certain functions for the capitalist mode of production at the centre.

If we took Laclau seriously when he suggested that Frank was intellectually naive and that his errors were errors of definition, then I think we would be doing Frank a gross injustice. Far from being ignorant of Laclau's apparent sophistication, Frank vigorously rejects the very position for which Laclau is arguing; ie., that an investigation of relations between the producer and the non-productive appropriator is a logical starting point for the analysis of underdevelopment. Let me quote some examples to substantiate this point: "if all non-cash nexus relations in agriculture are <u>by definition</u> non-capitalist and all money-contract payments capitalist, then the traditional Marxist theses about the conditions of agricultural employment are of course true by definition. But in that case they teach us nothing about reality And the reality of Brazilian agriculture is that the thousand and one variations and combinations of agricultural working relations are intermixed in all areas..."[8] "Which of these forms of the exploitative relationship, or their combinations, will obtain in a given case depends above all on the interest of the owner. And these in turn are determined by the capitalist economy of which he is a part."[9] "Evidently capitalism admits of, nay, requires, a variety of such relations corresponding to the variety of capitalist circumstances and development."[10]

Here Frank points to the inflexibility of Laclau's approach, for the latter certainly does equate the emergence of a rural proletariat with wage payment and land tenancy with 'servile obligations'.[11] These passages also indicate that Frank is hardly insensitive to the existence of different forms of productive relations. All that he denies is that they are in any sense fundamental. It is true, as

Laclau puts it, "that Frank totally dispenses with relations of production in his definitions of capitalism and feudalism"[12], but what Laclau omits to say is that Frank, far from being ignorant of his 'error', vigorously defends his dispensation. It is not as 'surprising' as Laclau suggests. For Frank "the owner-worker relationship, far from being the starting point of the chain of determination - or the fundamental contradiction to use Marxist terms - is only an extension and a manifestation of the determinant economic structure and relation. That structure is monopoly capitalism ..."[13] Furthermore, Frank argues that the words 'feudal' and 'capitalist' should be reserved "to refer to what is really central, the economic and social system and its structure itself, rather than applying them to all sorts of associated features"[14] (i.e., relations between owners and workers, behaviour and motivation of people, productive and distributive techniques, etc.).

This is the core of the debate between the two - what is 'fundamental' to Laclau is merely a 'manifestation' an 'associated feature' to Frank. Having decided that the question of productive relations is at best secondary, Frank's solution is to throw the baby (mode of production) out with the bathwater (relations of production). Nevertheless, Frank identifies a real problem, and his whole theoretical framework is best understood as a reaction to this problem. If productive relations are purely conditional upon the economic calculus of the 'formal capitalist' - if they are just another 'production possibility' curve - then their causal weight is slight indeed. Ranjit Sau, for instance, has given us a good example of the exact situation to which Frank is directing our attention. Referring to the Green Revolution in India, he points out that "... the farmers with the new technology prefer to use attached labourers, or permanent labourers, rather than casual labourers. They even go to the extent of giving some land to the workers to keep them tied. Such phenomena may tend to give the impression of resurgence of semi-feudalism..."[15] Frank tells us that, for Brazil, "various owner-worker relations are found intermixed all over the country, in each region, on many single farms, within many worker families; and they often change back and forth even from one growing season to another: .. is this because the degree of feudalism or of capitalist penetration concomitantly differs from one place, or family, or year, to another?"[16] On the contrary, he asserts that 'commercial determination' orders the forms of productive relation, and this is, in turn, a reaction to the economy at large. The type of crop is important, as is the degree of fluctuation in production and the amount and reliability of labour. What appear as 'feudal features' are facades for commercial exploitation. In short, capitalism does not necessarily imply the cash-nexus.

Now there is no doubt that Frank is grappling with a very

real problem here, but his solution to it is far from satisfactory. Instead of trying to specify the possible variation of productive relations within the capitalist mode of production, Frank opts for generality. He takes steps backwards until the problem which he identified has disappeared from sight. In this sense, I feel that Frank's emphasis on "the contradiction of continuity in change"[17] is disastrous, and that the true task of marxist analysis should be to highlight specific differences rather than to obscure them. Revolutionary strategy must be based on something more specific than a general appeal to 'the oppressed'.

The best we can say for Laclau's solution to Frank's dilemma is that it returns us to Frank's starting point, where everything is true by definition. For beneath the immediately apparent conceptual precision of Laclau lurk a number of thorny problems. Take, for instance, the feudal mode of production which he identifies in the Latin American countryside. Despite the fact that Laclau avoids the simplification of 'dualist' theories by linking the existence of this mode to the capitalist mode of production at the centre, the problem arises as to why we should even consider this 'feudal mode' to be a mode of production. It clearly lacks any dynamic of its own, and it is merely a reflective reaction to the rate of profit at the centre. If we are to investigate modes of production on the assumption that by doing so we learn something about the 'laws of motion' of the social formation within which it occurs, then Laclau's conceptualization seems totally beside the point, for his 'feudal mode' has no autonomy. In a paradoxical way, Laclau simply scores a point for Frank - who has argued all along that 'the centre' determines what goes on in 'the periphery' - and the differences between the two are thereby reduced to semantics.

Secondly, there is this rather odd concept of Laclau's - the economic system. This appears, at best, to be a grab-bag of ideas necessarily introduced by Laclau in order to hold together his various modes of production. It has concertina-properties, expanding to encompass the globe and in the next instance, shrinking down to a regional level. Not only that, but it can unite together economic sectors (industry, etc.) with modes of production (capitalism, feudalism, etc.) and productive units (individual farms, multinational corporations, etc.). If Frank's metaphor of the world-embracing octopus sucking out capital seemed bad, it at least had the virtue of being intelligible.

Let me summarise my argument up to this point. I have suggested that Frank's theories can be seen as a reaction to a crucial problem - the problem of correspondence between productive relations and modes of production. Frank solves it by scrapping the terminology altogether and opting for a 'model' of capitalism based on the monopoly of the centre vis-à-vis the periphery. Laclau reads Frank's 'solution' without seeing the problem to which the solution pertained, and therefore he returns us to the original starting point. We have now gone full circle, and in this sense Laclau's critique is a pre-Frankian one.

I would also maintain that the 'model' of capitalism which Frank employs has almost nothing to do with marxism, and that the task of an 'internal critique' of Frank still remains to be done, although important parts of it have been sketched out by Giovanni Arrighi. As with Laclau, Arrighi argues for the predominance of productive relations, but his critique at least takes the effort to read Frank through his own 'model'. Arrighi argues that Frank postulates the dominance of the colonial structure over the class structure, and that the resulting model has strong elements of determinism built in, which leads Frank to emphasize the continuity of the peripheral experience.[18]

An internal critique of Frank would also have to come to grips with his terminology, which is exclusively based on the use of polar opposites - appropriation/expropriation, metropolis/satellite, dependence/autonomy, etc., The latter concept dependence - offers, I feel, much more of an insight into the true nature of Frank's works than Laclau provides us with, and it is perhaps the key to correctly situating Frank. This concept has its origins in the works of Prebisch, but it is a common feature of much of the writing originating from the Third World which proclaims the irrelevance of neo-classicism to the problems of underdevelopment.[19] It tries to encapsulate 'the views from below' and it is in part a reaction to the cosmopolitan nature of metropolitan-born theories of imperialism and development.

Originally 'dependence' was seen as a national affliction common to the 'third world' and the concept achieved its highest level of development in this guise in the works of Osvaldo Sunkel.[20] Frank, of course, never endorsed this 'nationalist' formulation of dependence theory, although it was not always too clear in his earlier works. However, he increasingly aligned himself with Theotonio Dos Santos[21] who, operating with a clear grasp of the maoist dictum that "the fundamental cause of the development of a thing is not external but internal"[22], rejected the notion of external dependence and referred to dependence as "a conditioning situation" which "cannot be understood without reference to the articulation of dominant interests in the hegemonic centres and in the dependent societies."[23]

The two questions that need to be asked are (1) whether or not this "radical" version of dependence theory really amounts to anything essentially different from Frank's so-called 'bourgeois dependence theorists' (Furtado, Prebisch, Pinto, Sunkel), and (2) whether the concept of dependence can have any explicable content.

To take the latter question first, it is noticeable that, of late, a number of radicals have begun to voice their disapproval of the concept, although their reasons have rarely been clearly articulated. Hamza Alavi has recently said that dependence theory obscures the structural differences between those 'third world' countries in which some degree of national industrialization is taking place and those where it is not.[24] James Petras objects to 'the dominance of the colonial structure', as Arrighi terms it, and argues that class forces must be taken into account.[25] Both of these author's, however, seem to equate dependence with external dependence, and their criticisms say very little that Dos Santos would not endorse. We must, I feel, keep firmly in mind the fact that dependence was advanced as a concept precisely to account for the essential unity of the experience of the 'third world' which, it was asserted, was characterised by its 'dependent insertion' into the world system. Dependence conceived in this manner was a qualitative variable which drew the line of demarcation between the 'developed' and the 'underdeveloped'. Furthermore this qualitative variable assumed different forms throughout history[26] - financial dependence, industrial dependence, technological dependence, etc.

Few attempts, however, have ever been made to define the concept. Dos Santos' conception of dependence as a 'conditioning situation', while superficially attractive, is not precise enough. That the world is not composed of 'autonomous agents' be they countries, classes, or multi-national corporations, on the one hand, and those who are 'conditioned' (i.e., are limited by their environment) seems too obvious to belabour. 'Being limited' is a common affliction, although there are, equally obviously, different degrees of limitation. If, however, dependence is a question of degree and not of kind, then the notion that dependence is a qualitative variable seems to be challenged. Perhaps this calls for the invocation of the famous law of the transformation of quantity into quality.

A second tack would be to exclude the 'developed' world from the 'dependent' world. Havelock Brewster does this. Having defined dependence as "a lack of capacity to manipulate the operative elements of an economic system", and having characterised the symptoms of dependence as "as absence of interdependence between the economic functions of a system" (which implies the lack of an internal dynamic, the impossibility of planning, and the localization of political revolt), he then proceeds to define Great Britain out of his field of investigation.[27] This sort of game is not much help.

It seems to me that the notion of dependence really implies nothing more or less than the lack of some factor. Technological dependence is simply the lack of technology, financial dependence the lack of finance, etc. Now these 'lacks' have to be explained in class terms, no doubt, and related to the mechanisms of capital accumulation which govern the dissemination of technology, etc. But to invoke dependence as an explanation for underdevelopment seems to me to be profoundly mystifying; all that we are doing is stating what we already know in a different way. The task of naming should not be confused with that of explanation.

But to return from this long detour to the original question - just what is the distance between radical dependency theory and its 'bourgeois' parent? The answer is - not much at all. Prebisch, for instance, related 'underdevelopment' to the declining terms of trade for the 'third world', and this, in turn, was explained by the monopoly/monopsony powers of the metropolis. To get from Prebisch's model to Frank's, two quite simple transformations are involved:

1) Generalization of Prebisch's metaphor of centre/periphery so that, instead of there being only one centre and one periphery, we get a hierarchy of centres and peripheries.
2) Generalization of the monopoly powers which accrue to the centre. For Prebisch the centre had monopoly powers over the price setting mechanism - hence his political strategy, acted out in UNCTAD, was based on countering this.

For Frank the centre has a monopoly 'on everything', and he maintains that this has been so since colonial formation.[28]

If this can be accepted, then I think we have a much more sound basis for situating Frank and his contribution to the study of underdevelopment. It avoids the mistake which Laclau makes - of reading Frank as a theoretically naive marxist. It also challenges the almost universally accepted conflation of Baran and Frank.[29]

NOTES:

1. E. Laclau. "Feudalism and Capitalism in Latin America", New Left Review. No. 67.

2. A.G. Frank. Capitalism and Underdevelopment in Latin America, Penguin. Harmondsworth, 1971) p.37.

3. A.G. Frank, "Dependence is Dead, Long Live Dependence and the Class Struggle: An Answer to Critics", Unpublished Paper. I understand that this paper has subsequently been published in French in Partisans, No.68, 1972.

4. Reprinted in part as Chapter 15 of A.G. Frank, Latin America: Underdevelopment or Revolution (M.R.P.,New York,1970).

5. This is certainly the case in Frank's earlier works. However, in a recent article by Frank ("Development and Underdevelopment in the New World: Smith and Marx vs. the

Weberians", Theory and Society, Vol.2 (4), Winter 1975) there is clear evidence of a shift in this regard, for he begins to talk about "the diversity of modes of production in the New World", which is clearly an advance upon his blanket use of 'capitalism' common to his earlier works. However, even here, his usage of 'mode of production' has little in common with Laclau and is perhaps more closely linked to the concept of 'productive system' as employed by Kari Levitt, Lloyd Best and George Beckford, amongst others.

6. See A.G. Frank, Capitalism and Underdevelopment, op.cit., p.45.

7. I. Wallerstein, "The Rise and Future Demise of the World Capitalist System: Concepts for Comparative Analysis", Comparative Studies in Society and History, Vol.16(4), 1974, p.394. Wallerstein's work constitutes a much-neglected and highly original development upon the Frankian perspective of 'capitalism as a process'. For a good summary of his work, see R. Aya, "The Present as 'Jumbo History': A Review Article", Race and Class, Vol.17(2), 1975.

8. A.G. Frank, Capitalism and Underdevelopment, op.cit., p.262. My emphasis.

9. ibid., p.293

10. ibid., p.294

11. E. Laclau, op.cit., p.31 for the best evidence of this.

12. ibid., p.25

13. A.G. Frank, Capitalism and Underdevelopment, op.cit., p.292. My emphasis.

14. ibid., pp.267-268 My emphasis.

15. R. Sau, "Political Economy of Indian Agriculture, Economic and Political Weekly, 19.5.73, p.913. P.H. Prasad observes the same attachments of labour, but infers from it exactly what Sau warns us against - the existence of feudalism. See his "Production Relations: Achilles Heel of Indian Planning"; Economic and Political Weekly, 12.5.73, pp.869-872.

16. A.G. Frank, Capitalism and Underdevelopment, op.cit.,p.292.

17. ibid.,pp.36-38

18. G. Arrighi, "The Relationship between the Colonial and the Class Structures: A Critique of A.G. Frank's theory of the development of underdevelopment", paper presented at the conference on Imperialism - it's place in the Social Sciences Today, Elsinore, May 1971.

19. An excellent paper which centres upon this theme is N. Girvan, "The Development of Dependency Economics in the Caribbean and Latin America: Review and Comparison", Social and Economic Studies, Vol.22(1), March 1973.

20. See O. Sunkel, "National Development Policy and External Dependence in Latin America"; The Journal of Development Studies, Vol.6(1), October 1969. Sunkel's later works, of course, reject this position.

21. The clearest indication of this is given in J.D. Cockcroft, A.G. Frank and D.L. Johnson, *Dependence and Underdevelopment: Latin America's Political Economy* (Anchor, New York, 1972), p.xiv. See also A.G. Frank, *Lumpenbourgeoisie: Lumpendevelopment* (M.R.P., New York, 1972), p.9.

22. Mao Tse-Tung, "On Contradiction"; in *Four Essays on Philosophy* (F.L.P., Peking, 1969), p.26.

23. T. Dos Santos, "The Crisis of Development Theory and the Problem of Dependence in Latin America, in H. Bernstein (ed), *Underdevelopment and Development: The Third World Today* (Penguin Harmondsworth, 1973), p.78.

24. H. Alavi, "India and the Colonial Mode of Production", *Socialist Register*, 1975, p.193.

25. J. Petras, "New Perspectives on Imperialism and Social Classes in the Periphery", *Journal of Contemporary Asia*, Vol.5(3), 1975, p.305.

26. Samir Amin provides as clear a statement of these various forms as anyone. See his *Accumulation on a World Scale*, (M.R.P., New York, 1974).

27. H. Brewster, "Economic Dependence: A Quantitative Interpretation", *Social and Economic Studies*, Vol.22(1), March 1973.

28. See, for instance, A.G. Frank, *Capitalism and Underdevelopment*, *op.cit*., pp.205-206, where Frank describes the changing forms this monopoly has taken throughout history. It should be obvious from this passage that what Frank means by 'monopoly capitalism' is in no way comparable with the commonly accepted usage.

29. This conflation is shared by proponents and critics alike. Ted Wheelwright, for instance, wants to lump the two together. According to him, Frank developed upon "the rich legacy left by Paul Baran" and was "directly influenced by Baran". See his *Radical Political Economy: Collected Essays* (A.N.Z. Sydney, 1974), pp.249-50. John Taylor, from a highly critical perspective, is even more emphatic: Baran and Frank share the same problematic, the same theoretical or ideological framework. See his "Neo-Marxism and Underdevelopment - a Sociological Fantasy", *Journal of Contemporary Asia*, Vol.4(1), 1974, pp.7,10,12.

Chapter Eight

GUNDER FRANK IN RETREAT?

Jairus Banaji

Frank's work and the "dependency school" were basically products of a specific historical conjuncture in the accumulation of capital. The massive structural reorganization of the world economy bound up with the postwar restabilization of capitalism entailed a period of forced economic liberalization for those backward countries which had already experienced a certain accumulation of capital. Starting in the fifties, regimes which prefigured a form of capitalist democracy for Latin America and whose stability was linked to an older national capitalism entered a period of crisis and decomposition.

Opposition to "imperialism" became the common platform of the older national-protectionist capitalism and of the revolutionary wing opposed to capitalism as a whole. In some sense, the significance of Frank's work was its conscious attempt to break loose from the characteristic themes of petty-bourgeois democracy and create an independent platform for the revolutionary element. To do this, Frank chose to argue that agrarian backwardness was not something separable from the domination of world capitalism but an intrinsic part of it.

If Capitalism and Underdevelopment (cu) argued this specifically with reference to Chile and Brazil, World Accumulation (WA) attempts a loose generalization of this argument across space and time. Frank defines his theme as "a historical account of the process of capital accumulation"(p16).

I shall deal with the book chiefly in two parts. Firstly, insofar as Frank's study claims to form a historical summary of major developments that define the period of early capitalism (16-18th centuries), I shall take up issues related to his historical framework. Secondly, insofar as Frank claims to analyse these developments from a Marxist point of view, I shall concentrate on the way he tackles some of the theoretical issues involved.

1. THE HISTORICAL FRAMEWORK

> "I would say much less about the new mode of production. An enormous gulf always separates it from the facts you speak of, and presented in this direct form it appears as a pure abstraction which does not make the thing clearer but rather more obscure."
> (Engels to Kautsky, 1889)

(i) Cycles of accumulation?

Wallerstein's conception that "It was in the 16th century that there came to be a European world economy based upon the capitalist mode of production" (1974 p.67, emphasis mine) is also the starting-point of Frank's book. Its basic presupposition and stated object of enquiry is the accumulation process of capital as a world process, and this is described mainly in terms of major historical cycles in the epoch of early capitalism.

What is the nature of these cycles? Although this is never clearly specified at any single point in the book, Frank strongly suggests that these massive cyclical fluctuations that define whole centuries are intrinsic to the movement of the accumulation process. Let us see in what sense exactly. On p.65 of *WA*, initiating his chapter on the "seventeenth century depression", Frank writes, "the crisis and depression of the 17th c. may - and should - be traced and related to the earlier economic expansion: the development of capital accumulation in the 16th c." Therefore, when Frank goes on to write, "It is clear that the depression of the 17th c. followed the growth of the 16th c." (p.65), "followed" is implied in more than merely a chronological sense. Frank is arguing that between the cycle of expansion of one century and the supposed cycle of depression of the next there is a logical connection. On p.98, "During the 17th c...the previous expansion and accumulation of capital underwent a crisis of adjustment". And later, referring to 1762-89, "the entire"..international economy was going through a long crisis of accumulation" (p.171, emph. mine).

That crises are intrinsic to the accumulation process, that the accumulation of capital inevitably leads to an over-accumulation of capital, to a failure of valorisation, which is reflected cyclically in the form of periodic crises, is a basic and absolutely correct understanding of the economic cycle of developed capitalism (Grossmann, 1970; Mattick, 1974). But how far is it valid to suppose that this is the kind of cycle which accounts for the more complicated rhythms of early capitalism? (e.g. Van der Wee 1963) In other words, how far does any study of the epoch of early capitalism deal with a process of accumulation which has already evolved in its classical shape, and therefore with cycles which reflect the intrinsic movement of this process?

In short, what is the nature of the "capitalism" in question? Is it true, as Wallerstein and Frank suppose, that the world market of the 16-17th centuries was "based upon the capitalist mode of production"? In Vol.3 of Capital Marx writes, "whereas in the 16th and still partially in the 17th centuries the sudden expansion of commerce and emergence of a new world market decisively contributed to the downfall of the old mode of production and the rise of capitalist production, this process was, conversely, only carried through on the basis of the capitalist mode of production. The world market itself forms the basis for this capitalist mode of production. On the other hand, the immanent necessity of this mode of production to produce on an ever-expanded scale tends to extend the world market continually, so that it is not commerce in this case which revolutionises industry but industry which constantly revolutionises commerce". (Marx 1959 p.328, transl. modified, emph. mine. Cf. Marx p.470)

The meaning is quite clear, Marx contrasts two distinct stages in the historical development of capitalism. During the first it is "commerce", the "world market", or the general process of commodity expansion, of the penetration of commodity-forms of production, which forms the basis for the capitalist mode of production - that is, creates the conditions that enable it to develop. During the second, the stage characteristic of developed capitalism, capital in the technological shape of large-scale industry and mass production, rebounds on the world market and constantly revolutionises it. The latter, industrial capitalism or the "specifically capitalist mode of production" finds its own "material foundation" in machinery (Marx 1976 p.554) which in turn implies both the real subordination of labour to capital (the reconstruction of work process by capital) and the production of relative surplus-value (the drive for increases in productivity).

A world market "based upon the capitalist mode of production", i.e. a world economy founded on the rhythms of large-scale industrial capitalism and of the accumulation process linked to it, was still three centuries distant from the nascent world market of the 16th-17th centuries. Indeed, as the best historical work clearly suggests, 16th c. capitalism bore a predominantly speculative financial and commercial character.[1]

As if this is not clear enough, Marx himself explicitly states, "the peculiar cyclical path of modern industry, which occurs in no earlier period of human history, was also impossible when capitalist production was in its infancy. The composition of capital at that time underwent only very gradual changes. By and large, therefore, the proportional growth in the demand for labour corresponds to the accumulation of capital..." (1976 p.785). On the other hand, under developed capitalism the accumulated mass of capital always becomes, periodically, too large in relation to the given degree of exploitation, or there is not enough surplus-value to valorise the given capital, resulting in crises.

In which case, what was the character of the "cycles" that defined the epoch of commercial capitalism when the sole form of modern capitalist production was the manufactory? There are places in WA where Frank sustains a weaker position, ascribing to the cycles in question a "precapitalist" character (p.260). Yet Frank requires the postulate of specifically capitalist cycles to sustain a central assumption of the model of incorporation which I shall refer to shortly, with the result that the entire framework of theory around which the book is constructed is permeated by a sense of uncertainty and confusion. The notion that the cyclical fluctuations of early capitalism were cycles of accumulation in the sense of movements intrinsic to the nature of the accumulation process finally loses its implicit status of a basic argument and organising principle of the study to become only a series of question-marks. "Can we go further and find fluctuations in investment and profitability which could be termed cycles in that the downswing is caused by the upswing itself?" (p.260-61). (But obviously one has to if one is going to talk about "crises of accumulation", as Frank does, p.171.) "If there was an "investment cycle", how so?" (p.265). "If these events already represent cyclical fluctuations in productive investment, how did this prehistory of capital differ from its history?" (p.266), and so on.

Any attempt to reconstruct the history of early capitalism in terms of images derived from the history of developed capitalism is bound to run into massive problems of historical interpretation. Let us look for a moment at the way the so-called "depression of the 17th c." is handled.[2] Frank argues, "Most of the 17th c. was marked by a worldwide depression" (p.65). Two separate causal chains appear to be involved in his conception of this 17th c. "crisis". In the first place, the 16th c. price revolution had ended, leading to a "drastic decline in the rates of inflationary increase" (p.67). Moreover, "Along with the decline in prices, there was undoubtedly a decline in rates of profit" (p.67 emph. mine).

How far does this picture stand up? First, what is the nature of the (supposed) connection between declining prices and declining profitability? Frank suggests, as we have seen, that the 17th c. depression was a classic type of capitalist crisis rooted in the accumulation process of capital. However, if one accepts a notion of this sort, then the decline in commodity prices to which Frank draws attention cannot simultaneously be accepted as the "cause" of the crisis or downswing. As Grossmann (1970) showed some time back, Marx demonstrated the law of the falling rate of profit and thus the cyclical movement of profitability under developed capitalism, in abstraction from the movement of competition, i.e., fluctuations in the level of commodity-prices (including the price of labour-power). Therefore Frank is right to be more cautious. He says, "the decline in prices" was only the most "visible manifestation of the crisis" (p.76). But what was the so-called "crisis" due to?

Moreover, was there a "crisis" of accumulation in this period or any later period defined by low prices? Lublinskaya points out, "for Holland, England and France", the three countries that would matter most for Frank's argument, "the beginning of the (17th) century was not accompanied by the appearance of conditions unfavourable to (capitalist) development, despite the reduction in the influx of precious metals and the fall in prices which had already begun" (Lublinskaya 1968 p.13). In France, "low prices did not affect industry adversely...the first decade of the 17th c. was a period of boom in manufacture, craft production and agriculture..." (op.cit. p.13). In fact," both periods of particularly low prices (1600-15, 1660-80) were at the same time periods of marked boom and growth of capitalism in those countries where one can in general talk of such a phenomenon in the seventeenth century, namely, England, France and Holland" (op.cit. p.15, emphasis mine).

Frank's "undoubted decline in rates of profit" suffers from a slight element of historical impressionism. What really underlies the dogma of a 17th c. crisis is simply the contrast between this century and the previous one.

A second chain of causal connection is the collapse of the Baltic trade in the 1620s (on p.74 this "initiates the general crisis"). But in that case, what caused this collapse? Again, as Lublinskaya argues, a purely economic explanation appears to be ruled out. "What caused the reduction of imports of Baltic grain? In every case mentioned, the causes were purely political..." (Lublinskaya 1968 p.48). Although this is not an argument Frank would want to accept, in terms of an explanation of the "17th c. crisis" he has nothing else to go on.

The fact is that "it is anyway easy to find agreement that a "crisis" had in large measure overtaken Europe then no attempt is made to establish what the various authors understand by the word or whether their definitions coincide" (Polishensky 1974 p.12). Whereas a form of underconsumptionism underlies Hobsbawm's argument for the crisis (Hobsbawm 1954), Frank's notion of the crisis is more nebulous. If one accepts a Hamiltonian picture of the 16th c. (inflow of metals - price rise - profit inflation), one's theory of the economic cycle is fundamentally Keynesian (on the influence of Hamilton on Keynes, see Vilar 1956). On the other hand, Frank also suggests that it is the accumulation of capital itself that brings on the crisis.

What Frank anyway confuses are crises of capitalism as such and general economic crises through which capitalism seeks to remove the obstacles to its further development. Redescribing this methodologically, he confuses the conditions and presuppositions of capital created by the movement of capital itself with the conditions and presuppositions that belong to the history of the creation of capitalism (Marx, 1973 p.459 ff., Zeleny 1973 p.60 ff.). And this confusion is consistent with Frank's conception of the accumulation process as something historically given, as a pre-supposition of his analysis.

(ii) The second serfdom

However, there is a more specific reason why Frank chooses to organise his historical account of early capitalism in terms of cycles which are supposedly rooted in the rhythm of capital accumulation. On p.54 of WA he proposes the hypothesis that "institutional changes are primarily determined by what is "good business"... and ...as the historical examination in this book suggests,"external" contradictions appear to have more immediate importance when business is good and internal contradictions have more immediate importance when business is bad..." This is translateable into the argument that "during cyclical upswings such as those which were relatively predominant in the 16th c., merchant capital...achieved a relative predominance and contributed significantly through overseas trade (and of course pillage) to metropolitan capital accumulation .But during the cyclical downswings such as predominated particularly during much of the 17th c, capitalist development was promoted predominantly through changes in the mode of production..." (p.97-98).

In a sense this is the only substantive hypothesis proposed in WA. The most striking aspect of the argument is its manifest incoherence. For what else are "institutional changes" (supposedly linked to periods of boom, or "good business") if not "changes in the mode of production" (supposedly linked to conditions of crisis)? And what else if not these "institutional changes" or changes in the social organisation of production generate the "internal contradictions" that define periods of crisis?

That these equations are not arbitrary or gratuitous will be clear from Frank himself. Perhaps a major "institutional change" that occurred over the period Frank deals with was the enserfment of the peasantry in east Europe. To support the idea that this occurred basically in a period of world boom, Frank has to reinterpret the entire "second serfdom" more or less in the image first suggested by Hans Rosenbert (1943-44 p.233) for Brandenburg-Prussia specifically. "Gutsherrschaft, organised by express design as a commercial enterprise and managed in a fashion which effectively used land and people as capital", Rosenberg wrote, "was the Junker's answer to the Price Revolution." Frank therefore has to accentuate the world market aspects of the second serfdom, ascribing to these - the powerful expansion of demand for Baltic grain - the basic role in precipitating the vast continental movement of feudal restabilization. What this fails to notice is that fundamentally it was not the export of commodities but the production of commodities, not the world market as such and its supposedly capitalist pressure, but the market or the general process of commodity expansion, of the penetration of commodity forms of (feudal) production, that inspired the landowners from one end of east Europe to the other to introduce those changes in the productive organisation of the estate which we call the 'second serfdom' it had practically nothing to do, directly, with world market conditions, but did, nonetheless, relate centrally to the expansion of demand in their home markets. If the neo-feudal economies of Prussia, and, to some extent, of Poland were directly integrated into the world market boom of the 16th c., in Lithuania (Pokhylevych 1957), Bohemia (Polishensky 1974 p.88, Valka 1965), Hungary (Pach 1972, p.118, Kirilly and Kiss 1968, p.1212, p.1223) and Russia (Blum 1957, p.832, Blum, 1968 p.205, Confino 1963, p.136) it was basically the expansion of domestic markets that produced the turn to manorial production of grain on the basis of labour-service. Indeed, Topolski (1974) argues that this is basically also true of Poland.[3]

Precisely because the chief momentum behind the enserfment of the east European peasantry derived not from the cyclical fluctuations of the world market, but from processes of commodity expansion within their individual countries, it was possible for Kula to come up with the finding that in Poland feudal incomes actually expanded in the course of the 17th c. while the peasantry was further impoverished (Kula 1970 p. 95f.). Frank writes, "his (Kula's) analysis implies that the process of enserfment continued throughout the 17th c. on into the 18th c., despite the 17th c. depression in Western Europe...(this) would lead one to suppose as Blum's own interpretation suggests, that enserfment proceeded equally in times of depression and times of economic expansion" (p.61). Frank draws a more or less correct conclusion, but it is not one that fits with his hypothesis that "institutional changes" characterise only or mainly periods of world boom, and so he adds, "This would be hard to believe"(!).

What is "hard to believe", on the contrary, is that the world economy of the period of early capitalism had already developed a dynamism sufficiently strong to account for the basic internal evolution of a whole range of countries - regardless of the degree of development of capitalism within them. In this respect the world market expansion of the 16th-18th centuries stands out in sharp contrast to that of the 19th century. The sort of picture that Frank attempts to draw for early capitalism only gains validity once industrial capitalism comes into being and begins to determine the fundamental motion of reproduction throughout the world. In short, Frank's historical framework is difficult to accept as it stands. Its basis is a world market abstractionism[4], which is, however, crucial to what I shall now describe as the model of incorporation.

2. INCORPORATION MODELS AND THE NOTION OF WAGE-LABOUR

> "Only at a certain stage of the development of capital does the exchange of capital and labour become in fact formally free"
> (Marx 1973 p.770)

The epoch of early capitalism is definable as an epoch dominated by the law of the transformation of precapitalist into capitalist relations of production and forms of social life. It is an epoch whose historical tendency is therefore given by the dissolution of all prior modes of production. A historical analysis of early capitalism must therefore deal not only with the conditions under which the law penetrates and revolutionises the various countries of the world, but also, and mainly, with the forms and specific stages of this process of penetration. In Marx's work the portions dealing specifically with "so-called primitive accumulation" (the formational process of wage-labour), with the formal/real subsumption of labour into capital (the technological forms of the subordination of wage-labour to capital) and with "usury" (Marx 1973 p.853, pp.509-10, 1959 p.239, 1971 p.487, p.530. Banaji 1977a) all bear directly on this historical process of the penetration of capitalism.

An "incorporation model" of the growth of world capitalism can then be defined as a model that studies the development of capitalism not as a process of penetration of capitalist relations of production in historically concrete forms, but as a process that creates the conditions under which penetration becomes possible. It advocates the general thesis that integration into the world market represents the general form of incorporation into world capitalism. It is therefore crucially dependent on the assumption that the world market of early capitalism is already, in some fundamental sense, a form of world capitalism.

In the debate around Frank's work this model has taken two basic forms. (a) Following (early) Frank and Wallerstein, one posits a "single world capitalist system" that instantly reconstructs relations of production through incorporation into the world market (world capitalism). This is why Wallerstein is committed to defending the absurd notion that the Polish nobility of the 17th c., represented a class of "capitalists". In Hegel's terms one might say that the principle that regulates this form of the model is the abstract identity of world capitalism. (b) Following some of Frank's critics like Laclau, one posits a definite or indefinite multiplicity of precapitalist modes of production incorporated into world capitalism (the world market) and internal to its process of reproduction. (Here capital is purely negativity; it reproduces modes of production other than itself.) In its dualistic form (b), this model directly contradicts the thesis that the epoch of early capitalism is an epoch of the dissolution of all antecedent modes of production.

In this form it is therefore unacceptable in principle. On the other hand in its early-Frankian, antidualist and undifferentiated form (a), it is methodologically unacceptable, because it treats capital as a fixed essence, something incapable of the development of form and therefore intrinsically devoid of form. (For this reason it can say nothing about the State, beyond repeating the most general and perfectly useless formulas.)

Now despite its obvious elements of continuity with the rest of Frank's work, WA represents a certain novelty. It concludes by shifting hesitantly from an incorporation model of type (a) to one of type (b). Unlike CU with its directly polemical thrust against dualism and the theory of stages, WA is prepared to argue that the "single worldwide process of accumulation" embraced both "wage-labour" and "other relations of production", i.e. precapitalist (p.240-41) or non-capitalist (p.241 f.) relations

According to Frank, "superexploitation" formed the fundamental link between metropolitan capitalism and the incorporated sectors of world economy. By "superexploitation" Frank means a reduction of wages below the value of labour-power (except that for him this appears to represent a third form of surplus-value production which is neither relative nor absolute, whereas for Marx it is a form of absolute surplus-value production). "This superexploitation occurs both through wage-labour and through other relations of production" (p.240) which are not capitalist.

Frank is at least consistent. The (absurd) notion of a non-wage labour based accumulation of capital has two consequences. On the one hand, Frank has to argue, "accumulation, then, could not be said to have been directly based on surplus-value insofar as it was not produced by free wage-labourers" (p.241). On the other hand, as regards the process of primitive accumulation, "a considerable mass of the capital amassed...before the Industrial Revolution was produced with relations of production that did not imply, require or even permit the wage-labour divorce of producers from their means of production" (p.242), emphasis mine).

From a Marxist point of view both these views are logically inadmissible. It is quite meaningless to assert that accumulation, grasped conceptually, is nothing other than the conversion of surplus-value into capital, hence logically presupposes 'surplus-value'. Secondly, "primitive accumulation is nothing else than the historical process of divorcing the producer from the means of production" (Marx 1976 pp.874-75, 1971 p.271, p.311). It is the very process of formation of wage-labour, and to suppose that it did not "imply, require or even permit" this process of the "wage-labour divorce of producers from their means of production" is to suppose that it did not occur.

An epoch whose historical tendency is given by the transformation of precapitalist into capitalist relations of production (hence also by the primitive accumulation of capital) cannot simultaneously be one in which capitalism "coexists with", much less "maintains" or "intensifies" non-capitalism occurring "on the basis of" precapitalist relations of production; it arises out of their dissolution - the proletarianisation of the mass of independent producers, the break-up of their forms of economy, etc. What one has to analyse in studying this period "of the dissolution of the earlier modes of production" (Marx 1973 p.506) are the forms in which wage-labour is created, on the one hand, and the forms in which it is initialliy subsumed into capital, on the other. (And in this study there are no models to guide us. This study is entirely non-aprioristic, insofar as it is historical)

Yet there is a sense in which Laclau's dualism was attempting to come to terms with a real and deeply significant fact, which is this: capitalist relations of production can take on forms of appearance that contradict the formal equality of labour and capital. Whereas Frank maintains that "accumulation could not be said to have been directly based on surplus-value insofar as it was not produced by free wage labourers", one finds, on the contrary, (i) that every process of accumulation pre-supposes surplus-value, (ii) that wage-labour need not be "free" in the specific sense of presupposing the formal equality (of exchange) between labour and capital.

Frank is pushed into supporting the notion of a non-wage-labour based accumulation due to the circulationist definition of "wage-labour" which is so widespread in Marxist writings. Wage-labour is defined by him (and by 90% of Marxists) fundamentally in terms of properties that describe the situation of the commodity-owner, insofar as the wage-form pertains to the sphere of simple circulation. I have already argued elsewhere (Banaji 1977b) that this is scientifically a false or one-sided conception of wage-labour, because "only at a certain stage of the development of capital does the exchange of capital and labour become in fact formally free" (Marx 1973 p.770). This is why Marx can write, in the recently published Appendix (Marx 1976 p. 1064), that although the wage-form (the formal transactional equality between wage-labour and capital) is a "form of mediation intrinsic to" developed capitalism, "there are those who regard this superficial relation, this essential formality, this deceptive appearance of capitalist relation at its true essence". They thereby gloss over the essential nature of the relationship" (emphasis mine)

Frank's shift from the earlier tendency of Gunder Frankism acquires its sharpest outline at this point. Gunder Frankism gained its popularity, after all, because it suggested that capitalist exploitation, the enslavement of mankind by capital, is not a novelty in the so-called backward countries, that in these countries the impoverishment of the masses is not some eternal historical inheritance, but specifically a product of capitalism. Today, however, after ten years of solid pedagogical criticism, Frank finds himself compelled to retreat from that earlier conception into the doctrinally much safer position that if labour is not "free", it cannot be "wage-labour", therefore cannot produce surplus-value (or capital, for that matter).

In which case, however, let us take the most coerced and unfree form of labour that the modern world knows - slavery. Were the plantation owners of the southern states or of the Caribbean not capitalists? (Cf. Marx 1959 p.784, 1968 pp.302-303: Grossman 1970 p.400 f., p.406 f.) Frank himself would like to think that they were, that their exploitation of slave labour was fundamentally capitalist in nature, but his own framework of theory logically precludes any such conception. Therefore Frank runs into a further contradiction at this level. In some sense it is obvious to him, as his pages on slavery (p.120 ff.) show, and as some of the best studies argue or suggest (Fraginals 1964, Fogel and Engerman 1974, Aufhauser 1973), that the American or Caribbean plantations were capitalist enterprises - yet their basis was slave labour, the unfreest form of unfree labour.

The alternatives are inescapable. Either one sticks to the dead formalism which defines wage-labour not in terms of the relation of living labour to capital, but through images derived from the sphere of circulation, that "very Eden of the innate rights of man" (Marx 1976 p.280) - and in this case capitalism is exonerated of the massive brutalities which it inflicted on mankind prior to the birth of the modern working class (modern industry) and of the society shaped by its struggles; or one accepts that capitalism is compatible with the most brutal and barbaric forms of labour, that wage-labour, labour which produces capital, can take a series of unfree forms, implying various degrees of coercion and bondage.

The latter position, which is the one I accept, has an important methodological result. It becomes necessary to distinguish between (a) the immediate forms of exploitation of living labour and (b) the underlying relations of production of which they are a historically given expression.

And this conclusion is inevitable even if one's picture of capitalism as a historical system is confined to the pages of Volume One. The child labour incorporated into capital under 19th c. English capitalism was by no means labour "freely sold" to capital. (In fact nowhere in the world is child labour incorporated-into-capital, exploited-by-capital, "freely sold".) On the contrary, Marx wrote, "Previously the worker sold his own labour-power, which he disposed of as a free agent, formally speaking. Now he sells wife and child. He has become a slave-dealer" (Marx 1976 p.519). Even if this is too simple, the essential point that Marx is making stands.

Frank (p.247) refers to "household labour" as a proto-typical case of "non-capitalist relations of production" sustaining the accumulation of capital. But under capitalism domestic labour forms not a distinct mode of production sui generis but part of the circuit of reproduction of social labour-power for social capital. Women who work at home do not enter into any special set of "relations of production"; their relations of production are those of capital, mediated through the reproduction process of the total capital, insofar as they produce labour-power for capital (See Hensman 1977, Innes and O'Meara 1976). For this reason alone, if for no others, women who work at home are part of the working class in a much more fundamental sense than simply the fact that they are married into and dominated under working-class families.

In short, Frank's confusions here - and the retreat they force on him - stem from the fact that the forms of exploitation which mediate the essential relations of (capital) production, as historical forms or moments of the latter, are reified as substantive and independent "relations of production", so that he is perpetually trapped in the logical contradiction that the accumulation of capital, which can only occur as a set of capitalist relations of production takes place, for him, "on the basis of "non-capitalist" relations of production". And here again, because Frank senses the defect of his argument, senses the need for a distinction between (i) the immediate forms of appearance of labour which produces capital and (ii) the fact that this is labour which produces capital - he repeatedly returns to this problematic without any final sense of resolution (p. 244).

WA tends to end up with a position much closer to Laclau's - a single world capitalist system that supposedly embraces a variety of modes of production subordinate to, and reproduced by, the logic of the accumulation process (p. 251). Even if the shift is carried through only reluctantly, it is forced on Frank by the element of methodological continuity between his two major books, WA and CU. This can be defined as a certain formalism, and described, with Hegel (1966 p. 40), in the following terms: "they (the formalists) seem to subordinate everything to the absolute idea", Frank's world capitalism, " thus gives the appearance of being traceable in everything. But if we take a closer look at this expansion of content, it turns out that it has not been achieved through one and the same principle, the law of the transformation into capitalist relations, "acquiring various forms, but it is the shapeless (gestaltlose) repetition of one and the same idea", world capitalism, domination, dependency, etc. etc., "which is applied in a purely external way to a range of material and which obtains the tedious and fictitious appearance of diversity. The idea ... in fact always remains where it started if its development consists in nothing other than such a repetition of the same formula."

Frank is therefore left with nothing solid to counterpose against those "marxists" who maintain that "feudal" relations of some sort still prevail in the countries of the third world. "In terms of the criteria proposed above, this conclusion is, of course, entirely unacceptable", Frank states (p. 255). But what "criteria"? Frank has not developed any framework that would allow him to argue any differently from the way he does, i.e., to support any position other than the confused and equivocal one that the process of world accumulation entailed a "diversity of forms" of production relations. "I argue that their analysis as part of a single worldwide process of capital accumulation also requires more attention" (p. 255). For one who pioneered the polemic against dualism this is a terribly weak statement, and tantamount to a compromise with dualist positions of one form or another.

Yet Frank's shift is determined fundamentally by the inherent limits of all incorporation models, whatever the form of their argument. (For a good criticism, see Swainson 1977). In failing to analyse the process of the penetration of capitalist relations of production, hence indigenous processes of primitive accumulation and the growth of an indigenous capitalism which is not simply an agent of "foreign capitalism", the model of incorporation ultimately downgrades the class struggle between bourgeoisie and proletariat. The whole theory of dependency is still today fundamentally a petty-bourgeois theory which is inherently incapable of breaking loose from the platform of national capitalism. (With Samir Amin's arrival on the stage of "Marxist theory", it has become fashionable to advocate "disengagement from world capitalism". But this is tantamount to a programme of isolationist state capitalism, and has nothing at all to do with the revolutionary interests of the working class, which at all stages are bound up with the world market and its further development.)

"Dependency" is at best a (possible) description of the relationship of two individual capitals which, as such, belongs to the sphere of the competition of capitals, and, as this moement in their process of competition, describes an intrinsically unstable and fluctuating relation. Bengal and various other parts of India may very well have been "raped" by British imperialism, as Frank supposes, but today India ranks as the tenth largest industrial power in the world, it has seen an enormous and powerful development of industrial capitalism, and this industrial capitalism is today strong enough to make rapid strides into the world market. In the rapidly changing conditions of world capitalism today, the slogan of "national liberation" which Frank claims to advocate can be the expression only of one of two class ideologies - either of the conscious and cynical pragmatism of the big bourgeoisie which seeks to bolster its competitive position on the market, or the tired and worn-out radicalism of a "progressivist" petty-bourgeoisie i.e., which picks up the discarded slogans of national capitalism and imagines it is thereby fighting for revolutionary socialism. If a revolutionary Marxist theory of world capitalism is to make any progress at all in the 1980s, it must start by rejecting the entire framework of "dependency theory" and shifting its focus radically to the working class and its real practice of self-emancipation from capital.

NOTES

1. This is a clear image of the 16th-17th c. capitalism in historical studies. E.g., Braudel 1969 p. 65 "capitalisme marchand", p. 148 "un certaine capitalisme, plus financier et speculatif que marchand"; Polishensky 1974 p. 26 "commercial and financial capitalism"; Vilar 1971 p. 65 "the unstable capitalism of ports and markets".

2. Wallerstein 1978 proposes an argument about the 17th c. which is similar to Frank's in its general tenor. The conception of a world-wide rationalisation process of capital in the 17th c. is an attractive one. Unfortunately it remains a pure historical fantasy. If Frank at least hints at possible explanations of the "crisis", Wallerstein dispenses even with this formality. Why did world economy "stagnate" for close to 150 years? Because "demand is sluggish and profits decline " (p. 67). Secondly, related to this absence of any serious explanation is the fact that Wallerstein nowhere explains the nature of his 300-year cycles. Is it a cycle intrinsic to capitalism? It appears to be, because Wallerstein states that these 300-year cycles "are themselves evidence for a capitalist world economy" (p. 66 emph. mine). But in that case, what about the cycle extending from 100 to 1450 when, as Wallerstein states, "the feudal mode of production dominated Europe" (p. 67)?

3. Topolski argues with a rare sense of historical balance and caution: "Exports from the Baltic ports constituted from 20% to 25% of marketed production in the 16th c. If one were to include the Ukrainian territories and

the Grand Duchy of Lithuania in the calculations, one would obtain even lower percentages". Nevertheless, "that the port of Gdansk received around one-seventh to one-third of the total marketed surplus implies a figure high enough to support the theory of colonialism". By this Topolski means the theory which maintains that "through the mechanism of external trade, the Baltic countries were reduced to the position of "economic colonies of the West" (p. 248). "But if we take account of the fact that a considerable proportion of the grain sold on the Baltic ports (at least around 30%) never left the Baltic zone, we shall see that the percentage of grain (rye and wheat) that flowed beyond the limits of this zone represented, towards the end of the 16th c., around 17% of the total marketed surplus of grain in the Baltic...the view according to which exports were the chief of changes adverse to the economic growth of the Baltic countries (mainly Poland) does not appear to have a sufficient basis" (p. 431-32). (All emphases mine.)

4. This world market abstractionism is shared by Wallerstein. The notion that in the 16th c. there was a "single world system" that was fundamentally capitalist is a pure assertion founded on crude impressionism and weird deductions. Take the following argument, for example: "Michel Morineau points out that in medieval Europe wheat prices rose and fell in direct response to harvests. What happened in the 16th c. was not so much that bullion raised prices but that it prevented their fall. Indeed, Carlo Cipolla is skeptical that there was any real price rise at all. Rather he believes that what is truly significant about the financial structure of the 16th c. was not the rise of prices but the decline of the interest...Bullion cheapened money. What this seems to indicate is that the critical factor was the emergence of a capitalist system...The key variable was the emergence of capitalism as the dominant mode of social organisation of the economy" (1974 p. 76-77). Wallerstein does not bother to explain how he arrives at such a massive conclusion. But he continues, "Probably we could say say only mode in the sense that once established other "modes of production" survived in function of how they fitted into a politico-social framework deriving from capitalism" (p. 77. Emph. mine). For a start, if Wallerstein wants to establish that world capitalism from now on fundamentally determined the internal evolution of all other countries, then reference to the "politico-social" framework of capitalism is beside the point. As his own citation from H. Stahl indicates (p. 91), capitalism conquers the world market through its economic laws, the simplest and most fundamental expression of which is the law of value. Secondly, one "can" say anything one likes, the point is on has to demonstrate it. Needless to say, apart from terminologically reconstructing the feudal lords of eastern Europe into "capitalists" and other such purely verbal shifts, no

demonstration ever follows. E.g., on p. 305 we come across the following deduction: "Let us now compare the role of wheat production in Russia at this time. Let us start with Mankov's assertion about 16th c. Russia: "one can speak at this time only of an internal cereals market". That is, although almost no wheat is exported, "there existed already in the 16th c. a link between local markets, sometimes very far apart from each other." Thus capitalist agriculture emerged at this time, and in similar forms, both in Poland...and Russia". " Thus"?

REFERENCES

R.K. Aufhauser 1973 "Slavery and scientific management", Journal of Economic History 33.

J. Banaji 1977a "Capitalist domination and the small peasantry: the Deccan districts in the late 19th century", Economic and Political Weekly, Vol. 12 (Special No.).

J. Banaji 1977b "Modes of production in a materialist conception of history", Capital and Class (3).

J. Blum 1957 "The rise of serfdom in eastern Europe", American Historical Review 62.

J. Blum 1968 Lord and Peasant in Russia (New York)

F. Braudel 1969 Ecrits sur l'histoire (Paris)

M. Confino 1963 Domaines et seigneurs en Russie vers la fin du 18e siècle (Paris)

F.W. Fogel, S.L. Engermann 1974 Time on the Cross (2 vols., Boston)

M.M. Fraginals 1964 El Ingenio (Havana)

H. Grossman 1970 Das Akkumulations - und Zusammenbruchsgesetz des kapitalistischen Systems (Frankfurt, 2nd edition. Summarised in English as The Laws of Accumulation and Breakdown of the Capitalist System, Platform Publications no. 2, 1979).

G.W.F. Hegel 1966 Préface a la Phenomenologie de l'Esprit (Paris)

R. Hensman 1977 "Wage-labour - the production and sale of the commodity labour-power", Bulletin of the Communist Platform, no. 1.

E.J. Hobsbawm 1954 "The general crisis of the European economy in the 17th century" Past and Present 5-6 (two parts)

D. Innes, D. O'Meara 1976 "Class formation and ideology: the Transkei region", Review of African Political Economy no. 7.

Z. Kirilly, I.M. Kiss 1968 "Production de céréales et exploitations payannes en Hongrie au 16e et 17e siècles", Annales 23, nov.-dec.

W. Kula 1970 Theorie économique du système féodale. Pour un modele de l'économie polonaise 16-18e siècles (Paris)

A. Lublinskaya 1968 French Absolutism - The Crucial Phase 1620-29 (Cambridge)

K. Marx 1973 Grundrisse (trans. M. Nicolaus, London)
K. Marx 1976 Capital, Vol. One (trans. B. Fowkes, London)
K. Marx 1959 Capital, Vol. Three (Moscow)
K. Marx 1968 Theories of Surplus-Value, pt. 2 (Moscow)
K. Marx 1971 Theories of Surplus-Value, pt. 3 (Moscow)
P. Mattick 1974 Krisen und Krisentheorien (Frankfurt)
Z.P. Pach 1972 "Sixteenth century Hungary: commercial activity and market production by the nobles", Economy and Society in Early Modern Europe: Essays from Annales (ed. P.Burke, London)
D.L. Pokhylevych 1957 Krest'iane Belorussii i Litvy v XVI-XVII v. (L'vov)
J.V. Polishensky 1974 The Thirty Years War (trans. R. Evans, London)
H. Rosenberg 1944 "The rise of the Junkers in Brandenburg-Prussia, 1410-1563", American Historical Review 2 (pt. 2)
N. Swainson 1977 "The rise of a national bourgeoisie in Kenya", Review of African Political Economy, no. 8.
J. Topolski 1974 "Commerce des denrés agricoles et croissance économique de la zone baltique aux 16e et 17e siècles, Annales, 29 mars-avr.
J. Valka 1965 "La structure économique de la seigneurie tchèque au 16e siècle", Deuxième conference Aix-en-Provence 1962 t.2.
H. Van der Wee 1963 "Typologie des crises et changements de structures aux Pays-Bas (15-16e siècles)". Annales 18.
P. Vilar 1956 "Problems of the formation of capitalism", Past and Present 10
P. Vilar 1971 "The Age of Don Quixote", New Left Review 68
I. Wallerstein 1974 The Modern World System. Capitalist Agriculture and the Origins of the European World Economy in the 16th century (New York and London).
I. Wallerstein 1978 "The Crisis of the 17th Century", New Left Review 110.
J. Zelenyi 1973 Die Wissenschaftslogik Und 'Das Kapital' (German-trans., Frankfurt).

Chapter Nine

FRANK AND WALLERSTEIN REVISITED: A CONTRIBUTION TO BRENNER'S CRITIQUE

Haldun Gülalp

Robert Brenner's article that appeared in New Left Review No. 104 was a devastating critique of the recent currents in the theory of underdevelopment and the study of the transition to capitalism that he justifiably labelled neo-Smithian.[1] However, the discussion that one would have expected this article to bring about has not yet arisen. Besides, his critique was more related to the question of the transition to capitalism than the question of the origins and persistence of underdevelopment, although the two are of course closely interrelated. The present essay aims to further Brenner's critique with respect to the latter question.

The two writers that are at issue are again Frank and Wallerstein. It may be thought that enough has already been said about Frank. Although this may be true in a sense, it is nevertheless a fact that as long as ideologies form the basis of theories, the controversies never end. Now it is without doubt that in the social sciences no theory is free of ideology. Furthermore, the dependency school, or more generally the neo-Marxist approach to underdevelopment, that was founded by Frank rather than by Baran as is commonly supposed, has an ideological basis that is different from Marxism. The two schools, Marxism and neo-Marxism, with their different ideologies and thus different methods, form the two sides of the controversy.[2] Even a superficial glance at some of the controversies in the social sciences reveals that in essence they have been repeated through quite unexpected lengths of time. The history of thought in social sciences is full of examples of theories that reappear in different guises every time they are thought to have been refuted for good. This inevitably leads to a situation where the search for the similarities in essence behind the differences in guise of such theories begins to assume an important dimension as part of scientific enquiry.

Coming back to the present issue, if enough had been said about Frank, there would not have been a writer so influential as Wallerstein. Although Frank seems to have left the ground by stating: "I have never had the temerity myself to claim to be a Marxist".[3] Wallerstein, apparently unaware of this, is determined to keep the spirit alive by claiming that "both Sweezy and Frank better follow the spirit of Marx if not his letter".[4] It is interesting to note that it does constitute a real issue whether a writer who claims to be Marxist is really Marxist or not. If the reason for this is partly the considerations mentioned in the preceding paragraph, it probably also lies in the essence of Marxism itself, since Marxism involves an ideology that preaches revolution. Although this is not a question that is to be pursued here, it may be pointed out that this concern tends to become especially important in such cases as that of neo-Marxism which has mistakenly been considered a Marxist school that deals with a question neglected by "classical" Marxism, i.e. the question of underdevelopment,[5] and which has therefore caused a great deal of confusion.

The present essay aims to develop a refreshed critique of Frank together with the critique of Wallerstein. The latter will be especially in relation to what Wallerstein has in common with Frank and in relation to his theory that concern the analysis of underdevelopment. Since the emphasis will be on Wallerstein's theory, the review of Frank will be limited to revealing his basic conceptual framework.

FRANK

Frank acknowledges his debt to Baran, but he borrows the less important point made by Baran at the expense of the crucial one. He ignores Baran's conceptualization of the distinction between actual and potential surplus which is related to the analysis of the mode of utilization of the economic surplus in the underdeveloped society, which in turn is precisely the result of the internal class structure, but instead focuses on the point about the outflow of the economic surplus. Basing his theory on this point, Frank explains the process of underdevelopment by the continuous drain of surplus from the bottom to the top of a hierarchy of "metropolis-satellite" relationships. In fact he concludes that "underdevelopment was and still is generated by the very same historical process which also generated economic development: the development of capitalism itself".[6] Since for Frank the whole world is characterized by "capitalism" in a process that develops one pole at the expense of the rest, this conclusion is the reversal of the classical Marxist perspective on the role of capitalism. For Frank, the "historical mission" of capitalism is to "underdevelop" the world at large. It is this conclusion that marks the break with the early Marxist thinking and hence the founding of the neo-Marxist school.

Frank's point about capitalism being the cause of

underdevelopment is in fact related to his conceptualization of "capitalism". His concept of capitalism is totally different from the Marxist concept of capitalism as a "mode of production", just like his various other concepts, like "exploitation", etc., all of which constitute the significant aspects of his difference from the Marxist method. Although, as indicated above, Frank "should be correctly situated outside of Marxist theory", he has always been considered a Marxist which of course has caused a great deal of confusion.[7] On the one hand, Frank's critics have tried to correct his "errors" within a Marxist framework. Such is the criticism by Laclau who reminds Frank about the concept of the mode of production and the prominence of the "relations of production" in defining that concept.[8] This is a very basic criticism the implications of which, however, were not clearly seen by Laclau. Although its implications reach far beyond the question of the specification of the mode of production in the underdeveloped social formation, its major effect has been to originate a controversy in the literature on this latter issue. Similarly, another basic criticism directed to Frank is that he explains underdevelopment as the result of an external phenomenon, i.e. that of satellization and the consequent drain of surplus, by ignoring the internal class structure of the underdeveloped society.[9] Again, however, the implications of this criticism were not clearly seen, since at a more general level they are related to the concepts that Frank employs, notably that of "capitalism". Hence Frank can reply to such a criticism by arguing that he <u>does</u> consider the "internal structure" since he proposes that the metropolis-satellite structure of "capitalism" is reproduced in the underdeveloped society as long as it is a part of the world capitalist system.[10]

On the other hand, Frank has been very influential on the literature and has gained many followers who have basically used his method to reach, like him, "apparently" Marxist, i.e. revolutionary, conclusions. Hence the whole body of the school called "neo-Marxism" that has almost exclusively dominated the literature on underdevelopment until very recently.[11] The tenets of this school require a detailed discussion that cannot be undertaken within the bounds of this essay although a brief characterization that also involves the specification of the basic confusion in the neo-Marxist school could be made as follows: the use of Marxist "terms" instead of "concepts", based on an underlying theme that the role of capitalism is to create underdevelopment; hence the pseudo-Marxist conclusion that confuses the struggle against underdevelopment with the struggle against capitalism.[12]

The Marxist appearance, in terms of revolutionary conclusions, can become quite misleading because it is precisely the reliability of those revolutionary conclusions that should be at stake. Therefore, the whole conceptual framework should be analyzed with a view to this question. For Frank, the crucial element is the monopolistic structure of capitalism which constitutes the main contradiction of the system that causes underdevelopment as well as bringing about the transfer of surplus. But because his concept of monopoly is a vague one that only signifies the power to transfer surplus through a mechanism that is not clearly specified, the transfer of surplus turns out to be the sole cause of underdevelopment. Furthermore, the notion of monopoly is replaced by the concept of exploitation which leads to the conceptualization of capitalism as the hierarchical structure of monopolistic powers to transfer surplus. But since the notions of capitalism and exploitation are used as ideological concepts, the outcome is confused ideological conclusion. This can be seen by a closer examination of Frank's basic theoretical schema, i.e. his characterization of the contradictions of capitalism.

The first contradiction that characterizes capitalism is the "expropriation of economic surplus from the many and its appropriation by the few".[13] This is due to the monopolistic structure of capitalism. According to Frank, "it is this exploitative relationship which in chain-link fashion extends the capitalist link between the capitalist world and national metropolises to the regional centres (parts of whose surplus they appropriate), and from these to local centres, and so on to large landowners or merchants who expropriate surplus from small peasants or tenants, and sometimes even from these latter to landless labourers exploited by them in turn. At each step along the way, the relatively few capitalists above exercise monopoly power over the many below, expropriating some or all of their economic surplus and, to the extent that they are not expropriated in turn by the still fewer above them, appropriating it for their own use" (pp.7-8). This passage exposes Frank's main thesis which is repeated throughout his theoretical discussion. A close examination however, would reveal all its shortcomings and inconsistencies. First, capitalist exploitation for Frank is the expropriation of the surplus, and it may take place between countries, regions, or individuals; therefore it is totally devoid of class content. Secondly, this exploitation is not because of production relations, but because of monopolistic powers that are employed. What precisely this monopoly power signifies and through what mechanism surplus expropriation takes place are not specified. Therefore, for instance, a merchant is considered a capitalist who exploits the small peasants by expropriating the latter's surplus through his monopoly power. Thirdly, all the links in the chain are considered homogeneous. Therefore the USA is considered a capitalist that exploits Chile just like the merchant who exploits the peasants. Fourthly, since these links extend in chain-like fashion, the capitalists at various levels may both be exploiting and exploited at the same time. In other words, the relations of exploitation are between capitalists that only differ from each other according to the level each has in the hierarchy depending on its monopoly power.

The foregoing do not exhaust the list of the aspects of the mess that Frank's theory leaves one in. Without any further elaboration, however, his specification of the second contradiction of capitalism can be considered. The second contradiction that characterizes capitalism is the "polarization of the capitalist system into metropolitan centre and peripheral satellites" (p.8). This appears as only a repetition of the first contradiction since it is the metropolis-satellite relationship that implies the expropriation-appropriation relationship where the metropolis is the exploiter and the satellite is the exploited. A question that follows is, of course, what happens with the expropriated surplus. According to the passage quoted above, the capitalists, if they are not in turn expropriated, appropriate "it for their own use". Repeating the same point with the new terminology, Frank says that "the metropolis expropriates economic surplus from its satellites and appropriates it for its own economic development" (p.9). The change in the terminology, however, signifies the conceptual leap that Frank takes, which is not at first apparent, but which has important implications. Therefore, the formulation of the second contradiction is not simply a repetition of the first contradiction, but it is bringing it to a different plane. What is meant by this and also its implications must be shown clearly.

First, capitalism is defined as an exploitative system. The non-specification of this exploitative relationship allows capitalism to be generalized to include various forms of exploitation. Based on this capitalist exploitation is defined as the expropriation of surplus. Because this definition is necessarily vague, it constitutes the first step in the conceptual transformation. If made precise, this definition refers to the relationship between goegraphical regions or, more specifically, between countries. Before this is spelt out however, in the first contradiction the relationships are formulated as capitalist relationships that take place between economic agents within a single nation or internationally. Defining each layer as capitalist and each link as a capitalist relationship thus loosens the definition of "capitalist" to include various agents like merchants, peasants, etc. Based on this, again, the definition is narrowed down to the individual country as the constituent of the capitalist link. This final conceptual transformation is achieved by the introduction of the metropolis-satellite schema. Since one cannot speak of the "economic development" of a peasant by appropriating the surplus of landless labourer for his own use, nor define an "economic surplus expropriation" relationship between a merchant and a small landholder (let alone defining it as capitalist exploitation), the discussion of the second contradiction can only be comprehensible if the units of analysis are countries. The concepts of "economic surplus" and "economic development" can only be used with reference to countries. Thus the economic agents of the initial schema that Frank suggests as defining the capitalist structure are replaced by countries, and this is how the discussion of the second contradiction is carried out (pp.9-13). Therefore, it is only through the above described conceptual muddle that Frank can emerge with the conclusion that the relationship between countries is one of capitalist exploitation that causes one's development by the other's underdevelopment. With respect to the latter, Frank makes the following point: "The satellites remain underdeveloped for lack of access to their own surplus and as a consequence of the same polarization and exploitative contradictions, which the metropolis introduces and maintains in the satellite's domestic economic structure" (p.9). However, the internal existence of the "capitalist contradictions" in the satellite could not have caused its underdevelopment since the same contradictions exist in the metropolis which does develop. Besides, according to Frank, once the external ties of the satellite with the metropolis are weakened, as in a period of crisis or war, the satellite does manage to develop, and has actually done so; again, despite its internal contradictory structure. Therefore, cleared from its inconsistencies, Frank's theory seems to amount to a single point that is neither substantiated nor clearly explained. It is that the transfer of the economic surplus from one country to another develops the latter and underdevelops the former. In addition to this Frank makes the ideological point that this relationship is one of capitalist exploitation. Hence his conclusion that "development and underdevelopment are the same in that they are the product of a single, but dialectically contradictory economic structure and process of capitalism" (p.9).

It is after this stage of the argument that Frank introduces the third contradiction of capitalism, i.e. "continuity in change". According to him, the fundamental structure of capitalism has remained the same since the sixteenth century and it is this aspect that should be emphasised as he has, i.e. as the "exploitative" relationship between countries. This point does not mean the formulation of another contradiction of capitalism. It only allows him to focus more on the above mentioned single point that he makes, by ignoring the internal structures as well as the structures of the external relationships and their transformations.

Viewed in the light of the above discussion, the criticisms made of Frank by Laclau and Dos Santos that were mentioned before can be reconsidered. Since Frank's definition of capitalism relates to the external link of surplus transfer between countries, both criticisms point to the same problem. In other words, it is precisely because of his concept of capitalism, which Laclau criticises, that Frank ignores the internal structures, a procedure which Dos Santos criticises. However, even when forced to consider the internal structure, Frank can avoid the concept of the mode of production. This he does by his double use of the concept of capitalism as explained above. Therefore, by switching back and forth between his two schemes he can get round the criticisms. Although this procedure does not save Frank from the criticism that he ignores the relations of production, Laclau's neglect of this procedure causes him to fail to see the implication of his criticism.

WALLERSTEIN

Wallerstein's theory can be considered an attempted revision of Frank's theory in the context of the historical origins of capitalist development. Although it does not involve the conceptual mess that Frank had entered into as described above, it certainly involves the neo-Marxist concepts. Clearing Frank's inconsistencies, as it were, from the ultimate theory that the transfer of surplus between countries causes development/underdevelopment, as well as a refined attempt to explain and substantiate this point, is what comprises Wallerstein's revision. In the latter, the terms metropolis and satellite are replaced by the terms core and periphery. Although they denote the same concepts, they no longer extend in chain-like fashion nor do they refer to anything other than countries.

Still, it is not very clear that for Wallerstein the ultimate cause of development/underdevelopment is the transfer of surplus because, while trying to substantiate this point, he also attempts to answer questions that the theoretical framework of Frank could not tackle. This attempt, however, leads Wallerstein to develop an analysis that becomes a source of confusion for the establishment of the specific role of surplus transfer within the world-economy. It will be shown that this is the weakest point in Wallerstein's theory remaining <u>within</u> his own conceptual framework. The <u>limits</u> of the latter is of course a different matter. Thus Wallerstein attempts to answer questions like the following:- What is the basis of the division of labour that defines the present world-system? How does this division of labour determine the internal structure of each country? What is the relationship between the latter and the place a country has in the world-system? What is the mechanism of the transfer of surplus? Why are the core countries dominant in the world-system? What is the essence of this dominance? etc.

The starting point for Wallerstein's analysis is the concept of "social system" which is explicitly defined with reference to the circuit of commodities. Based on the concept of an exchange system involving an independent division of labour between the "areas" that take part, there can only be two kinds of social systems: the closed, self-sufficient economic nodule; and the world-system.[14] The world system, in turn, can have two forms: world-empire; and world-economy. Both kinds of world-systems have the common characteristic that they are, in essence, systems of surplus transfer from the periphery to the core of the system. The world-empire, with its centralised bureaucracy, appropriates the surplus of the periphery by force. Although this involves a more direct mechanism of surplus appropriation, the weight and expense of such an extensive central bureaucracy cannot but lead to the eventual disintegration of the system (MWS, Ch.1, Ch.5). In the world-economy, however, the political structures are decentralised, avoiding the weight and expense of the central political authority and allocating it to the level of individual nation-states, while the economic mechanism becomes central. The economic mechanism, on the other hand, is the system of exchange. "It was only with the emergence of the modern world-economy in sixteenth-century Europe that we saw the full development and economic predominance of market trade. This was the system called capitalism" (RFD, p.391). The essence of the world-economy, however, is not different from that of the world-empire. "What capitalism does is offer an alternative and more lucrative source of surplus appropriation" (MWS,p.16).

The question that follows is, what precisely is the structure of the capitalist world-system, what is the difference of the world-economy from the world-empire? The answer to this question may be said to comprise the main subject of Wallerstein's analysis. With some anticipation of what is to appear in the following exposition, the crucial variable in determining the difference of the world-economy from the world-empire and in constituting the mechanism whereby surplus is appropriated by the core turns out to be the decentralised political structure with a hierarchical structuration of the strength of individual nation-states. The allocation of the political authority to the individual nation-states does not simply become a means of avoiding the expense of a central bureaucracy but instead becomes the very essence of the system such that it is precisely based on the existence of such individual states with different strengths that the capitalist system acquires any meaning, i.e. that of developing a mechanism of surplus transfer from the periphery to the core.

The origins of the modern world-economy lie in the crisis of feudalism, the causes and the specifity of which do not directly relate to the present discussion. The important point to note is that the response to this crisis has been in the form of territorial as well as commercial expansion that has resulted in the generalization of trade relations. "The expansion of the sixteenth century was not only a geographical expansion. It was an economic expansion...It marked the establishment of a regular trade between Europe and the rest of the inhabited world" (MWS, p.102). A point to be noted in this connection is that for Wallerstein feudalism does not signify a self-sufficient closed economy (MWS, pp.17ff). Although this is contrary to Frank's contention, it is necessary for Wallerstein's argument. This is because in Wallerstein's schema, the systematization of trade and the ensuing interdependent geographical division of labour on a world scale is prior to the formation of the capitalist system. In fact, the formation of a capitalist world-economy as such is the outcome of it. However, this constitutes an important loose end in Wallerstein's analysis as will be seen presently.

According to him, the establishment of the geographical division of labour as a result of the commercial expansion comes about through the pattern of "response" each country has to the expanding commerce. Thus some countries like England "responded by creating an industrial base" while others, like eastern Europe, responded by developing what he calls "coerced-cash-cropping". The pattern of response, on the other hand, is determined by profit maximization considerations. Thus in the case of both the landowners in western Europe and those in eastern Europe, there is the same question: "where was he to draw the largest and most immediate profit?" Now the landowner could either turn his land into pasture or lease for money and invest in trade and industry, or alternatively, he could intensify the production of staple and invest in trade. Western Europe chose the first alternative and eastern Europe chose the second (MWS,pp.111-112). In other words, according to Wallerstein, the development of capitalism is based on the already existing capitalist rationality of the economic actors that take part in the process of the formation of the capitalist world-economy.

This is where the thrust of Brenner's argument comes in, and the loose end in Wallerstein's analysis that was mentioned above.[15] But Brenner does not stop here and goes on to remind Wallerstein that capitalist rationality can only exist if there exists the 'capitalist class structure based on free-labour'. For Wallerstein, however, there is no such necessary relationship. In this world-economy, "not all these capitalists 'forms' (of production) were based on 'free' labour - only those in the core of the economy. But the motivations of landlord and labourer in the non-'free' sector were as capitalist as those in the core" (MWS,p.126). Thus even the formation of a 'capitalist class structure based on free labour' itself is the result of a rational choice for profit maximization as a response to the commercial expansion.

Given the capitalist rationality for all economic actors, the differences in response must be explained by the differences in the objective conditions of profit maximization. These objective conditions lie "in part in past history, in part in current geography" (RFD,p.403). To be more specific, they are technical conditions like tht then existing land/labour ratio, the extent of the internal market, the geographical location of the country, etc., that determine what particular product it is most profitable to specialize in. But given these objective conditions, the choice of the product also determines the "labour-control method" that is most suitable for its production. For instance, high population density requires intensive agriculture, and the latter requires more skilled manpower which is not suitable for coerced labour. In such a case, "the coercion has to be more indirect, via market mechanism" (MWS,p.101). This means the development of the wage-labour form of production. In the case of eastern Europe, for instance, geographical location, as a factor among the others, turned Poland into the "greatest exporter of wheat". "The rise of a Polish wheat-exporting economy meant...the rise of large domains with coerced cash-crop labour". Moreover, "it meant also the rise of the political strength of the nobility". (MWS,p.304). In other words, the geographical division of labour that is established as a response to the commercial expansion also determines the class structure of each country. Thus in contrast to the eastern European countries, the western European countries that have specialized in industry have developed the wage-labour form of production leading to the rise of the bourgeoisie.

The geographical division of labour thus determines the occupational division of labour which determines the place each country has in the hierarchical structuration of the world-economy. According to Wallerstein, in the formation of the world-economy, core areas emerge as countries where the bourgeoisie got stronger and the landlords weaker, and the periphery as vice versa (MWS,p.302). The important relationship that determines whether a country is to be a core country or only peripheral, is the strength of its state. According to him, those countries that could achieve the process of "statism", i.e. the concentration of power in the central state, became the core countries of the world-economy, (MWS,p.147). On the other hand, "the strength of various state-machineries at specific moments of the history of the modern world-system" is to be explained "in terms of the structural role a country plays in the world-economy at that moment in time" (RFD,p.403). In other words, an industrial country with the bourgeoise in power has a strong state, while a country with the nobility in power has a weak state. "While the sixteenth century was a period of the rise of state power in western Europe, it was an era of decline for state power in eastern Europe, both cause and consequence of the latter's economic position. As the landed aristocracy of Poland grew stronger...and the indigenous bourgeoisie grew weak, the tax base of the state frittered away which meant that the king could not afford to maintain an adequate army". (MWS,p.309).

A strong state, on the other hand, enables "the country as an entity to get a disproportionate share of the surplus product of the entire European world-economy" (MWS,p.309). This comes about through the transfer of surplus between countries, which is the essence of the capitalist world-economy. "Once we get a difference in the strength of the state-machineries, we get the operation of 'unequal exchange' which is enforced by strong states on weak ones, by core states on peripheral areas" (RFD,p.401). This point is based on Wallerstein's general conception of the state. According to him, "in a capitalist world-economy, political energy is used to secure monopoly rights (or as near to it as can be achieved). The state becomes less the central economic enterprise than the means of assuring certain terms of trade in other economic transactions". (MWS,p.16).

This brings the discussion back to the question of the difference between the world-empire and the world-economy. What this distinction signifies for Wallerstein's argument must now be clear. According to him, "an empire cannot be conceived of as an entrepreneur as can a state in a world-economy. For an empire pretends to be the whole. It cannot enrich its economy by draining from other economies, since it is the only economy" (MWS,p.60). "That is why the secret of capitalism was in the establishment of the division of labour within the framework of a world-economy that was not an empire rather than within the framework of a single national state" (MWS,p.127).

To recapitulate the above exposition in Wallerstein's own words, it would be appropriate to quote the following passage that excellently reveals his conceptual framework:

> "Why different modes of organizing labour - slavery, 'feudalism', wage labour, self-employment - at the same point in time within the world economy? Because each mode of labour control is best suited for particular types of production. And why these modes concentrated in different zones of the world-economy - slavery and 'feudalism' in the periphery, wage labour and self-employment in the core, and as we shall see sharecropping in the semi-periphery? Because the modes of labour control greatly affect the political system (in particular the strength of the state apparatus) and the possibilities for an indigenous bourgeoisie to thrive. The world-economy was based precisely on the assumption that there were in fact these three zones and that they did in fact have different modes of labour control. Were

this not so, it would not have been possible to assure the kind of flow of the surplus which enabled the capitalist system to come into existence." (MWS,p.87).

From the above exposition it must be clear that for Wallerstein, just as it is for Frank, it is capitalism as a universal system that explains both development and underdevelopment. Moreover, Wallerstein reaches this conclusion through a conceptual framework which is very similar to that of Frank. To show this, a brief review of Wallerstein's main concepts is necessary.

To start with, the concept of "capitalism" itself may be considered, since it is the crucial concept in the formulation of the main conclusion. It was shown before that Laclau's criticism of Frank with the charge that Frank's definition of capitalism was based on the relations of exchange ignoring the relations of production was not a complete criticism since Frank's concept of capitalism could not in fact be comprehended within the terms of the Marxist concept of "mode of production". However, Wallerstein occasionally appears to define capitalism as a mode of production. He says "capitalism is a mode of production, producing for profit in a market..." (RFD,p.399). He rejects the view that capitalism is the capital/wage-labour relationship: for him it is "production for sale in a market in which the object is to realize the maximum profit" (RFD, p.398). It must be noted that this is the only definition Wallerstein gives when he defines capitalism as a "mode of production". However, this definition is both internally insufficient and inconsistent. Since, as noted before, Wallerstein contends that production for exchange in a market is not only limited to capitalism, the distinguishing feature must be the realization of profit. But the concept of "profit" can only be meaningful if there is the capital/wage-labour relationship. Therefore, the above quoted definition must necessarily imply a mode of production in which capital and labour-power are commodities. But the latter specification is clearly contrary to Wallerstein's contention. It follows that by "capitalism" he must understand something that is not sufficiently characterized by the above definition.

It must be borne in mind that capitalism for Wallerstein is something more general than what the concept of mode of production designates. Therefore his conceptualization must be comprehended in its own terms. Capitalism, according to him, is a variant of "world-system"; it is a "world-economy". "Capitalism and a world-economy (that is, a single division of labour but multiple politics and cultures) are obverse sides of the same coin. One does not cause the other. We are merely defining the same indivisible phenomenon by different characteristics" (RFD, p.391). World-system, on the other hand, is a variant of the general concept "social-system". It was emphasised before that Wallerstein defines a social-system with explicit reference to the circuit of commodities. With such a general defining characteristic of the concept of social-system, his procedure of taking it as the unit of analysis for the study of social change is a claim for totality (MWS, Ch.1 and Ch.7; RFD, pp.387ff). But as Laclau notes, it "is not a rich and complex totality of theoretical determinations, resulting from a progressive process of approximation to the concrete, but exactly the opposite: it is a vacant and homogeneous totality created by eliminating differences instead of articulating them".[16] It must be clear from the above review of Frank's theory that exactly the same thing could be said for him too.

Yet it is this concept of totality that constitutes the departure point in Wallerstein's position with regard to the controversy on the "modes of production". According to him, the "substantive issue" in this controversy "concerns the appropriate unit of analysis for the purpose of comparison". (RFD, p.393). There is no need to emphasise that in relation to this controversy, Wallerstein's position is the same as Frank's ; viz, once the world-system is capitalist, what appears as different forms of production and exploitation are in fact capitalist in essence because capitalism can and does embrace various forms of production. Moreover, and this is the important point, capitalism is a system that is precisely based on the existence of these various forms. This last point shows that the similarity between Frank and Wallerstein concerning the above question is not only limited to a general conception of the universality of capitalism since the sixteenth century, but it extends further. To explain this, a few examples may be given from the arguments of Wallerstein. He asserts that "slavery and so-called 'second serfdom' are not to be regarded as anomalies in a capitalist system...This is a relationship in which labour-power is a commodity (how could it ever be more so than under slavery?)..." (RFD, p.400) and again, "the point is that the 'relations of production' that define a system are the 'relations of production' of the whole system, and the system at this point in time is the European world-economy. Free labour is indeed a defining feature of capitalism, but not free labour throughout the productive enterprises. Free labour is the form of labour control used for skilled work in core countries whereas coerced labour is used for less skilled work in peripheral areas. <u>The combination thereof is the essence of capitalism</u>. When labour is everywhere free, we shall have socialism" (MWS, p.127 - emphasis is added).[17]

The first point to be derived from these examples is something that has been touched upon before. It is impossible to comprehend Wallerstein's analysis within the terms of Marxist concepts. The differences must be obvious in his use of the terms like "free labour". "Labour-power as commodity", etc. These, to note, are not unimportant concepts that could easily be stretched into various meanings; they are the most crucial concepts of the historical materialist study of capitalism. Therefore, Wallerstein's use of these concepts as in the above quoted passages means that he has a totally different conceptual framework. This being the case, it does not seem to be a fruitful effort to correct the "errors" that he has committed within a Marxist framework. Brenner, too, seems to have indulged in this effort in his criticism of Wallerstein.

It was pointed out before that for Wallerstein capitalism is a system that is precisely based on the existence of various forms of exploitation and this is explicitly repeated in the underlined statement in the above quotation. This is the result of his conceptualization of a world-system, which with certain characteristics becomes a world-economy. Having reviewed his analysis in some detail, there is no need to go over the same material except to note that the world-economy, i.e. the capitalist world-system, is a system/mechanism that regulates the transfer of surplus from some countries to the others, and this mechanism works precisely because of the differences in the forms of production that appear in these different countries that take part in the system. It is in the light of this that the three conditions he poses as the necessary requirements for the establishment of capitalism can be understood: "an expansion of the geographical size of the world in question, the development of variegated methods of labour control for different products and different zones of the world-economy, and the creation of relatively strong state machineries in what would become the core-states of this capitalist world-economy" (MWS, p.38)[18]. As it turns out, Wallerstein's concept of "capitalism" is essentially the same as Frank's. It is the hierarchical structure of monopolistic powers to extract surplus. The only difference, as noted before, is that while for Wallerstein it is only countries that constitute the "layers" of this hierarchical structure, for Frank it is more general, including also the individual economic actors. This was shown to be a credit on the part of Wallerstein in terms of conceptual consistency.

Therefore, for Wallerstein, as well as for Frank (and to be sure it is a lot clearer in the case of Wallerstein), the main element in the conceptualization of capitalism is the notion of surplus transfer between countries. The division of land that defines this system "which is not merely functional - that is, occupational - but geographical...is a function of the social organization of work, one which magnifies and legitimises the ability of some groups within the system to exploit the labour of others, that is, to receive a larger share of the surplus" (MWS, p.349). In such a conceptualization, the "exploiter" and the "exploited" are countries, and capitalism is that system which brings this relation of exploitation about. It was pointed out before, while reviewing Frank, that this replacement of classes by countries is a main feature of neo-Marxism which may be called a form of nationalistic third-worldist ideology.

A less subtle example of this procedure of replacement in Wallerstein's method, is his analysis of the "semi-periphery". He starts with the following question. "Both kinds of world-system, the world-empire with a redistributive economy and the world-economy with a capitalist market economy, involve markedly unequal distribution of rewards...Why do not the majority who are exploited simply overwhelm the minority who draw disproportionate benefits?" (RFD, pp.403-4). The answer is that "it is the normal condition of either kind of world-system to have a three-layered structure" (RFD, p.404). Therefore, the role that the middlemen play in a world-empire is assumed by the semi-periphery in a world-economy. "This semi-periphery is then assigned as it were a specific economic role, but the reason is less economic than political...The existence of the third category means precisely that the upper stratum is not faced with the unified opposition of all the others because the middle stratum is both exploited and exploiter" (RFD, p.504.)

It does not seem necessary to go into a detailed discussion of this piece of analysis. The problem is simply that the replacement of classes by countries blinds Wallerstein to the elementary facts that a country or nation is not a homogeneous unity whose members have common interests, but rather they are composed of classes with contradictory interests. Therefore he seeks the 'political stability' of the world-system in the concept of a 'bumper' in his model of the hierarchical structure instead of the concept of collaboration between the dominant classes of each nation that make up the world-system. This latter point is related to the question of his concept of totality. The world-system may indeed be the appropriate unit of study, but only if its constitution is analysed through the smaller social-systems that can be defined on criteria other than the circuit of commodities. In other words, it is again the individual social formations with specific class structures that interact and integrate to make up the world-system that Wallerstein eliminates and reduces to the simple categories that he employs. This is because he lacks the vision of class contradiction, and therefore the different forms of exploitation that exist in his model of the world-economy do not designate class structures but simply different techniques of organization of production. But once the circuit of commodities is taken as the defining criterion of a social-system, the question may arise as to the necessity of bringing in the discussion of the variety of forms of production. As it seems, these various forms of production are brought in simply as a deus ex machina to develop the analysis of the mechanism that explains the basic category in

Wallerstein's conceptual framework, i.e. the transfer of surplus. However, it will be shown below that it is precisely this procedure that constitutes the basic problem with Wallerstein's theory.

Wallerstein's neglect of the existence of classes with contradictory interests is also inherent in his analysis of the state. It was shown above that according to him, the state is an "instrument" that must be conceived in terms of its operation in an international context of transferring surplus from the periphery to the core. The class basis of the state disappears in this analysis and it becomes an instrument to intervene in the free operation of the market to impose certain terms of trade in international transactions (RFD, pp.400ff., MWS, Ch.1, Ch.4.). Therefore the state is not conceived in terms of class struggle but is conceived in terms of the struggle between nations. From this it follows that the nation with a strong state wins the struggle of being a core country. Hence Wallerstein cites the example of Sweden: "as a peripheral state with a weak bourgeoisie, it was an arena in which the political power of the aristocracy grew with the economic expansion of the sixteenth century...The nobility hence needed conquest and for that they needed a strong, not a weak, state. Once they had the strong state, they would be able in the seventeenth and eighteenth centuries to use mercantilism as a lever of industrial advance, and hence be spared the fate of Poland" (MWS, pp.312-313). Such an argument is clearly due to his disregard of the concepts of class and class struggle. Thus he can easily conclude that a state based on the political power of the nobility transforms itself into a state that is based on the mercantilist interests of the bourgeoisie once it becomes "strong".

On the other hand, such an argument, which is based on his concept of the state as an instrument of struggle between countries, is inconsistent with his general model that explains the strength of the state, and the resultant inflow of surplus, with the labour-control method that the given country employs. In other words, it is not clear whether a strong state leads to industrialization or the wage-labour method leads to a strong state. This impasse in Wallerstein's analysis is in fact due to the insufficiency in his conceptual framework. This point has been partly grasped by Brenner in terms of Wallerstein's confusion between "labour-control method" as a technical determination and "class structure" as a political phenomenon. Brenner says that according to Wallerstein labour-control systems are results of the specific geographic position of the country in question in line with the requirement of the product that it specialises in. Thus the character of the state is determined. But Brenner adds that also, according to Wallerstein, it is the strength of the state that determines the country's position in the world market. Then the question is, does the state determine the country's role in the world-economy, or the other way around? Brenner comments, "to view the labour-control system as a class structure of exploitation precludes its being conceptualized in essentially technical-functional terms. Since from this viewpoint, the region's class structure conditions the very development of its productive forces, and thus by extension its role in the world-economy, the region's class structure, in determining the structure of the state, cannot be viewed as merely 'transmitting' the pressures of the world market and division of labour".[19]

Yet this observation does not reach the crux of the matter. It fails to realise that Wallerstein nowhere relies on the historical materialist concept of class structure so as to confuse it with the technical concept of labour-control method. The difficulty has to be conceived at a more general plane. In order to avoid the above confusion in the direction of causal determination between his different variables, Wallerstein has to show simultaneously that a core country has an industrial base, employs the wage-labour method, and has a strong state. But with such an approach to the problem, not only the relations of determination become unclear, but also these various elements of characterization appear only as descriptive categories. And this is precisely the essence of his model. Thus to show, for instance, that in a core country industrialization and the wage-labour method go hand in hand, he has to slur over the fact that agriculture too, in a core country, employs the wage-labour method.[20]

To understand the problem, it has to be placed in a broader perspective. It was stated before that the aim of Wallerstein was two-fold; i.e., to develop a framework that substantiates Frank's point that it is the transfer of surplus that explains development/underdevelopment and that, at the same time, attempts to answer questions that Frank's theoretical framework could not handle. In this context, the crucial element in Wallerstein's framework appears to be the category of forms of production. It was mentioned above that the variety of the forms of production in Wallerstein's world-economy is in a sense brought in as the deus ex machina to explain the reasons for surplus transfer. But choosing this specific deus ex machina, as it were, is not at all an arbitrary choice. For Frank has almost nothing to say on the subject; and the neo-Marxist school in general, although arguing that the capitalist mode of production embraces various forms of production, cannot explain why the core countries have the wage-labour form while the peripheral countries have the 'pre-capitalist' forms.

This is precisely where the originality of Wallerstein comes in. Within his own conceptual framework he can explain the 'distribution' of the forms of production on the world scale in the context of an international division of labour, by avoiding the concept of class struggle. And this he does by relying on a neoclassical analysis. Accordingly, it is the ahistorical and universal notion of profit-maximising rational individuals that explains in technical terms what method of labour-control is to be employed according to the given geographical distribution of resource endowments that determines the optimal allocation on a world scale not only of resources but also of the organization of production; and all this comes about through response to the market such that the relations of exchange appears to be the determinant relations.[21]

What is meant by this could be explained in a little more detail. The point is that the main features of neo-classicism can be detected in Wallerstein's analysis. First of all, it was briefly pointed out before that Wallerstein assumes capitalist rationality before capitalism itself. This is the typical ahistorical nature of the analysis. Together with it comes its static nature. Accordingly, the development of industry in certain countries, but not in others, is because the conditions of profitability dictate to them respectively what line of production to choose. This implies two things that both relate to the essence of neo-classicism. One is that it is the given objective conditions determined by nature, i.e. by resource endowments and the like, that dictate what line of production is to be chosen. This is simply an apology for the existing division of labour. It is all the more so, since Wallerstein also derives the nature of the social stratifications from this choice based on the given conditions. In other words, social phenomena are explained by the grace of nature and hence there is no room (and no need) left for class struggle. The other implication is that whatever is the outcome, it has been chosen by the participating economic actors and therefore implies an optimality. In other words, given the objective conditions, the participants in the world-economy have chosen what is most profitable for themselves and thus have brought about the existing division of labour. Given the objective conditions and given the rational behaviour of the participants, the outcome could not have been otherwise. Apart from its apologetic nature, it must be noticed that this is more of a description than analysis.

With such an approach to the problem, the following question world-system, could there be some rich (developed) and some poor (underdeveloped) Countries? It must be amphasised that in a formulation such as Wallerstein's, the concepts of development/underdevelopment do not have much substance since the rich and the poor Countries are hemogeneous but only different in terms of their place in the heirarchy. In other words, he cannot differentiate between these countries in terms of their modes of production, i.e. the specific combination of productive forces and production relations, and their articulation. This being the case, he has to refer back to the transfer of surplus to answer the above question. But then he has difficulty in explaining how the transfer of surplus could have been the reason for development/underdevelopment. If it is the transfer of surplus that is the explanatory variable, he has to show that this surplus is utilised for development. But to do this he has to refer to the class structure. In other words, if by some reason or another, surplus were to flow from England to Poland, instead of the other way around, it is not clear how Poland was to develop, within the reasoning of Wallerstein. Therefore, with his scheme of a given geographical division of labour that already explains the hierarchical structure of the world-economy, the transfer of surplus can explain nothing. In other words, his neo-classical analysis appears as an alternative explanation of development/underdevelopment within his own conceptual framework that does not require any reliance on the notion of surplus transfer. Wallerstein's attempt to substantiate the point that surplus transfer causes development/underdevelopment leads him into an analysis that renders the notion of surplus transfer useless. However, it was shown above that this alternative explanation is a mere juxtaposition of descriptive categories together with the notion of surplus transfer. With such a circular scheme of descriptive elements that he poses as causal relationships, his theory of the surplus transfer causing development/underdevelopment cannot be considered to have been substantiated. Therefore, Wallerstein seems to have been left with the same single point that Frank was left with, neither substantiated nor adequately explained.

POLITICAL IMPLICATIONS

The political implications of the neo-Marxist theories cannot in fact be divorced from their method of analysis which in turn is closely related to the underlying ideology. The Marxist appearance in terms of revolutionary conclusions, yet using Marxist terms in a totally different conceptual framework is what brings about the question of the reliability of these conclusions. Without going into a detailed discussion of the Marxist method, its most basic feature that distinguishes it from "vulgar economics" in general can be briefly stated. Marxism sees through and goes beyond appearances to reach real social relations. It does not stop at analysing the market relations where the appearances show but analyses the relations of production. In contradistinction, "vulgar-economics" cannot go beyond appearances and its analysis is locked up in the sphere of circulation. It cannot see that the relations between things are in fact relations between men in their productive process. However, this fetishism inherent in the nature of "vulgar-economics" is just a reflection of the alienation inherent in the nature of capitalism. Therefore, it is precisely by seeing through and criticising "vulgar-economics" that Marxism can see through and criticise capitalism. It is precisely this method that unites science with revolution in Marxism.[22] Therefore, a science that cannot go beyond the appearance of the capitalist reality cannot have a sound basis for revolutionary conclusions. This is what seems to be the case with neo-Marxism. Its revolutionary conclusions seem to be mere ideological slogans that are not based on its scientific analysis.

That the revolutionary conclusions involve ideological confusion can in fact be easily seen by reconsidering the main thesis and the accompanying political conclusion of neo-Marxism, i.e. that capitalism causes underdevelopment and that a socialist revolution is necessary. Clearly, these are two separate points and the only logical link is that if capitalism causes underdevelopment it must be replaced by socialism in order to solve the problem of underdevelopment. In other words, the latter does not derive from the former unless socialism is conceived as a system that brings about development. And this seems to be precisely the case in neo-Marxism. However, this is never put so crudely, and the justification for the link between these two separate points is argued through the conceptual mess that has been described above. A quick review of its elements would reveal that all the misplaced concepts form a consistent whole around this main thesis.

The argument that the whole world is characterized by capitalism leaves no doubt that underdevelopment is due to capitalism and also that a socialist revolution is not only possible but also necessary. What class or classes are to carry out this revolution, however, is not at all clear. On the contrary, classes are replaced by nations. This derives from two misplaced concepts. One is the concept of exploitation that refers to the transfer of surplus between national economies and the other is the concept of capitalism that refers to this system of "exploitation". It follows that it is because of capitalism, i.e. the international system of exploitation, that the exploited nations become underdeveloped, i.e. remain deprived of their own surpluses. To give an end to exploitation, therefore, the exploited should revolt against the exploiter. Hence the notion of proletarian nations, and the third-worldist approach to socialism, and the conclusion that the periphery should revolt against the centre to transcend capitalism, without giving due regard to the internal class forces, in the periphery as well as in the centre, that are to lead the socialist revolution. But because capitalism is not conceived as a mode of production, socialism cannot be conceived as a mode of production either. It is rather ambiguously conceived as a system that makes possible independent national development.

The origins of this development ideology can in fact be traced through the evolution of the literature of which neo-Marxism is the descendent,[23] i.e. the structuralist literature. The starting point of the structuralist school was the problem of underdevelopment; and this reflected its ideological formation which was not based on the tradition of class struggle of developed capitalism given the underdeveloped socio-economic and undifferentiated class structure of those societies where this literature was developed. The initial critique of the conventional development theory was an anti-imperialist critique finding the problem in the external orientation of the underdeveloped countries, and finding the solution in their internal orientation. This implied the replacement of the underdeveloped structure by an independent capitalist structure. Therefore the structuralist school was the spokesman of the "national bourgeoisie". It was when the "national bourgeoisie" went into collaboration with metropolitan capital that the structuralist theory and the development model fell into a crisis. Faced with the pressing social need for independent development and the realization that it was not possible in a capitalist system, the "socialist" alternative was seen as the solution. This found expression in "Marxifying" structuralism. Thus "the immediate effect of 'Marxifying' radical structuralism was to shift the implied solution to the problem of underdevelopment from economic nationalism to <u>socialism</u>, and to shift the means from utopian recommendations of radical structural reforms to <u>revolutionary struggle</u>."[24]

But if this is the case, then the class basis of this ideology seems rather dubious. It was suggested above that the neo-Marxist concept of socialism is not the Marxist concept of socialism that is a mode of production beyond capitalism and that is to be established by a proletarian revolution. It appears rather as a policy preference to achieve national and independent development. But then there is the question of whose preference this is supposed to be. Clearly it cannot be based on the anti-imperialist and anti-monopolist ideology of the "national bourgeoisie" although it might be tempting to think so. First, the "national bourgeoisie" has proved collaborationist, and secondly, the solution envisaged is socialism, i.e. the abolishment of capitalism altogether. The answer sought seems to lie in the following neo-Marxist evaluation of the petty-bourgeois: "This category has often had a residual flavour in Marxism, but its importance for neo-Marxism is considerable...admitting that the bourgeoisie and the working-class are either non-existing or not obviously militant, while the peasant masses are not spontaneously revolutionary, (neo-Marxism) places great stress on the role of petty-bourgeois intellectuals as originators of revolutionary ideas by virtue of their relative deprivation in the colonial social structure".[25]

NOTES

1. R. Brenner, "On the Origins of Capitalist Development: A Critique of Neo-Smithian Marxism", NLR 104.

2. For elaboration of this point, see my "Imperialism and Underdevelopment", MA Dissertation, University of Manchester, 1978.

3. A.G. Frank, "Dependence is Dead, Long Live Dependence and the Class Struggle: An Answer to Critics", World Development, 1977, p.362.

4. I. Wallerstein, "The Rise and Future Demise of the World Capitalist System: Concepts for Comparative Analysis". Comparative Studies in Society and History, 1974, (Hereafter referred to as RFD).

5. A. Foster-Carter, "Neo-Marxist Approaches to Development and Underdevelopment" in E. de Kadt and G. Williams (eds.), Sociology and Development, Tavistock, 1974. Also in Journal of Contemporary Asia, Vol.3, No.1 (1973).

6. A.G. Frank, Latin America: Underdevelopment or Revolution, Monthly Review Press, p. 9.

7. See, however, R. Leaver, "The Debate on Underdevelopment: On Situating Gunder Frank", Journal of Contemporary Asia, 1977, where the above quotation is from. It is rather amazing that this has only recently been realised and still not universally.

8. E. Laclau, "Feudalism and Capitalism in Latin America", NLR, 1971.

9. See, e.g., T. Dos Santos, "The Crisis of Development Theory and the Problem of Dependence in Latin America" in H. Bernstein (ed), Underdevelopment and Development, 1973.

10. See Frank's 'Preface' to his Capitalism and Underdevelopment in Latin America, Monthly Review Press, 1967.

11. For a recent survey, see G. Palma, "Dependency: A Formal Theory of Underdevelopment or a Methodology for the Analysis of Concrete Situations of Underdevelopment?", World Development, 1978. An earlier exposition of neo-Marxism from the neo-Marxist point of view is Foster-Carter (1974). Two important volumes in the same tradition are Bernstein (1973) and I, Oxaal, T. Barnett and D. Booth (eds.), Beyond the Sociology of Development, R. and K., 1975.

12. See, e.g. P. Sweezy, Modern Capitalism and Other Essays, Monthly Review Press, 1972: "..the principal contradiction in the (capitalist) system...is not within the developed part but between the developed and underdeveloped parts" such that "the relations of the one to the other...are fundamentally exploitative" (p.13) and "Against this background the real meaning of the communist revolutions of the twentieth century becomes clear" (p.23). Thus neo-Marxism replaces the basic Marxist vision of the conflict between classes by the conflict between nations.

13. Frank (1967), p.6.

14. I. Wallerstein, The Modern World-System, Academic Press, 1974 (Hereafter referred to as MWS), p.348.

15. See Brenner (1977)

16. E. Laclau, "Postscript" Politics and Ideology in Marxist Theory, New Left Books, 1977. p.45.

17. Incidental, both of these passages have also been quoted by Laclau to show Wallerstein's "errors" - a procedure that Laclau still seems to insist on. So it should not be very surprising that Laclau expresses his surprise about how Wallerstein could have committed these "errors". See Laclau (1977), p.45 and p.46 fn.6.

18. It may perhaps be appropriate to remember that the three conditions posed by Marx for the establishment of capitalism were as follows: development of commodity production that accompanies a division of labour, emergence of a class of free labourers, accumulation of capital. See. E. Hobsbawm (ed.), Karl Marx: Pre-capitalist Economic Formations, Lawrence & Wishart, 1964.

19. Brenner (1977), p.64.

20. See the related point in Brenner (1977), p.61, and also his excellent argument on p.62.

21. See also Laclau (1977) and Brenner (1977) on the neoclassical aspect of Wallerstein's theory.

22. L. Colletti, "Marxism : Science or Revolution?" in R. Blackburn (ed.), Ideology in Social Science, Fontana, 1972.

23. See Dos Santos (1973); P.J. O'Brien, "A Critique of Latin American Theories of Dependency" and D. Booth, "Andre Gunder Frank: an Introduction and Appreciation" in Oxaal et. al., (1975); C. Leys "Underdevelopment and Dependency: Critical Notes" Journal of Contemporary Asia, 1977.

24. Leys (1977), p.98.

25. Foster-Carter (1974), p.88.

Chapter 10

CAPITALIST INDUSTRIALIZATION IN THE FOUR LITTLE TIGERS OF EAST ASIA

Clive Hamilton

In the ideological battle the rapidly-industrializing countries of the Third World have been the trump card of orthodox economics. For those immersed in the dependency theorizing of the fifties and sixties - which argued for a rigidly structured relationship between industrial centre and agricultural periphery - this was a difficult trick to win. The infusion of dependency concepts into Marxist thought presented the latter with the same problem - how to reconcile the apparent industrial development of certain countries of the Third World with imperialist domination. Too often the reply lay in moral censure rather than detailed historical analysis. Of course there was never any shortage of bourgeois economists eager to flatter Brazil or South Korea for their growth figures, and thus themselves for the rightness of official economic theory. For them these countries were virtuous because industrial output multiplied, and the processes of class formation and repression which underlay the statistics were wholly ignored as outside the field of economic theory. For Marxists and dependencias these countries were opprobrious because they were repressive and this condemnation relieved them of the burden of analysing the growth of industry.

The broad consensus of radical economic analysis was that capital in the imperialist centres was alone capable of self-expansion and that any sporadic industrial growth in the periphery occurred solely at the behest of transnational corporations. The centre, by this means or by trade, managed to extract from the periphery its surplus product and thus deprive it of its own funds for accumulation. This comfortable conception was boldly and vehemently attacked by Bill Warren who marshalled an array of statistics to show the extent of industrial development in the Third World and drew from these some very radical conclusions, namely that the imperialist powers favoured Third World industrialization, that in any case their ability to restrict the latter had been and is being markedly eroded, and that imperialism will disappear.[1] But while Warren did a valuable service in assailing the 'impossibilists', he at the same time resurrected the 'inevitabilists'. The error of Warren was to remain always, like the apologists, at the level of appearances rather than to broach the material processes at work. In other words, Warren failed to locate the appearance of industrialization of a certain form and at a certain time and place in the changing structure of class relations, and these set within the international capitalist economy.[2] In consequence, industrialization has no historical foundation and no modus operandi and as such it has neither contradictions nor limits. This essay is a contribution to the critique of the impossibilist-inevitabilist problematic.

1. THE INTERNATIONAL DIVISION OF LABOUR

From one perspective, the world economy consists of a collection of industries, or production processes, which are distributed unevenly around the globe. The existence of transnational corporations means that this distribution does not correspond to the distribution of the capitals which own and organize production. Within an industry, competition among capitals allocates to each one a space in the world economy. On the world market, capitals jostle each other in an unceasing attempt to annex a larger space, and the methods by which this struggle is carried out provide the moving force behind the development of the international division of labour. If we think of a country as a collection of capitals which occupy spaces in some industries but not in others, then its development will depend very largely on what these spaces are. This is so because certain industries at certain stages of development offer more opportunity to capitals in their quest for self-expansion. The history of the world capitalist economy has left capitals indigenous to the Third World more or less wholly excluded from the broad range of industries which we associate with an advanced industrial economy.

In recent years, however, it has been possible for capitals in a few select 'newly industrializing countries' to occupy a larger and more diversified space in the world economy by specializing in the production and export of light consumer goods, industries traditionally monopolized by firms in the advanced capitalist countries. Well over half of this new production has taken place in four countries of east and southeast Asia; South Korea, Taiwan, Hong Kong and Singapore - the 'four little tigers'.[3] Not all of the growth of manufacturing production in these countries has been due to the ability of indigenous capitals to penetrate the Western monopoly for part represents the transfer of production processes by TNCs. Nevertheless, the share of TNCs in the manufactured exports of the Four has been relatively small, with the notable exception of Singapore. For the early seventies the figures were for Hong Kong 10%, South Korea at least 15%, Taiwan at least 20% and Singapore nearly 70%.[4]

The fact that, except for Singapore, indigenous capital has been responsible for the great bulk of manufactured production, and an even greater proportion of total output, is essential to the argument of this essay.

The state of the world economy has been fundamental to the industrial development of the Four because for export-dependent capitals it is the primary determinant of the amount of economic space to be commanded. Indigenous capital, which has accounted for the bulk of export production, has therefore expanded by annexing space in the world economy and doing so at the expense of other capitals. Other countries have industrialized largely on the basis of new spaces in the form of growing domestic markets, but in the Four rapid growth was induced from abroad. As a result they are subject to powerful and uncontrollable external forces, as the history of the clothing and textile industry in Hong Kong illustrates. In the early sixties textile exports to the USA and EEC were restricted by quota, and this was later extended to clothing exports. From 1974 the Multi-Fibre Arrangement placed strict limits on textile exports in particular. Hong Kong capital has been forced to shift into the clothing and finishing sectors, which in 1977 comprised fully 40% of Hong Kong's exports, while the textile sector had declined from 18% in 1959 to less than 8% in 1977.[5]

Incipient indigenous capital does not find it equally easy to break into every industry. While this much is obvious, to specify the characteristics of the industries which present openings is not so straightforward. The indigenous capital of an underdeveloped country must enter the international division of labour by evicting an already-established capital, or at least by restricting the growth of other capitals. It must be asked, then, under what circumstances can foreign capital be 'persuaded' to relinquish its grip on a given industry. To dislodge the well-established competitor the indigenous capital must match the conditions of advanced development of the productive forces which prevail in developed countries. In the case of TNCs which operate in the Third World, they must only recreate the productive conditions which prevail at home. This is necessary only in certain sectors, and the characteristics of these sectors will be elaborated on presently. Suffice it to say here that as a general rule, these sectors are those which, as a result of technological and organizational factors, do not require large agglomerations of capital to operate efficiently. This establishes a relation between the form of capital (its size, spread and organizational history) and the type of industry in which it can develop. Clearly, this fact gives TNCs a great advantage. The implication is that, because of the histories of capital accumulation in the Four, industrialization has been spearheaded by a very few industries with singular features.

Within the extensive and overwhelmingly apologetic literature on the development of the Four there runs the implicit argument that a 'country' industrializes as a result of the decisions of the state, without ever stopping to ask what the state represents or to analyse the material context in which the state performs its functions. The literature implies that Singapore industrialized because Lee Kuan Yew had read Samuelson. These writers in fact replace the anarchy of capitalist production, at a local and world level, with a wholly planned and autarkic economy. This voluntarism is closely bound up with the use of the concept of a 'country' - 'Korea decided to industrailize' or 'Brazil had an import-substituting strategy' - conceived of as a homogeneous social totality with a single will, a will expressed by the state. In fact, capitalist development expresses the will of capital, but not a collective will, merely the aggregation of the profit-oriented activities of many capitals. Where the word 'country' is used in this essay it is shorthand for a geographically specified collection of accumulation processes along with all of their contradictions and determinations.

The present study of the East Asian newly industrialized countries will examine the structure of classes in detail and ask how its development was compatible with industrialization. In particular we ask:

i. How is the social surplus product generated; by feudal, capitalist, colonial or other production relations?

ii. How is the surplus used, or who gets it? Does foreign capital channel it overseas, or reinvest it in plantations or industry? Does a landlord class consume it wastefully or invest it in agricultural improvements? Does merchant capital invest it in trade, or industrial capital in industry?

iii. In what specific ways is the class structure affected by integration into the international division of labour? In particular, is the influence of imperialism on class relations such as to inhibit the development of indigenous industrial capital?

2. COLONIAL CLASS STRUCTURE

The attempt to understand capitalist industrialization in the Four begins with the obvious structural fact that industrial capital dominates the production of surplus value. This raises the fundamental question of how this process of class transformation came about, for it is within this process that industrial growth occurs. The political histories of the Four are unique to each country but need to be understood together and we start from the commonplace observation that the foundations of social transformation after the Second World War were laid in the pre-war colonial period. In each case the national economies of the Four were organized and, to varying degrees, built to serve the economic interests of the Japanese and British colonialists.[6]

The twentieth century occupation of Korea and Taiwan by Japan was an extension of the new eastern power's industrial development. The dependent and distorted economies which emerged were integral segments of the Japanese economic empire. Under strict administrative control they were organized so as to provide growing quantities of agricultural products to supply the burgeoning Japanese proletariat. The extraction of the agricultural surplus was achieved by different means in Korea and Taiwan but the purpose was the same.

In Korea, the Japanese took much greater direct control of agricultural production by acquiring large tracts of land, to the extent that by 1942, 80% of forests and 25% of cultivated land was in Japanese hands.[7] The reorganization of land ownership led to a major increase in tenancy; the proportion of households that were pure tenants increased, according to Kuznets, from 29% in 1913-17 to 56% in 1938.[8] The traditional Korean landed aristocracy was seriously weakened by colonial occupation and annexation of land, but it was not destroyed. It continued to exist effectively in alliance with the colonisers and was to suffer the opprobrium of this collaboraton in the future. The twin exactions of pre-colonial feudalism and Japanese colonialism caused widespread agricultural pauperization; 56% of farm households were left with only 5.6% of the land and rice consumption was halved between 1912 and 1936.[9] While the Japanese were diligent in pursuing improved agricultural productivity, they were equally diligent in syphoning off the rural surplus, and more, through high rents and taxes.

The Japanese chose not to intervene so directly in Taiwanese agriculture and found it expedient to leave much of the rural social structure intact. With the exception of lands turned over to sugar-cane production, the application of labour to the process of cultivation was little changed. However, under the policy slogan 'agricultural Taiwan, industrial Japan', the colonialists sought to expand agricultural production to provide for exports to Japan. To this end the colonial Government-General carried out a cadastral survey and then a land reform in the first years of this century. The land reform simplified the ownership system by eliminating sub-tenancy and absentee landlords but it did little to improve the lot of the cultivator. The purpose was to encourage production for the market, to force peasants to look beyond the immediate needs of family and village, where self-sufficiency reigned. Raising productivity was the key to this and the growth and spread of Japanese business in Taiwan essentially served that purpose by introducing capital into agriculture. A stiff land tax added large revenues to the colonial treasury. After the first two decades of imperial rule, in which means of raising the peasants' output were carefully studied, productivity began to rise and continued to do so until the war. The primary reason for this was the introduction of new seeds, particularly the innovatory horai strain of rice, but also in the application of fertilisers, crop rotation and deeper ploughing, and in the 1930s especially in the spread of irrigation and farm machinery.

One observer has commented: 'The output of the island was gradually shaped so as to furnish a net contribution of agricultural and semi-processed food and related commodities every year to Japan'.[10] The same may be said for Korea if we add mineral products to its exports. Certainly, both of these colonies came to have very high levels of per capita foreign trade, higher in the 1930s than any other Asian country except British Malaya.[11] Moeover, trade was highly concentrated, Japan taking 85% of Taiwan's exports between 1911 and 1940 and supplying 74% of its imports, these imports being mainly fertiliser, machinery, manufactures and fishery products. Much of the fertiliser that was indispensable to Taiwanese agriculture originated in other parts of the 'Yen Bloc', Korea and Manchuria. This centre-periphery trade was very lucrative for Japanese capital for, at the same time as it reinvested locally-generated profits on a large scale, there continued to be very substantial net exports to Japan, of the order of 25-30% each year.[12] This was achieved by expanding local output while restricting local consumption.

While both colonies remained primarily sources of agricultural produce throughout the Japanese interregnum, in the 1930s as the Japanese war machine geared up for greater imperial adventure, some industry developed in both Korea and Taiwan, albeit as little more than an adjunct to the coloniser's industrialization. In Taiwan a boom occurred in 1936-42 and in addition to the earlier-developed food-processing factories, which until this time produced three quarters of all Taiwanese manufactured products, some industry emerged (machine- and ship-building, petroleum refining). Up to this time the proletariat, which worked mainly in the sugar mills, had grown no faster than total employment. On the eve of the war manufacturing contributed only about 18% of national income.[13] Needless to say, this industry was firmly controlled by Japanese capital, and in fact the locally-owned industry which had existed, mainly handicrafts and cottage productions, declined in the twenties and thirties, in Taiwan as in Korea.

The post-Depression colonial period in Korea also saw industrial development, chiefly in the northern part of the country, but again it was of an enclave character. Here the emphasis was on mineral extraction to fuel Japanese industry, and industrial growth was quite substantial. The manufacturing share of output was 43% at the outbreak of war and, remarkably, agricultural and industrial exports comprised 30% of gross domestic product.[14] Korean capital's participation in all this was minimal throughout; it owned a mere 11% of total industrial capital in 1938 and even this declined to 3% by 1943.[15] Moreover, industrial production was highly concentrated with several large Japanese concerns, comprising

1.2% of factories, producing 60% of total factory output in 1939.[16]

The colonial administration took measures strictly to circumscribe indigenous capital accumulation in the early part of its rule (for a period around the First World War it forbad new locally-owned enterprises altogether), measures that were superfluous subsequently, and the effect was to confine the inchoate classes of Taiwanese and Korean capitalists to the interstices of the Japanese colonial economy. The Korean mining boom of the twenties had provided some small scope for indigenous entrepreneurial expansion beyond the traditional boundary of textiles and trade, but local capital was everywhere out-gunned by the stronger and favoured Japanese businesses. Most Korean and Taiwanese capitalists hedged their bets by holding large tracts of land to guarantee a steady income, for they competed not simply against colonial capital but against colonial capital in alliance with an administration which sedulously regulated all areas of business activity. The latter favoured the development of oligopolies. In the Taiwanese sugar industry, where the policy was perhaps most marked, government intervention in support of Japanese business took the form of direct subsidies, marketing advantages and access to superior, imported equipment which more or less excluded local participation in the industry. (The sugar cartels were in a position to compel Taiwanese farmers to grow sugar rather than rice by withholding irrigation water.)

All in all, colonial domination in the two countries had a fundamental impact on domestic class structures the full significance of which would only emerge after decolonisation. It severely weakened the traditional governing class and landed aristocracy, robbing them of much of their political power, appropriating large portions of their material base and causing them, particularly in Korea, to be tarred with the collaborationist brush. During the period of intense colonial rule there was no potential, indigenous leadership stratum to speak of, except perhaps for scattered cabals of intimidated nationalists. No strong merchant class could develop, nor was indigenous industry allowed to flower. Enclave industrialization did breed significant numbers of industrial proletarians, especially in Korea where by 1943 industrial workers numbered perhaps 750,000, but skilled workers were encouraged to emigrate to Japan or Manchuria. Many did, along with thousands of unskilled labourers who were required to perform the lowest-paid and meanest jobs in and around Japanese industry.

Moving south to Hong Kong and Singapore we find that the nature of their economies and their strategic location meant that imperialism had entirely different effects. The British empire built up these cantons as trading depots to service the lucrative Far East commerce and both developed into prosperous international free ports based on both British and Chinese capital and local labour. While the merchant business of Hong

Kong opened up the vast Chinese hinterland, Singapore dealt in the tropical produce of neighbouring regions and imported manufactured goods from the west. Linked to this trade were numerous European agency houses, shipping companies and insurance and banking institutions owned mainly by London-based capital. The local Chinese, on the other hand, controlled retail trade, transport, goods-handling, and secondary industries such as pineapple factories and sawmills. Chinese capital also managed to make significant inroads into finance and wholesale trade. In both Singapore and Hong Kong the colonial administration, with wanton disregard for the relative autonomy of the state, served the interests of the British trading companies, but did so with a kindly eye to the material well-being of local Chinese business.

3. FORMATION OF THE POST-WAR NATION-STATE

The dominant social force throughout post-war Asia was nationalism. Those nationalists in former Japanese colonies were fortunate to be in the domain of the war's loser since the first act of the victors was to strip Japan of its empire. In the face of a tangible enemy, pre-war nationalism could unite those who suffered under foreign rule and who turned to rebellion. Middle strata, industrial workers, peasants and the dispossessed combined to fight the Japanese and the Europeans in movements across the continent. Independence movements were driven towards policies of radical social reform as national liberation became increasingly associated with a new social order rather than sentimental atavism. Impending victory precipitated irresolvable divisions, as the imminent seizure of power undermined the cohesive strength of the goal of national self-determination. The division between Nationalists (now capitalized) aligned with landed and city capital and communists, pursuing the supersession of capitalism, dominated political and military struggles after the war. The popular victory in China in 1949 cast a long shadow over the ruling classes of the whole region.

The anti-Japanese nationalists in Korea were the forces most capable of taking control after the Pacific defeat, and these forces were dominated by communists. Emphatically in Korea, Japanese occupation destroyed the power and legitimacy of the traditional governing class. The vacuum left by Japanese capitulation was filled, in the southern part of the peninsula, by the seizure of factories by Korean workers. Pre-war Japanese enterprises were now operated either by workers on a profit-sharing basis or by the local People's Committee. When US forces arrived two months after the Japanese surrender, one of the first tasks was to appropriate all property of the former invaders, including the factories, and there began the process of crushing all popular political activity. But nationalism was an irresistible force, one which the US Army Military Government (AMG) could not ignore in its half of the country. Syngman Rhee combined impeccable nationalist credentials with a loathing of Communism and could be trusted to form a legitimate interim government in opposition to the left-leaning forces of the self-proclaimed People's Republic. Rhee was brought back from decades of exile in the USA to do this, and thus was initiated a process of rooting out and destroying the left opposition, although it was several years before the parliamentary liberal-left was wholly exorcised from the South Korean body-politic.

Rhee's faction was virtually the only one in Korea to support the US-UN proposal for separate elections in the south in 1948. The entire opposition sent its leadership to Pyongyang for a joint North-South conference which called for withdrawal of foreign troops and for separate elections to be abandoned. A popular uprising against the US-Rhee regime had been savagely crushed in 1946. There was little class basis for Rhee's government, his power deriving from the US alliance and increasingly his control over and loyalty from the indigenous repressive forces. His Democratic Party (from 1951 the Liberal Party) supporters comprised mainly landlords, some businessmen, and anti-communist nationalist professionals. Apart from the irreplaceable backing of the US forces, Rhee managed to retain power for 14 years because he won the allegiance of two powerful groups, the bureaucracy and the police. Both of these had strong links with the Japanese colonial era; they smelt of collaboration and feared popular reprisals. Rhee's police were vital in destroying the remnants of the left and parliamentary opposition in the South.

The US-Rhee alliance was an unstable one throughout. An early point of contention was land reform. There was strong mass commitment to land reform and it had been the cause of peasant revolts, the killing of landlords and land seizures. When the landlord-dominated Interim Assembly refused to act on land reform in 1948 the AMG began distributing to tenants government holdings confiscated from the Japanese. The AMG, initially suspicious of land reform, followed McArthur's lead in Japan. After the elections of that year, the National Assembly in 1949 enacted, against Rhee's presidential veto, the first part of sweeping land reforms aimed at abolishing tenancy. When Rhee's forces suffered a crushing defeat at the 1950 elections, elections Rhee had fought the US to abandon, his position was saved only by the outbreak of war.

The influence of the AMG and then the US State Department after formal independence was pervasive and irresistible in South Korea, as it was in Taiwan after the Nationalist retreat. These two areas formed the frontier of the US empire in Asia. In the military, US hegemony extended to all important decisions; advisors were scattered throughout, and large numbers of officers were sent to US military schools for training. Military aid was massive, and so was economic aid. In both countries, aid constituted the largest portions of national budgets for several years. Moreover, economic advisors directed economic strategy and the State Department, in South Korea especially after the civil war, planned 'self-supporting' economies with the ability to sustain large military forces. Foreign direct investment was extremely low in both countries until the late 1960s. The effect of US intervention was not only to sustain conservative, anti-communist regimes but also to foster the development of nascent bourgeoisies whose members profited from close ties with US instrumentalities and in particular from special purchasing and selling rights for US aid commodities.

The process of post-war class formation in Taiwan was not quite so convoluted. The establishment of the Republic of China under Kuomintang (KMT) leadership was itself an act of annexation since the Taiwanese had a distinct cultural identity and resented dominance by mainlanders. The defeated Nationalists traced their origins to Sun Yat-Sen and the twenties when the movement represented progressive elements in Chinese society indignant at European incursions and then Japanese invasion. However, the KMT had become increasingly reactionary in the struggle against socialism. The million or so refugees who fled to Taiwan made up a good portion of China's capitalists, managers, professionals and dispossessed landlords. The accession to power of the KMT was initially precarious and consolidation relied on US support.

The Nationalist government was no puppet of the US State Department but the influence of the mission from the Agency for International Development (AID) in Taiwan over the economic organization of the island was widespread and in certain respects determinant. Economic stabilization and reconstruction was heavily dependent upon the torrent of US aid which began to flow in the early fifties. Even before then US influence was critical; in particular the Joint Commission on Rural Reconstruction, with both Chinese and American members, advised on and monitored the radical programme of land reform in the 1949-53 period. From the outset AID representatives and Chinese officials conferred in detail on the whole gamut of resource allocation decisions. They did so mainly through the offices of the Economic Stabilization Board set up in 1951. The AID mission saw its responsibility as one of using all its powers to ensure the implementation of US goals and the principal weapon at its disposal was control over aid funds. The goal was to promote development with a degree of self-sufficiency, both to create a stronger basis for Taiwan's military defense and to advance this Chinese territory as a showcase of capitalist development. The 1948 Bilateral Agreement stipulated that the government should promote agricultural and industrial production and ensure economic stability. AID used its control over funds to strengthen the influence of sympathetic political groups, not least the military, the foundation stone of early KMT rule. The AID mission did not hesitate to use its big gun - the threat to withhold aid - when conflict with the Chinese government arose. In one critical case in 1960 the mission threatened to withhold additional aid in order to push through the 19-Point Program, a document which reads like an IMF ultimatum to a desperate debtor: freeing of markets and exchange controls, denationalizations, liberalization of trade, anti-inflationary monetary and fiscal policies, removal of certain subsidies and so on. In another instance in 1962 the same threat was used to persuade the government to raise electricity rates.[17] Above all, AID consistently used its influence to promote, directly and through the government, the development of private industry and to restrict government enterprise. It did so by inducing the government to sell off nationalized industries, to facilitate private investment and to provide infrastructure for industry. Aid was a crucial element in founding and expanding such industries as glass, synthetic fibres, plastics, hardboard, cement, paper and textiles.[18]

The rapid reimposition of British colonial rule in Hong Kong and Singapore after the war deprived the nationalists there of the chance to seize power. In Hong Kong the colonial status quo has proved unshakeable to this day. Nationalism has never been the force it has been elsewhere, perhaps because national identity lies in China proper, where the revolution was fought. Hong Kong had always been a tight commercial enclave and the flood of refugees in 1949-50, along with later waves, only served to buttress and invigorate this status. The flood carried with it oppositionist elements - capitalists, professionals and the dottle of the old ruling class - many of whom felt at ease in the mercantile traffic of Hong Kong, British ruled or not. Moreover, the Nationalists had been mostly banished from southern China. All the same, there were firmly-rooted centres of nationalist sentiment and political activity among the Hong Kong working class, and trade unions divided between those controlled by the KMT and those led by communists aligned with Peking. But such was the solidity of the long-established alliance between colonial government, the British business houses and Chinese capitalists that, other than periodic rioting (energetically suppressed), anti-colonialism posed no serious threat.[19]

In Singapore things were quite different, for there nationalism was part of the wider Malayan movement and was extensively supported by indigenes of most social strata. The contradictions were sharpened as a result of decolonization in Burma, India and Ceylon in 1948 which left Singapore as one of the last bastions of the British Empire in the Far East. The nationalist movement was not led by a national bourgeoisie but by an alliance of middle-class professionals and labour-movement activists. Historically, the labour movement in Singapore had been broadly-based and militant. By the end of the Second World War the departing Japanese left behind a fierce anti-colonialism, and the returning British were met by demands for self-determination and a labour force in a combative mood. The response was a series of reppressive labour laws and security provisions which, enforced with great effect, emptied the labour movement of radicals by the time full independence was granted in 1965.

The main vehicle for the independence struggle was the People's Action Party (PAP) founded in 1954 by a group of English-educated 'non-communists' around Lee Kuan Yew. The members of this group many of whom could not speak Chinese) were from privileged backgrounds; professionals and civil servants rather than businessmen. It was apparent to them that the most powerful force for independence was the organized labour movement, but to gain this support would require an alliance with cadres of the Malayan Communist Party (MCP) whose influence dominated there. This was not an insuperable obstacle particularly since the MCP was in the process of reorienting its strategy towards the parliamentary road after serious defeats suffered using insurrectionary tactics. The PAP soon developed a mass base in the trade unions and Chinese schools. While the communist cadres commanded the rank and file organizations of the Party, the Central Executive Committee stayed in the hands of the Lee faction. Considerable conspiratorial effort was expended by the latter to maintain control of the higher Party organs, not stopping at approving measures by the British authorities to suppress radical dissent. In 1956, the arrest by the Government of 14 PAP office-bearers stayed an impending and popular communist dominance of the Party's central bodies, and in 1959 the PAP non-communists plotted with the parliamentary opposition to prevent the PAP communists from gaining a majority in the National Assembly. Not surprisingly, the Party split in 1961, the radicals, including non-communists, taking 60 to 70% of the membership into the new Barisan Socialis, an organization then systematically extinguished by Lee.

From the outset the PAP declared itself 'socialist' - said Lee in 1965, 'I am an unrepentent socialist' - but this brand of socialism meant no more than the pursuit of a more equitable, efficient and honest society. It did not represent a threat to capital as such, indigenous or foreign, and the British authorities came to look upon the Lee forces with increasing favour. The colonial master could transfer power to these socialists with confidence. The nationalism of the founders of the PAP was genuine enough, but so was their opportunism. In the mid-60s Lee put it candidly:

> Fourteen years ago a number of my colleagues and I organized the Government workers and others in a movement of protest to challenge authority, and trade unionism became a banner behind which we challenged the whole system. Now we have to re-educate not only our trade union leaders, but, even more important, the workers that this can no longer be.[20]

The study of the histories of class transformation in the post-war conjunctures of the Four indicates that domestic class structures took their shapes in conformity with and influenced by the interests of their respective imperial powers. The lack of a clearly dominant local class or coalition of classes at the end of the Pacific war was easily filled in the cases of Singapore and Hong Kong by the return of the former rulers, but in Korea and Taiwan it left a battleground which Nationalist forces, in these two countries if not elsewhere, managed to wrest for themselves. The class basis of Nationalist rule - the social forces which could sustain it in the long term - was yet to develop. Develop it did, without serious opposition in Taiwan but tumultuously in South Korea, and we must finally take up this next chapter in Korean history.

It was Syngman Rhee's inordinate nationalism which began to alienate his own support as the fifties progressed. His conservative backers became increasingly estranged by his obsession with the North and fanatical anti-communism, and Rhee exacerbated the rift by his autocratic leadership and savage use of police powers. The US also thought Rhee went too far and was additionally concerned, in unison with Korean business interests, with the regime's neglect of economic development.[21] The two were related, since the US had begun to evolve a new East Asian strategic plan which foresaw a strengthened Japan assuming some of the USA's commitments, economic and military, in the region. This, of course, would require rapprochement between Japan and Korea, something which was anathema to Rhee. Towards the end of the fifties, the economic position of South Korea began to decline and business was squeezed. Recession was compounded by a poor harvest in 1959-60. The US had been losing faith in its fractious protégé and in 1960 withdrew its support.

The student 'revolution' of April 1960 saw the Rhee regime collapse with remarkable speed. Elections in July caused the Democratic Party to be swept into office on the slogan 'Economic Development First'.[22] However, its leadership was not easily distinguishable in social background from that of its Liberal Party predecessor, and it had the additional problem of being hopelessly riven with factionalism. Disunity in government and unrest on the streets precipitated a military coup in May 1961.

Perhaps unusually in recent history, the US appears to have had no foreknowledge of the coup. It was carried out by a coterie of young colonels with Park Chung-Hee, a major-general, playing a leading role. The source of all of the original plotters was the 8th Military Class of 1948-49, men who, having borne the brunt of combat during the civil war, felt overshadowed by the more senior officers many of whom were tied up in the corruption of the Rhee regime. The sympathies of the conspirators lay with the indigent and increasingly distressed peasantry (three quarters of the coup's authors and subsequent military rulers were rural-born) and their first acts were to annul rural debts and extend agricultural credit. More generally, their economic orientation was nationalistic and aimed at less reliance on the US by encouraging heavy industry and agriculture to achieve self-sufficiency and export growth. This was not in accord with US plans for South Korea although there was relief in the fact that the colonels were less concerned with excoriating Japan for past crimes if co-operation would lead to economic progress. The US quickly recognized the new government and the aid flows continued.

The transition to formally civilian rule and the election of Park to the presidency in 1963 also witnessed the gradual emergence of a new leadership group. Park, involved in the coup but without the young colonels' reformist fervour, attracted the support of, from the US and business viewpoint, the more pliant (and more senior) levels of the military hierarchy.[23] The military was the most Americanised institution in Korea and had been thoroughly imbued with the ideology and techniques of American capitalist management. By 1961 roughly 6000 officers had been trained at military schools in the USA. The liberal writers Cole and Lyman have observed:

> In certain characteristics, particularly time orientation, work habits and management outlook, the military early became one of the most 'modernized' institutions in Korea, out of balance in this respect with most government and educational institutions.[24]

The wholesale import of Fordism into Korea could not itself form the basis of a new stage of national development but the fact that it was consistent with the dominant mode of capital accumulation was of considerable importance.

The accession to power of the Park faction had as its concomitant the dulling of the fire of the young colonels, who were gradually brought into line. President Park's economic strategy was altogether consistent with US designs, for it meant a dependent economy fully integrated into the international division of labour on the basis of relatively free trade and the pursuit of Korea's 'comparative advantage' in labour-intensive products. Integration was consummated in 1965 by the normalization treaty with Japan, a diplomatic meeting which sparked rioting throughout the land.

4. FORMATION OF THE CLASSES OF CAPITALISM

In the industrialization of the 'four little tigers' the role of indigenous capital accumulation varied from relative insignificance in Singapore to the main bearer in Hong Kong, Taiwan and Korea. True enough, in the last two cases domestic accumulation was to a very large extent stimulated by the circulation of US money- and commodity-capital in the form of grants, loans and military spending. Nevertheless, our understanding of this industrialization requires more thorough discussion of the forces that generated the capitalist classes which would carry out indigenous accumulation. While accumulation in the fifties was slow by later standards, it was highly formative. The study of the Four reveals that the primitive accumulation of capital is as much a political process as an economic one.

The processes were very similar in Korea and Taiwan. A reorganization of their economies took place after the Japanese defeat as newly-formed states took possession of former Japanese property. (In Korea, as we saw, the US AMG appropriated factories from Korean workers.) In Taiwan the Government assumed control of enterprises accounting for 90% of the total capital of Taiwanese enterprises. In the following years, heavy industry was to be developed with the benefit of US investment aid, while light industry was rapidly sold off to dispossessed landlords and monied classes. Non-agricultural private capital tended, in the early post-war period, to be concentrated in commerce and small-scale industry, with large investments (including infrastructure) undertaken by state-owned concerns. The proliferation of small manufacturing and commercial businesses was augmented by influxes of refugee capitalists who were quick to establish profit-making operations where opportunity arose. In Korea, those big capitals which had managed to prosper during the Japanese occupation, few as they were, invested mainly in the profitable 'three white industries' - spinning and textiles, flour milling and sugar refining.

In the early 1950s state-owned enterprises occupied the commanding heights of these economies - in Taiwan they contributed 55% of total industrial product - but large portions were then sold off to private capital - by 1964 the previous figure had fallen to 38%.[25] The KMT Government gave a major boost to private capital in the 1950s by transferring to private ownership four major public corporations - the Taiwan Cement Corporation, the Taiwan Paper and Pulp Corporation, Taiwan Agricultural and Forestry Development Corporation's Canned Pineapple Division (a very big export earner), and the Taiwan Industrial and Mining Corporation (iron, steel, machinery, coal and spinning). These and other windfalls accruing from the close relationship between state and private capital were one of the most important sources of accumulation in both Taiwan and Korea. Jones and Sakong commented on the latter country in these terms:

> ...a major characteristic of Korean entrepreneurship in the 1950s was that it was far easier to make money from government-derived favors than from productive competitive activity, and entrepreneurs naturally followed their pocket books.[26]

In their study of the 'Fifty Groups' - South Korea's fifty most influential industrial groups, consisting of over 500 firms nearly 60% of which are in manufacturing - Hyung and Shin tell us that most of the present big enterprise groups evolved in the 1945-61 period (31 of the 50, compared to 13 before 1945 and 6 between 1962 and 1976).[27] Serious shortages of consumer goods provided favourable circumstances for enterprise and particularly for those businessmen who could procure a foreign exchange allocation since, with prices high, importation itself guaranteed big profits, although preference in loans was given to exporters who used local raw materials and domestic producers who relied on imports of capital goods. In effect the Special Foreign Exchange Loan provided an impetus for the formation and development of new businesses because new firms of the right sort could attract these loan, 'and this access to loans rather than production itself must have been the backbone of profitable capital accumulation at that time.'[28] Thirteen of the fifty groups began their businesses in foreign trade. After foreign trade the most common line of business on which the groups developed was textiles (8 of the 50), although most of those in the former category moved into textiles as well before diversifying in the seventies into heavy and chemical industries.

The structure and purpose of British colonialism in Singapore and Hong Kong differed radically from the Japanese imperial idea in the more northern colonies. British capital sought in these two strategic ports only centres for its great eastern entrepôt trade, and garrisons to protect it, and did not conceive of these outposts of empire as extensions of its economic territory in the way that Taiwan and Korea were integral to the industrial configuration of Japan. It followed that British colonial administration did not deliberately constrain the development of business by local capital; indeed, British traders were reliant on it for vital activities such as cargo handling, local transport and simple processing. Indigenous capital had developed strong roots in both colonies and was threatened neither by the re-establishment of British dominion nor independence under the PAP in Singapore. These local capitalist classes were expanded in the turbulent post-war decade by waves of refugees escaping from instability and expropriation. In Hong Kong particularly, a large segment of Shanghai's business community, notably those in the textile trade, escaped to the crown colony before and after the popular victory of 1949. This led one commentator to observe that a 'significant component of Hong Kong's "growth" was simply a transfer of economic activity from one industrial centre to another, and as such it should not be compared with the more indigenous growth found in other countries'.[29]

The prosperous years of the fifties could only enrich those engaged in international trade, as many were in Hong Kong and Singapore, and in the latter wealth flowed also in the form of British military expenditure as Singapore took on increased strategic importance. But Hong Kong capital went beyond its traditional involvement in entrepôt trade, and in fact was forced to do so by the closing of China's economy after the US ban of 1950 and the UN embargo of 1951. By these moves Hong Kong's main source of re-exports was choked off. Many local businesses were compelled, in order to avoid failure, to begin manufacturing commodities, to sustain turnover by adding value locally. Several of the big British trading companies followed suit. In Singapore, too, it became increasingly necessary for local capital to be transformed from a merchant to an industrial circuit. The state took a leading role in this, although on the whole local capital was neglected in favour of transnational corporations. Local investors, tied up in commercial enterprises, were accustomed to making short-term investments with quick returns. Moreover, few bankers had the experience to assess the value of industrial machinery which could serve as collateral for industrial loans. The Finance Division of the government's Economic Development Board attempted to overcome this difficulty by itself offering medium- and long-term loans for industrial investments and by underwriting the issue of stocks and bonds by industrial enterprises. Bankers in Hong Kong were less hidebound and by lending against the insubstantial collateral of personal standing laid the foundation of the textile industry and thus industrialization.

Clearly, the state has played an indispensable role in the process of early capital formation in both Taiwan and Korea. The state - in the shape of the government, its individual members, its statutory bodies and public corporations - was intimately involved at all levels of primitive accumulation. The importance of the process lay not in the amassing of fortunes by individuals or firms but in the creation of conditions in which capital could be accumulated industrially; in other words, it was the process of transforming capital from agricultural and merchant forms into industrial form. No matter how large fortunes grow, capital will continue to be invested in land and trade as long as it is more profitable and secure to do so. That was the case in post-war Taiwan and Korea where high rents and the security of land kept the bulk of private capital rooted in the soil - the figurative soil of exploitative agrarian social relations. The transformation and expansion of capital in the fifties came about in response to the twin pressures exerted by the growing unattractiveness of investing in land and the increasing profitability of building industry. There were two essential agents in this process of primitive accumulation; the revolution in agrarian relations (and its implications for industrial labour) and the ingestion of US aid funds.

i. The Impact of Land Reform

Both Korea and Taiwan had far-reaching land reform programmes in the early fifties and in the former, as we have seen, this course was forced on the Rhee regime by popular demand and US coercion. In Taiwan land reform was a product of the populist streak in Chinese nationalism but the KMT leadership was not averse to such a change partly because they attributed their defeat on the mainland to the inequality of land ownership and partly because they themselves were no longer tied to the land. Taiwanese landlords were not closely affiliated with the new ruling élite, and the AID mission gave its persuasive blessing to this 'modernization'. The three-stage reform programme of 1949-53 began by substantially reducing rents and giving tenants greater security, and in 1952 the government sold off public lands to landless farmers. The final stage required private owners to sell to the government all holdings above three hectares in exchange for government bonds and shares in state enterprises. The government subsequently sold the land, for purchase price, to the tenants. In fact many landlords sold up before the third stage as the rent reductions cut deep and expropriation on poor terms appeared imminent. Whereas in 1952 owner-cultivators comprised 38% of the agricultural population, by 1965 this had risen to 67%.[30] Business speculators travelled the countryside to buy the dispossessed landlords' new share-wealth at low prices, but it was mainly the smaller landlords who thus suffered. The essential point is that after the land reforms it was no longer profitable or safe to invest in land, and there began a shift into industry and commerce (which continued into the sixties) the upshot of which was to leave the social and economic position of the landlord class seriously weakened.

In Korea the process was remarkably similar. High rents had established agriculture as the most profitable roost for capital. The object of the 1949 reforms was to make all farm land owner-occupied and the legislature approached the problem directly by simply outlawing tenancy. The reforms were not confiscatory, for the landlords were paid in land bonds which could be employed to buy formerly-Japanese industrial and commercial property. However, this exchange was unalluring to many and options on Japanese factories were often taken up at knock-down prices by urban professionals and technicians some of whom had been employed in the same factories before the war. The reforms, which also set an upper limit of three hectares, redistributed 40% of total arable land and affected the majority of farm households. By 1974 70% of farm households were fully owner-operated.[31] The economic and subsequently the social dominance of the landlord class was greatly undermined and droves of rural families of wealth left the land in the fifties and sixties.

If the land reforms ended the era in which agriculture was the most secure environment for the accumulation of wealth, we must now ask whether the rural sector provided a stimulus to the primitive accumulation of industrial capital through the flow of its surplus product. This is not an easy question to answer because of its complexity and the lack of data. Turning first to productivity, it appears that Taiwanese farm production roughly doubled in the 1951-63 period (representing 5% growth per annum with a modest rise in the input of farm labour) but rice output increased by only 42%. Nevertheless it appears that the independence of the tiller did encourage greater production despite the fact that the average amount of arable land per household was very small and often divided into tiny plots. (Gallin reports an average plot size in the southern village of Hsin Hsing of under 0.3 hectares.) This made the efficient use of machinery difficult. However, the application of more capital in the forms of irrigation, fertilizers, seeds, pesticides and improved techniques increased output enough to feed Taiwan's growing population. US aid, it should be said, financed 59% of net domestic capital formation in agriculture over 1951-65. Still, most of the benefits took some years to filter through for Gallin reports from Hsin Hsing that in the late fifties it was fairly common for more than half of the local farmers not to realize any cash for their crops and thus to remain at subsistence level. (Villagers also said that they were better off under the Japanese.)

In Korea the farmer appears to have fared worse. The land reform did not solve the serious problem of land fragmentation and intensified the proliferation of small and miniature farms. In 1962 miniature farms (under 0.5 hectares) comprised 44% of the total and small farms (0.5 - 2.0 hectares) 51%. Agriculture was neglected in government plans and this for the good reason that huge shipments of grain (mostly wheat, barley and rice) arrived from the USA under the PL 480 scheme. (In Taiwan, PL 480 surplus agricultural commodities amounted to one quarter of all US aid over the aid period.) There is no doubt (and here a US Congressional Committee agreed) that these shipments when coupled with the government's grain price policy retarded the growth of Korean agriculture. Between 1962 and 1973 Korean food self-sufficiency fell from 93% to 69%, in that half of the peninsula which had once been the food bowl of the entire country. Throughout the sixties grain imports rose and by the end of the decade 9% of previously cultivated land lay fallow. Thus although agricultural value-added grew in the sixties at about 5% each year with extensive irrigation, emphasis on fertilizers, etc., at the same time farm household income levels deteriorated sharply in comparison with city households.[32]

The explanation for the apparent paradox lies in the government's policy of directing the agricultural 'surplus' out of the countryside and into industry at a rate that was debilitating for millions on the land. The elements of this policy have been much the same in Korea and Taiwan. In Korea, by means of compulsory payment of rents and loans in grain and, when necessary, the occasional legislated state monopoly of grain purchase, the government has ensured that the bulk of produce has passed through its own agencies. Moreover, it has been bought at prices below the market price and often below cost-price, and sold to the urban workforce cheaply. Shipments of cheap grain from the USA have formed an integral part of the policy. In Taiwan the government has forced the growing of rice by withholding essential fertilizers, over which it has a monopoly, to farmers who do not co-operate. Land taxes must be paid in rice and a portion of each harvest is compulsorily acquired by the state's agencies at an official price which is perhaps only 70% of the market price.

ii. Formation of the Proletariat

Through the government policy of low food prices for urban workers, industrial capital has profited from the agricultural surplus. But the state's agricultural policy was imperative to industry for another reason, the stimulation of migration from farm to factory. That trend, history tells us, is inevitable in any process of industrial expansion and in Britain's case much has been made of the effects of enclosure in this respect. But even the British rural diaspora and the reconstitution of the landless in the industrial cities was sedate by comparison with Korea and Taiwan. While land reform was a progressive step and represented a victory for popular agitation and insurrection, the consequent rural ownership structure opened the countryside to the state's exploitative policies. In Korea, as grain imports rose and land was left untilled, between 1967 and 1972 the rural population fell from 16 million to 13 million which, with natural increase, meant that about 7 million people left the land for the cities, in the space of 5 years. The long-term effect of land reform had been to drive both the richest and the poorest from the villages. A similar though less dramatic process of spawning a proletariat occurred in Taiwan. The farm population began to decline absolutely in 1967. Many farm workers have been forced to supplement the family income by taking work in Taipei or one of the other industrial centres, to the point where in the late fifties agriculture furnished perhaps only 65% of village income.[33]

The state's agricultural policies in Korea and Taiwan, by encouraging rural-urban migration and providing cheap food for city workers, has vitally assisted the transformation of agricultural into industrial capital by making industrial investment more profitable. Here we touch upon what has been world-wide perhaps the most important state function in the industrialization process - the provision of a workforce of adequate size and temperament for the multiplying factories. The genesis of industrial capital is, pari passu, the formation of an industrial proletariat. Moreover, the sort of industrial development which has dominated society in Taiwan, South Korea, Hong Kong and Singapore has been acutely dependent on an unceasing flow of cheap labour. The rows of industrial workers came from three sources - immigration, farms and population growth. In each case immigration was a principal ingredient.

In Taiwan the post-war 'population explosion' was due more to expatriation than copulation, and the same may be said for Korea in the fifties. The surges of immigration into Hong Kong from China continued into the sixties, and while in these countries the motives for accepting such large numbers of refugees were initially political in character the importance of their role in subsequent economic growth is incontrovertible. The Singaporean government set out quite deliberately to attract immigrants from Malaysia to swell the industrial ranks and one estimate put their numbers at 10% of the 1972 workforce.

But sheer numbers are not enough. A new proletariat must be adequate to the rigours of factory work, but a great deal can be tolerated when there is no alternative means of livelihood. With the continuing purge from the land the dependence of the working person on a factory job intensified. Unemployment was substantial well into the seventies - in 1976 a Korean minister said that the first priority was to increase employment.[34] The pressure to accept the terms of employment gathers additional weight from the almost total absence of social security provisions. Within the factory the ranks of labourers have been augmented by a great influx of women workers. In Hong Kong in 1967, 47% of the manufacturing workforce was female. In Singapore the figure stood at 44% in 1971 and this was expected to exceed 50% by 1973. The apologist Galli reports that in 1978 women comprised 25% of the total Taiwanese workforce but they 'are particularly well-represented in the labour-intensive, export-oriented textile, electronics, and plastic goods industries'.[35] The selection of large numbers of women workers, as well as immigrants and children, has been instrumental in maintaining the competitiveness and profitability of export producers. Lastly, one must refer to the 'wage-restraint' imposed by the suppression of trade unions and political opposition. The history of repression is so well documented as to make any further comment superfluous.

iii. Aid and Accumulation

The foundation of the rapid export-oriented growth of the late sixties and seventies in Taiwan and Korea was laid in the fifties - in the transformation of capital into industrial form, in the multiplication of that capital, and in the provision of conditions in which accumulation could take place. The second of the essential agents of this process was the deployment of aid funds provided by the USA. The importance of investment-aid was not so much that it directly bolstered agglomerations of private industrial capital but that it created conditions conducive to accumulation. It did so most bountifully through the promotion of infrastructure and agriculture, and the stimulus it gave to demand. After aid petered out in the mix-sixties its place was soon taken, especially in the early seventies, by foreign commercial loans and direct foreign investment. (In Korea net foreign borrowing began to exceed net foreign transfers in 1968.) The post-war period in Korea witnessed an inflow of $US4.5 billion in grant aid alone from the USA, much of it in the form of commodities.[36] For the larger part of the fifties and early sixties fully one half of Korean government revenue came from the USA. Aid was critical in providing the bulk of domestic investment funds and this was essential to finance a sound infrastructure on which private capital accumulation could proceed. According to reputable figures, the proportion of foreign capital (almost none of which was direct investment until the late sixties) in total investment was 42% in 1953 and 58% in 1955, rising to a peak of 65% in 1961.[37]

We are fortunate in having detailed information on the effects of aid on Taiwan's economic development in the book by Neil Jacoby.[38] The relatively slow growth of Korea in the fifties and early sixties contrasts with the quickened pace of output expansion in Taiwan. The latter, over the 1951-65 aid period, received a total of $US1.5 billion in aid (almost $100 million per annum), a figure a third that of war-torn Korea but spread over a population half the size. The war, of course, was extremely taxing on Korean resources, and the land reform proceeded far less smoothly than in its neighbour to the south. Over the 1951-65 period US aid to Taiwan contributed about 34% of total gross investment. More than a third of the total allocation to specific sectors ($1.1 billion) went to infrastructure with human resources (education, administration, housing, health, etc.) and agriculture receiving about a quarter each, leaving 15% for industry. The bulk of investment in Taiwanese infrastructure in the period was funded by US aid (74%) and more than half of agricultural investment came from the same source (59%). Industry, however, was built up mostly by private investment (aid contributing only 13%)[39] but there is no doubt that this private industrial investment was absolutely dependent on the aid-sponsored economies due to a well-developed infrastructure (especially electric power and transport systems) and the expansion of the agricultural surplus under the impact of aid projects.

Jacoby constructed a model of the Taiwanese economy and projected its path on the assumption of no aid at all. Noting the caution with which all such models should be treated, in essence he concluded that aid more than doubled the annual rate of growth of GNP, quadrupled per capita GNP and cut 30 years from the time needed to attain 1964 living standards. He argues that the critical impact of aid was in overcoming the shortage of foreign exchange (most aid was in the form of commodities). It was not any deficiency in domestic savings that provided the limit but the inability to buy foreign capital goods. Our argument here is that the importation of capital goods and their deployment in the development of infrastructure and agriculture were decisive in providing conditions conducive to the accumulation of private capital.

5. THE CONDITIONS OF THE DEVELOPMENT OF INDUSTRY

Having acquired sopme appreciation of the transformation of class structures in the Four and the emergence of industrial capital as the dominant economic force, we must now ask how the 'favourable condition' of capitalist production relations was in practice translated into capitalist industrialization. It will be argued that industrialization in the East Asian newly industrialized countries proceeded only with very heavy reliance on a few particular industries. We are led to focus attention on these sectors and to ask how it was that the Four managed to make major inroads into the world markets for these products.

In the course of his discussion of the general law of capitalist accumulation, Marx wrote:

> The battle of competition is fought by the cheapening of commodities. The cheapness of commodities depends, all other circumstances remaining the same, on the productivity of labour, and this depends in turn on the scale of production.[40]

Here is a useful clue. Marx's 'other circumstances' included the free flow of technology, an assumption more difficult to make when applying this idea to competition between advanced and underdeveloped countries, and the equalization of wages everywhere. The Four have relied on the differences of wages internationally, and the productivity of labour needs to be measured in cost terms, i.e. accounting for both physical productivity and wage levels. As a general rule, underdeveloped countries of the periphery cannot match the scale of production which prevails in industries of the centre, and this is due primarily to the absence of large, unified capitals, the inability to use appropriate technologies, a dearth of production expertise, and the high costs of transport when home markets cannot sustain large-scale production.

However, there are certain industries which are not subject to the tyranny of large-scale production and these are the natural allies of the 'country' which aspires to industrialization within the world capitalist economy. Marx again:

> ...with the development of the capitalist mode of production, there is an increase in the minimum amount of individual capital necessary to carry on a business under its normal conditions. The smaller capitals, therefore, crowd into spheres of production which large-scale industry has taken control of only sporadically or incompletely.[41]

The international division of labour can be conceived of as a structure of world production arranged on a scale according to the amount of capital needed to set up a competitive enterprise, a measure which might be proxied by the degree of concentration in each industry.[42] The industries at the bottom of the scale will be the ones into which smaller capitals, the indigenous capitals of the Third World, crowd. The object of these capitals is to create the conditions of advanced development of the productive forces which prevail in the advanced countries. Foreign capital which builds industry in a country of the periphery is, as a rule, much less subject to the constraints of size, experience and access to technology, and must only recreate the advanced conditions of production which exist elsewhere. In the next section it will be seen that this has great significance for the sectoral concentration of domestic as opposed to foreign capitals in the Four.

All this assumes that indigenous (and foreign) capital relies heavily on external markets. Integrating industrial development into the framework of the world market determines the form which growth will take, and the structure which emerges will be biased accordingly. Industrial growth based on expanding, protected, domestic markets - where protection conditions competition, the environment in which capital valorizes itself - presents an entirely different object of analysis.

It will be established in the next section that the reliance of indigenous capital in the Four on export markets was fundamental. Assuming this is so for the moment, then it is obvious that the state of the world economy in the key period of the sixties was decisive. Throughout that decade rapid growth provided expanding markets to be commandeered by new capitals. World production of manufactured goods grew at 7% per annum in the 1963-73 period while world manufactured exports grew more quickly at an average annual rate of 11%. This was considerably faster than in the fifties.[43] An increasing proportion of this trade was between developed countries but that did not prevent some peripheral countries from grabbing a share of growing markets. It should be noticed that for some Asian countries the Vietnam War provided a lucrative opportunity to increase exports. Wideman estimates that the war enriched Korea by about $1,205 million between 1966 and 1970, although a good proportion of this was attributable to the export of ROK soldiers and construction workers. Taiwanese firms became an important source of supply too - in 1966, of Taiwanese exports to underdeveloped countries 10-20% went to Vietnam.[44]

As a consequence of this general buoyancy and associated full employment in the West, protective measures were revised downwards. The Kennedy Round of negotiations in the early years of the decade brought the average Most Favoured Nation tariffs imposed by advanced countries down to around 7% in the EEC and 10-11% in the USA and Japan. However, those exports in which the newly industrializing countries specialized continued to attract tariffs considerably higher than the average, for these industries are always most vulnerable in the West. The cost advantages of low-wage producers still outweighed the effect of the tariffs and were regulated more effectively by quotas. But as long as full employment persisted, if imports drove some businesses, or sections of businesses, to the wall, other profitable pursuits could be found. In a period of sustained growth, new spaces in the international division of labour were constantly created. Tariffs, moreover, were by no means uniformly high on the exports favoured by capitals operating in the Four; some, such as electronics, remained comparatively low but these industries were the very same ones in which TNCs predominated in order to take advantage of low wages and tax concessions. Production could be exported to the periphery while still having access to the markets of the centre.

6. THE STRUCTURE OF INDUSTRY

As an essential component of the investigation of the relation between the structure of capital, industrial growth and integration into the international division of labour we will comment on four features of the industrialization process which were fundamental to the emergence of the Four.

i. A period of rapid growth

Rapid industrial growth escalated in the second half of the sixties, although the process had been gathering momentum from the early fifties in Hong Kong and early sixties in Taiwan. Each of Taiwan, Korea, Singapore and Hong Kong achieved annual average growth rates of real GDP of around 9% in the sixties, compared, for example, to West Germany's 4.6%.[45] These rates of growth of the Four were sustained and increased in the early seventies (except for Hong Kong) while the West declined. Most of the growth of output was due to expansion of manufacturing industry. In Korea, manufacturing output grew at 18% per annum in 1963-72 and its share of GNP rose from 15% in 1962 to 24.6% in 1969 and 31.8% in 1978. The economy had grown slowly in the fifties and early sixties even though awash with aid funds, and did not begin to expand rapidly until after the normalization treaty with Japan in 1965. It was not the treaty itself which sparked off rapid growth - although its terms provided around $800 million in loans and 'compensation' to Korea - but it revealed for all to see the revised strategy of the Park regime which pursued heavy integration into the world economy, of which Japan was the region's centre of attraction.

Taiwan, on the other hand, began a vigorous export drive in the early sixties although, as elsewhere, the most rapid growth took place in the latter part of the decade and the early seventies. The share of manufacturing in GDP grew from 16.8%

in 1960 to 26.4% in 1970 and by 1979 had reached 35%.

The expansion of Singapore's industry in the late sixties coincided with a large inflow of foreign direct investment and is almost wholly explained by this. Compared with a rate of 8% per annum in the 1961-67 period, GDP at current prices between 1966 and 1972 grew at an annual average rate of 13.9%, with value-added in manufacturing increasing at the tremendous rate of 23.4% per annum, a rate unmatched even by Japan at its most prolific. The contribution of manufacturing to total GNP increased from 15% in 1965 to 26% in 1977. In Hong Kong, too, the already very large manufacturing labour force grew - from 40% of the labour force total in 1961 to 47% in 1971. While Hong Kong industry grew steadily throughout the fifties and sixties here again the late sixties provided the greatest stimulus.

ii. <u>Heavy reliance on manufactured exports</u>

While export industries have come to dominate the economies of the Four, this growth has been based on ever-increasing imports of raw materials and capital goods both from the region and from the advanced countries. In fact import growth has for most of the period out-weighed export growth and together these have meant that the economies of the East Asian newly industrialized countries have been closely entwined in the world market. Between 1967 and 1971 the manufactured exports of Taiwan grew at an annual average rate of 38%, of Korea at 42% and of Singapore at 24%.[46] By 1973, one third of Korea's output of light manufactured goods was being exported and almost 90% of all exports were manufactures. The enormous growth of manufactured exports displaced traditional exports so that in Taiwan, for instance, whereas in 1952 manufactures accounted for less than 5 percent of exports over the 1964-68 period they amounted to almost 60 percent and much more in the seventies, even though in the early sixties there was a substantial expansion of agricultural and processed agricultural products.[47]

Industrialization in these countries should not be seen simply as a process of expanding export industries for their own sakes, since industrial growth has been extremely dependent on imports. The exporting firm is very often an importing one as well. The direct import content of South Korea's exports was about 42.5% in the 1967-73 period according to the Ministry of Finance. The circular nature of this is nowhere better illustrated than in Hong Kong where, it is estimated, in recent years 95% of manufactured output has been exported.[48] The shift from re-exports to domestic exports has not markedly diminished import-dependence.

Export industries came to dominate Singapore's economy in the 1968-74 boom period. In 1972 exports constituted 46.5% of total industrial sales and in major industries - such as petroleum refining, electrical machinery, clothing and textiles, and wood and cork products - the proportion was considerably higher.

It may seem that this argument understates the importance of domestic markets in industrialization and this suspicion receives some reinforcement in the case of Korea where, according to Balassa's figures, in 1969 'only' 18% of manufactures were exported, compared with 36% for Taiwan.[49] Undoubtedly, growing wages and unearned income provided expanding domestic demand but at least throughout the sixties and early seventies the squeeze on agricultural incomes and near-subsistence wages severely limited the domestic market. In 1967 Korean households were spending as much of their income on food as their counterparts in the Philippines and Sri Lanka.[50] Moreover, not only was Korea's 18% of manufactures exported much higher than other populous countries of the Third World (where it was something less than 10%), but Korea was in the middle of a tremendous expansion of manufactured exports which took it to far higher levels of dependence on world markets. By 1979 31% of all Korean manufactures were being exported and industries such as textiles, leather, rubber and non-metallic mineral products had export ratios around 60%.[51] The rapidity of industrial growth in the sixties and seventies in each of the Four was reliant on external markets since growth was dependent on extreme specialization.

iii. Dominance of specific export industries

More interesting than the simple observation that industrialization in these countries relied very heavily on international markets is the dominance over exports of a narrow and characteristic range of manufactured commodities. The narrowness of this range and the nature of the production processes involved reveal much about the structure of capital in these countries and the severity of the constraints exercised by the international division of labour.

Reliance on a limited range of export commodities is not a feature of the world economy unique to newly industrializing and underdeveloped countries, as the instances of Australia and New Zealand confirm, but when a country's industrial growth is as dependent on the expansion of export-oriented industry as, say, South Korea, this reliance takes on a far greater significance. In the Four, as in almost every industrial country, the role of the clothing and textile industries has been of outstanding importance and may be said to have spearheaded industrialization in Hong Kong, Taiwan and Korea. In Taiwan these industries in the early period were of unrivalled importance in terms of export and employment growth. In Hong Kong their place has been supreme for three decades accounting for from 40 to 50% of total exports and a similar proportion of industrial employment. Their lesser significance in Singapore has been due to the dominance of petroleum refining but they still managed in the 1967-72 period to contribute 9.2% of output growth and 23.2% of employment growth.[52]

In Taiwan in 1965 textile, leather, wood, paper and related products plus electrical machinery and apparatus accounted for 29% of exports. In 1970 this proportion had grown to 54% and stood at 50% in 1979. In the seventies there has been some shift to the latter group (comprising mainly radios, TVs, cassette recorders, calculators and sewing machines) as well as to miscellaneous products such as sports goods, cutlery, plastic goods, fittings and semi-conductors. In Korea the picture is similar, although there has been some diversification in the last decade. Nevertheless, in the 1971-73 period, clothing, textiles and footwear (mostly clothing) comprised, on average, 34% of total exports (down from well over half in the sixties) and if we add plywood, transistors, valves and the three-digit group 'other manufactures' the total exceeds 50%. In Hong Kong clothing, textiles, footwear, plastics and electronics accounted for 70% of domestic exports in 1965 and the figure has remained more or less unchanged ever since.

While these traditional export sectors have not been as dominant in Singapore as elsewhere, because of the place of petroleum refining and rubber and the overwhelming influence of foreign capital which tends to favour other industries, the concentration of exports in a few industries has been no less marked. This concentration developed rapidly in the second half of the sixties after the government discarded its policy of supporting import-substituting industries. By the early seventies electronics and electrical machinery, transport equipment (predominantly ship-building and repairs) and petroleum refining accounted for 53% of total value added and 63.3% of total exports. In the critical 1967-72 period these three industries were responsible for 60.3% of output growth and 42.3% of the growth of employment.

TABLE 1: US & Japanese Imports from Taiwan, South Korea, Hong Kong and Singapore - US$1,000

Imports from Taiwan

	1969		1973	
	US	Japan	US	Japan
A	332,553	28,095	1,652,430	473,749
B	190,517	16,629	908,479	249,291
B/A	.57	.59	.55	.53

Imports from Korea

	1969		1973	
	US	Japan	US	Japan
A	276,396	42,295	933,339	793,811
B	130,591	33,806	405,868	520,735
B/A	.47	.80	.43	.66

Imports from Hong Kong

	1969		1973	
	US	Japan	US	Japan
A	740,084	37,001	1,334,854	223,104
B	417,796	14,521	803,298	103,029
B/A	.56	.39	.60	.46

Imports from Singapore

	1969		1973	
	US	Japan	US	Japan
A	25,386	1,197	390,944	47,435
B	18,551	152	349,395	20,141
B/A	.73	.13	.89	.42

'A' represents manufacturing industry, sectors with SITC code numbers 5-8: 5 (chemicals), 6 (manufactured goods classified chiefly by material), 7 (machinery and transport equipment), 8 (miscellaneous manufactured articles).
'B' represents the SITC two-digit groups 65, 84 & 72: 65 (textile yarn, fabrics, made-up articles and related products), 84 (clothing), 72 (electrical machinery, apparatus and appliances).

Source: adapted from K. Yoshihara, 1976, Tables 4.13 & 5.11.

Table 1 gives a fair indication of the concentration of industrial exports to the most important foreign markets. Japan and the USA take over half of Taiwan's exports; about 40% of Korea's trade is with Japan alone; and Singapore's exports go mainly to the US and EEC. It should be noted that the industrial concentration of exports from Hong Kong and Singapore to the US and Japan increased over the 1969-73 peiod while that of Taiwan and Korea fell slightly.

iv. Role of Foreign Capital

The first part of this essay emphasized the critical role played by foreign aid and loans in the domestic accumulation processes of Korea, Taiwan and Singapore. But what can be said about the role of direct foreign investment in their periods of rapid industrialization? As a rule, direct foreign investment has been of no great significance and industrial development has been carried out largely by indigenous capital. The exception, which proves several rules, is Singapore where direct investment by TNCs has been of overwhelming importance. More recently, particularly in the early years of the 70s, there have been very considerable flows of foreign productive capital into Korea, Taiwan and Hong Kong, but these flows followed rather than initiated the widespread development of industry. Even these later flows have not overshadowed the accumulation of capital domestically - in 1976 direct foreign investment accounted for a mere 5.9% of Korea's and 3.9% of Taiwan's new gross fixed investment in manufacturing.[53]

Foreign involvement, it is true, can take forms other than direct investment in wholly-owned subsidiaries or joint ventures; contractual purchasing arrangements and licensing agreements are bread and butter for many local firms in the Four, and since the late sixties and particularly in the mid seventies there has been a great surge of commercial loans to domestic enterprises (usually through state organs). Subcontracting is very common in Korea, especially in electronics, and in Hong Kong's clothing trade. One of Korea's largest enterprise groups, Samsung, is closely tied to several foreign corporations - Sanyo and Nippon from Japan, Integrated Circuits International and Corning from the USA - mostly producing components for electronic products. Many of Samsung's orders are farmed out to 500 small, local firms. However, in the decade 1966-75 only about 20% of Korea's exports were bonded and this declined to about 13% in later years. Undoubtedly, these arrangements generate large profits, some of which flow overseas, but the fact remains that the capital which organizes the production processes is in the hands of indigenous firms. The same comments apply to commercial loans.

To iterate Nayyar's figures, it is estimated that in the early seventies foreign-controlled companies accounted for about 10% of Hong Kong's manufactured exports, at least 20% of Taiwan's, at least 15% of Korea's and nearly 70% of Singapore's. It is likely that these figures have risen somewhat since then, and we now have it from an official Korean source that the share of foreign-invested enterprises in total exports has gradually risen from 16.9% in 1974 to 18.7% in 1978. It is of central importance to the argument of this essay to show that foreign investors tend not to be as heavily involved in the traditional export industries of clothing, textiles, plastic products and the like as local firms, nor even in some heavy industries such as steel, basic chemicals and shipbuilding (dominated by state investment), but exhibit a preference for industries such as electronic and electrical assembly, some types of engineering and, in the case of Singapore, petroleum refining. The latter industries tend to be more capital-intensive in the design and construction stages and in certain segments of the fabrication processes while still relying on cheap labour for assembly. A deep capital structure is necessary to undertake whole production processes such as those in electronic appliances. Singapore's industrial structure testifies to this: in a newly industrializing country dominated by foreign capital one finds significant capital in heavy engineering, ship repair, oil refining, ball bearing production, aircraft componentry and industrial machinery, in addition to the usual light manufacture and assembly operations of electrical machinery, electronics and textiles. This difference in the sectoral orientation of TNCs in comparison to local firms is also illustrated in the types of industries which populate free trade zones.

As US aid began to peter out in the mid to late sixties, Korean industrialization was increasingly sustained by public and commercial loans from overseas. Between 1964 and 1971 Korea's foreign savings rate fluctuated between 35 and 50% but direct investment was of little significance. Between 1959 and 1966 it comprised less than 7% of total foreign loans, exceeding that figure marginally in the 1967-72 period and rising to 11% over 1973-75.[54] In the early seventies and mostly from 1973 there was a frenetic rush to invest in Korea, with most of the impetus coming from Japan, but this was well after Korea had established a substantial industrial structure. Overall, in the period 1962-79 direct foreign investment comprised only 1.2 percent of gross domestic capital formation, while loans accounted for 18.9% of the total.

The surge of direct foreign investment in the seventies was concentrated in a few industries: by 1980 chemicals had taken 19% (a value of US$218.9m), electrical and electronic projects 14%, machinery 8%, textiles and garments 7% and petroleum 6%. By the end of 1978 foreign-invested enterprises accounted for 14% of total value added in the Korean manufacturing sector. In 1978, while heavy and chemical exports made up 64% of total overseas sales by foreign-invested enterprises, the figure for all enterprises in Korea was only 42% of exports.

The pattern in Taiwan has been similar to that in Korea although foreign direct investment began to flow earlier, steadily throughout the sixties reaching a peak in 1970. While responsible for more of the industrial growth of Taiwan than of Korea, foreign investment was by no means dominant on the island. Almost 80% of Taiwan's exports throughout the sixties were attributable to locally-owned firms. In the 1965-68 period arrivals of foreign investment amounted to no more than 7% of gross domestic capital formation.

In the sixties the bulk of US capital in Taiwan co-operated in public enterprises particularly in the development of capital goods industries, while Japanese investors, strongly attracted to the Kaohsiung Export Processing Zone completed in 1966, favoured consumption goods industries and electrical and electronic products in particular.[55] A dramatic change in the direction of US direct investments in the late sixties and early seventies saw the electronics industry take 68% of total US investments by the end of 1973.

It is difficult to define foreign investment for Hong Kong. Industrialization was heavily dependent on 'foreign investment' in the form of refugee capital, capital which became domiciled on arrival. The long-established and now highly diversified British trading companies are regarded often as local companies despite the fact that their owners live overseas (Hong Kong remains a British colony). Those who report on the subject do not always make it clear although discussions usually refer to the newer, post-war waves of US, Japanese and European TNCs. Foreign capital is significant in most sectors of the economy including distribution and trading, banking and insurance, and utilities, but in the manufacturing sector local firms have always been predominant primarily because of the huge proportion of manufactured output which is due to exports of clothing and textiles. It is estimated that in 1969 foreign-owned firms employed about 8% of the manufacturing labour force and probably accounted for a larger share of output. In sum the part played by TNCs in the expansion of export production in the crucial decades of the fifties and more so the sixties was quite small. In the seventies, however, the rate of flow of foreign capital became swift. The inflow that did occur in the sixties was responsible for some diversification of the industrial structure, moving mainly into electrical goods and metals, but also into plastics and textiles. The surge of investment from the USA and Japan in the early seventies was concentrated in electronics. Textiles and chemicals were also favoured and the three industries accounted for 57% of total foreign investment in Hong Kong manufacturing in 1976.[56] Nevertheless, a survey showed that in 1974 foreign firms employed less than 10% of the industrial workforce and were responsible for less than 11% of total exports.

In sharp contrast to the experience of its more northern confreres, industrialization in Singapore occurred at the behest of transnational corporations. Foreign capital has so overwhelmed indigenous firms that the latter have played no role in most export industries and a small role in the rest. In 1965 export industries were relatively insignificant (although exports, mainly petrol, still accounted for about one third of manufacturing sales) as the new state and indigenous capital pursued import-substituting growth on the assumption of federation with Malaysia. The very quick industrial growth which was consequent upon the supersession of these policies was due almost wholly to foreign investment. In the period 1966-72 something like US$2.5 billion of foreign capital poured into Singapore.

As an indication of this sudden foreign hegemony, at the end of the fifties paid-up capital of foreign-controlled companies constituted 22% of the total capital of manufacturing firms. In 1973 this had risen to nearly 75%. Yoshihara's detailed and valuable work reveals that as early as 1970 wholly foreign companies accounted for 57% of total exports, and these together with joint ventures accounted for 83% of total exports leaving a mere 17% for domestic firms. The only industry in which the latter produced more than half of exports was food. Other than food, in the three biggest export industries of 1970 - petroleum products, electrical/electronics and transport equipment which together accounted for 58% of total manufactured exports - foreign-dominated firms accounted respectively for 97, 99 and 72% of exports. Between 1966 and 1972 the output index of wholly domestic companies rose from 100 to 274 while that of wholly foreign firms rose from 100 to 786. In sum, then, by 1978 foreign-dominated firms accounted for 52% of employment, 63% of value-added, 71% of output and 84% of manufactured exports.

Finally, it is necessary to get a picture of the direction of foreign investment in Singapore, and here again Yoshihara's study is invaluable. The best available measure of the industrial orientation of foreign investment is paid-up capital by industry in 1970. US equity capital is concentrated in petroleum and petroleum products, accounting for a little over half of total US equity capital. On the face of it US equity capital in electronics and electrical products (only 13% of the total) is small, but if investment is defined to include intercompany loans and accumulated profits (a large proportion in this particular industry) then the weight of electronics and electrical products is much greater (rising to 31% of US investment). Other significant industries for US investors were printing and publishing, oil related equipment, and chemicals (mostly batteries and plastic products).

Japanese capital in Singapore, about two thirds of the US total, is concentrated in shipbuilding and shiprepair (46% of the total), and, apart from the next most important, electronics (14%), no other industry stood out. British investment, amounting to a little less than the Japanese total, is not heavily concentrated in any industry and was absent from electronics and garments. Drugs have attracted the largest amount (17.5%) followed by food, wood and wood products and non-metallic mineral products. It should be noted, however, that Shell has a huge investment in petroleum refining and this investment was equal to 82% of total British and Dutch investment in Singapore in 1972.

In summary, foreign investment in Singapore in 1973 was concentrated in petroleum and petroleum products (25% of total paid-up capital of foreign-controlled companies), textiles and garments (13%), chemicals (10%), food, beverages and tobacco (10%), and electronics and electrical products (8%). Domestic paid-up capital was concentrated in food, beverages and tobacco (29%), shipbuilding and repair (19%) and metals (18%).[57]

7. THE STRUCTURE OF CAPITAL

The image which emerges from these sketches of various aspects of the industrialization processes of the 'Four Little Tigers' is one of swift and narrowly-based industrial development. The greatest industrial growth took place in the second half of the sixties and early seventies and, with the didactic exception of Singapore, was predominantly a process of indigenous capital accumulation. Industrialization was very largely contingent upon growing overseas markets and was based on extravagant growth in a very few industries. The specific characteristics of these industries are highlighted by Singapore's divergence from the norm, an infraction of law which hardens the evidence in favour of a relationship between the structure of capital and its specific place in the international division of labour.

It could reasonably be asked why the industrialization of the Four was not based on the growth of the machine tool, pharmaceutical and vehicle industries for instance. The reply lies in the nature of the indigenous capital which undertook industrialization, its features when compared to industrial capital in the West. Essentially, the local capitals in the sixties were relatively small and inexperienced. It was neither possible nor feasible to mobilize the large amounts of capital needed to employ advanced production technologies. Capital-intensive production processes demand large agglomerations of funds combined with extensive expertise. Indigenous capitals in the Four, per contra, with histories in trade, distribution and petty manufacture, were unaccustomed to such operations and could rely only on projects requiring relatively low fixed investments and with high capital turnover.[58] To undertake a major project involving large initial outlays, even if the financial structure had permitted, would have been extremely risky since economies of scale begin to apply only with large output. Their success would thus depend on capturing large segments of Western markets in competition with long-established and very big Western competitors. It was not so much access to technology that was the problem but the lack of experience and finance to apply it profitably. Therefore indigenous capitals crowded into those industries which required only small initial fixed capital outlays and involved technologies that were not subject to rapidly increasing economies of scale. These tended to be highly labour-intensive; big Western corporations had a firm hold on capital-deep production processes and even the advantage of very cheap labour could not ease the difficulty of loosening such a grip.

Ranadev Banerji has undertaken a very worthwhile study of the contribution of small-scale manufacturing enterprises at different levels of development.[59] He argues that scale economies are more important in some industries than others and that the small-scale sector varies in significance correspondingly. The predominance of small plants in certain industries cuts across groups of countries which differ according to levels of development and size. Although the proportion of small plants is much larger in low and middle income countries than in high income countries, in both groups there are some countries which have proprotionately fewer small plants regardless of industry, signifying the interplay of diverse factors. One pivotal result to emerge is that there are certain industries in which small-scale plants are highly efficient when compared to the average for all industry. These are food and beverages, apparel, wood products and furniture, printing and publishing, leather products, non-metallic mineral products (in high-income countries only) and diverse industries. Banerji observes that a common characteristic of these industries in that (except for printing) they have substantial direct backward linkages with agriculture and mining. If we add textiles to this group then the figures show that small-scale production (in high, middle and low income countries) is of far greater importance than in more advanced industries such as chemicals, petroleum, paper, fabricated metal products and machinery of all sorts. Essentially, then, there are certain industries (the first-named above) in which small-scale enterprises can effectively compete against larger companies, and these are the industries into which domestic capital in the Four entered.

These comments are reinforced by regard to the divergence of the industrial complexions of foreign and local firms investing in the Four. Foreign capital extended into both those industries favoured by local capital (textiles and clothing, plastics and metal products) as well as some which the latter could not easily enter (electronics and electrical products, chemicals, petroleum, engineering). That they entered the former is no surprise since foreign companies could most effectively respond to intensifying competition from newly industrializing countries by immersing themselves in the same conditions. Nor is it surprising to learn that many foreign investments in these countries are quite small. Generally, but not universally, big investments tend to be more capital-intensive and therefore less nourished by cheap labour. In the late sixties and early seventies a multitude of small Japanese investments (by small, medium and large companies) were undertaken throughout South and Southeast Asia. As we have seen, in 1974 Japanese investments averaged less than US$350,000 in Taiwan, Korea and Hong Kong but were considerably higher in Singapore (US$570,000).[60] Nevertheless, these foreign investments were undoubtedly higher than those of indigenous capitalists and it is these with which we are chiefly concerned. It was locally-owned and locally-organized production which set out to compete on the world market.

Information on the characteristics of local business in the Four is scarce and scattered and this makes it all the more difficult to draw comparisons with manufacturing firms in the OECD countries. Observers agree, however, that private industrial enterprises in the Four were, particularly in the early stages of industrial growth, small by comparison, they were often family businesses and, at least in Korea and Taiwan, were often short of capital.

These features stood out in Hong Kong, which exemplified most that was idiosyncratic in the manufacturing firms of the Four (although elsewhere the structure of business has advanced to a higher stage while that of Hong Kong persists). In Hong Kong a very high proportion of businesses were family-owned and capital to establish a business (contrary to conditions in the other three) was easy to borrow from local banks. A large proportion of funds was working capital, equipment was limited, simple and heavily used, and investment planning, such as it was, rarely extended beyond five years. Many local businesses survived on subcontracted work from overseas manufacturers or buying groups. The big British houses in Hong Kong tended to be concentrated in trade, shipbuilding, utilities and banking as well as manufacturing. But in manufacturing at least, competition was very severe.

A survey in 1968 revealed that 84 percent of industrial establishments in Hong Kong employed less than 50 workers, although half of the workforce in registered establishments were employed in workplaces with 200 or more workers (while only 16 percent worked in firms with over 1000 workers). Firms were thus small by international standards,[61] and this impression is reinforced by looking at the operations of TNCs in the colony. Most electronics companies are wholly-foreign subsidiaries whereas more than half of the US-affiliated companies in textiles are joint ventures. Correspondingly the scale of operation of the latter is much smaller. In 1970 there were only two US-affiliated textile companies employing over 500 workers while ten subsidiaries of US TNCs in the electronics industry each employed more than 500 workers (and two employed more than 2000 workers). Most US investors involved in joint ventures in the textile trade are wholesalers rather than major US manufacturers.[62]

In Taiwan and Korea, local private capital was, until recently, incapable or shy of large-scale investments. This was undoubtedly attributable to, among other things, the failure of companies to mobilize outside funds since even the biggest concerns were, almost uniformly, owned by individuals. By 1972 only 66 Korean companies had offered shares to the public. In order to channel domestic savings into productive activity the government had in 1968 legislated for preferential treatment - in the form of reduced taxes and accelerated depreciation - for companies which would go public. The failure of the 'big owners' to respond to this inducement led in 1972 to a law empowering the Minister of Finance to order the sale of shares to the public. Nevertheless, it was still the case in 1976 that 32 of the 50 Groups had big owners holding more than half of their companies' stock.[63]

In Taiwan, as in Korea, the inability of domestic companies to gather together large investment funds meant that big, capital-intensive projects - petroleum refining, electricity, fertilizers - depended on US aid and loans channeled through the state. Liu specifies five 'capital-intensive' industries four of which (the above three plus sugar) are state enterprises (the exception is cement, an industry previously sold off to private capital).[64] Privately-owned industry developed through labour-intensive and 'technology-intensive' industries (the latter combining relatively sophisticated technology with heavy reliance on unskilled and semi-skilled labour). The former led the export boom and were generally Taiwan-owned while the latter also relied heavily on export markets but developed largely as a result of joint ventures with Japanese capital.

8. MORE RECENT DEVELOPMENTS

The above inquiry has tried to describe the conjunctural forces which combined to sponsor the development of industry of a certain type in the four East Asian newly industrializing countries. The political condition which enabled industrial development was essentially that industrial capital exercised political control over both other segments of capital and the working population. This is not to argue that the state evolved as the direct political representative of industrial capital but that its social and historical foundations were ultimately and overwhelmingly favourable to the accumulation of capital through industrial development. Changes at the political level confirmed the transformation of the method of gathering, deploying and then producing the social surplus product. It must be emphasized that the investible surplus was multiplied by massive inflows of overseas aid into Taiwan, Korea and Singapore, and by large, but inestimable, amounts of refugee capital into Hong Kong. In the former these flows were both attracted by and sponsored the hegemony of industrial capital. In Taiwan and Korea, as well as in Singapore, the social surplus product deriving from foreign and domestic sources was to a very large extent mobilized in the state, and mobilized in such a way as to enrich private industrial capital. By this stage, concentrations of agricultural capital in Korea and Taiwan, an alternative pole of attraction for the surplus product, were all but extinct.

The political forces which underlay their industrial development were not just internal to the Four. On the one hand, the regimes which allied state apparatuses with the capitalist classes of Korea and Taiwan were decisively backed by the omnipotent United States, and Singapore's PAP regime emerged under the approving eye of the British colonial authorities. On the other hand, the foundation of industrial growth on export industries depended on the more general world political currents which were conditioned by, among other things, continued economic growth throughout the sixties and early seventies. The world political climate was such as to permit the Four to annex substantial portions of the global allocation of production in certain industries. The entry into the international division of labour has been largely on the terms laid down by the dominant capitalist powers, and in consequence the Four have been left with economies which are heavily biased towards a few consumer goods industries, except in Singapore where foreign capital has been responsible for a broader, but no more independent, industrial base.

This particular path to industrial growth has led the Four into an awkward situation, one exacerbated by the downturn of the world economy in recent years. Their spaces in the international division of labour depend heavily on relatively low wage levels, but the process of industrial growth carried with it, at certain stages, working-class organization, high demand for labour and thus pressure to increase wages.[65] Already the wage levels of the Four are significantly (but variably) above those of all other countries in the region with the exception of Japan, and not only is some foreign capital in footloose industries such as electronics beginning to move house to Thailand, the Philippines and similar places but domestic capital in the clothing trade, for instance, is itself beginning to go transnational. Moreover, the decline in the growth of world consumption has meant that the economies of the Four are supported by an eroding base and one subject to further erosion through political intervention, i.e. protection. This vulnerability has come about as a result of the structure of capital and its means of accumulation in the Four, since, it has been argued, the relative smallness and inexperience of indigenous capital left little alternative if industrialization were to be pursued by integration into the world economy.

The solution for indigenous capital appears to lie in the deployment of large masses of capital in industries of a more advanced nature in pursuit of greater self-sufficiency. The substantial development of heavy and chemical industries which has occurred already in Korea has required huge capital investments and has been largely under the direction of state agencies. However, these projects have been disproportionately sponsored by foreign, particularly Japanese, corporations seeking new territory in which to expand their operations. These industries provide backward linkages for the vital export industries lessening, for example, reliance on imported synthetic fibres, but they do so at the cost of a different harness.

Both Korea and Taiwan attempted in the seventies to diminish their reliance on light industrial exports and machine imports by promoting heavy and chemical industries. Traditional export industries were seen as too vulnerable and governments intervened in a major way to promote investment in heavy industry. Korean sources claim to have greatly diversified their export structure in the last decade, to the point where in 1979 45% of Korean manufactured exports were products of heavy and chemical industries.[66] Of these, iron and steel products (bars, sheets, plates, tubes and castings) and electronics were the most significant. The electronics industry is dominated by Japanese and US corporations and its exports consist mainly of consumer products the majority of whose parts are imported (especially televisions and recorders) and components such as integrated circuits and transistors. Machinery exports are relatively unimportant (4.4% of total manufactured exports) and consist predominantly of transformers, bulbs, cable, wire and resistors. All of these commodities, other than steel products, are produced by labour-intensive processes, and where advanced technology is involved it is mostly controlled by TNCs. Moreover, after the difficulties of competing with Western capital on its own ground in a sluggish market became apparent, there has recently been a shift back to emphasis on the traditional export industries and textiles in particular (after the mid-seventies decisions to 'close the textile phase').[67] Both countries embarked in 1981 on government sponsored reinvestment programmes in the clothing and textile industries in order to face the competition from both low-wage producers in the region and US companies which have invested massively in highly-advanced technology.

The ability to compete through capital investment has in the seventies increased in some sectors concomitant with the growth of large conglomerates in Korea and Taiwan. The concentration and centralization of capital has proceeded a-pace assisted by swollen profits and the development of financial institutions capable of assembing many small savings for use by industrial investors. But as long as domestic markets remain restricted, big capitals, reliant on exports, will find it difficult to expand. It is not so much access to technology, for if it is profitable to sell technology then it will be sold, as a rule. Instead one must ask whether indigenous capital in the Four is strong enough to enter those industries in a major way by forcing out other capitals, by annexing a portion of a relatively fixed space in the international division of labour. Given the present supremacy of Western capital over world markets for these products, this seems unlikely.

More than that, one must ask what effects the bigness of capital and the bigness of production facilities will have on the management of labour. It is already suggested that workforces in the larger, more automated and more impersonal factories of TNCs are more militant, despite the care taken in choosing workers who are least likely to rebel. An extension of industry to more sophisticated products will also require more-skilled labour making capital more dependent on labour, and that would demand redoubled repression of trade union oganization and political opposition.

NOTES

Thanks are due to Paul Ensor, Richard Luedde-Neurath, Gordon White and fellow students at the Institute of Development Studies. They do not necessarily hold the views expressed here.

1. Bill Warren, 'Imperialism and Capitalist Industrialization', New Left Review, 81, September-October,

1973.

2. Robert Brenner ('The Origins of Capitalist Development: A Critique of Neo-Smithian Marxism', New Left Review, 104, July-August, 1977) has written a superb article which reminds us with coercive logic of the centrality of class transformation in economic development.

3. Also the 'four little dragons'. This is another graphic expression to come out of China where, in the post-Mao era, the leadership has been sufficiently interested in the 'lessons' to be learned from these paragons of capitalism to set up a separate institute to study each of them.

4. D. Nayyar, 'Transnational Corporations and Manufactured Exports from Poor Countries', The Economic Journal, 88, March, 1978, Table 1.

5. Chen in D. Lethbridge (ed), The Business Environment in Hong Kong, (Oxford U.P., Hong Kong, 1980), p.25.

6. Marx wrote: 'In all cases of conquest, three things are possible. The conquering people subjugates the conquered under its own mode of production...or it leaves the old mode intact and contents itself with a tribute...or a reciprocal interaction takes place whereby something new, a synthesis arises...' Grundrisse (Penguin, 1973), p.97.

7. J. Gittings and G. McCormack (eds), Crisis in Korea (Spokesman Books, 1977). P. Kuznets Economic Growth and Structure in the Republic of Korea Yale U., Economic Growth Centre, 1977) p.17) says that if government property is included the Japanese may have controlled more than half of the land in Korea.

8. Kuznets, ibid. p.16.

9. Gittings & McCormack, ibid. p.74.

10. G.W. Barclay, Colonial Development and Population in Taiwan (Princeton U.P., 1954) p.19.

11. Ibid. p.33.

12. Ibid. p.21.

13. Mo-Huan Hsing, 'Taiwan: Industrialization and Trade Policies', in J.H. Power et al., The Philippines and Taiwan (Oxford U.P., 1974) p.154.

14. S.I. Cohen, 'Industrial Performance in South Korea', The Developing Economies, XVI, No.4, December, 1978, p.409.

15. Gittings & McCormack, ibid. p.75; also S. Cohen, ibid., p.409.

16. Kuznets, ibid. p.22.

17. On all this see Neil Jacoby, U.S. Aid to Taiwan (Praeger, 1966) chapter X.

18. Ibid. p.138.

19. The ideological justification for colonial rule was set out in a government report averring that the relationship between government and people should be consistent with the traditional Chinese concept, one 'analogous to that which should exist between parents and children, or between a shepherd and his flock...(T)he rulers of society...should be

men of learning, virtue and ability...(T)he traditional concept does not contemplate the direct participation of the population in the...processes of government'. This was written in 1966. Quoted in Keith Hopkins, Hong Kong: the Industrial Colony (Oxford U.P., Hong Kong, 1971) p.214.

20. Quoted in Hans Luther, 'Strikes and the Institutionalization of Labour Protest: the Case of Singapore', Journal of Contemporary Asia, Vol. 8 No. 2, 1978, p.219.

21. Some argue that it was not Rhee's neglect of development so much as his demands for a more autonomous strategy centering on import-substituting industries. This would have meant the shifting of US aid away from the dumping of consumer goods and into investment goods.

22. The new government pledged to 'utilize the industrious and intelligent labour of Korea to produce commodities for export, as successfully demonstrated by Japan in the early stages of industrialization and by Hong Kong more recently', and 'to make an all-out effort in normalizing relations with Japan with a view to promoting mutually beneficial economic arrangements'. Quoted in Cheryl Payer, 'Pushed into the Debt Trap: South Korea's Export "Miracle"', Journal of Contemporary Asia, Vol. 5 no. 2, 1975. A big devaluation, urged by the US, deepened the recession and was very unpopular.

23. The colonels were by no means anti-business, but they did take action to recover 'illicit fortunes' made in the welter of Rhee corruption in order to direct these funds into industrial development.

24. D.C. Cole & P.N. Lyman, Korean Development: The Interplay of Politics and Economics (Harvard U.P., 1971) p.36

25. Jacoby, ibid. Appendix Table C.11.

26. L.P. Jones & Il Sakong, Government, Business and Entrepreneurship in Economic Development: The Korean Case (Harvard U. Council on East Asian Studies, 1986) p.57.

27. Hyung Yoon Byun & Shin Haing Kim, 'Modernization of Private Enterprises in the Republic of Korea: A Study of th Fifty Groups' Development Pattern', Institute of Developing Economies, Joint Research Programme No. 7, 1978, p.8.

28. Ibid. p.10.

29. Owen in Hopkins, ibid. p.149.

30. Tchin-Ching Liu, 'The Process of Industrialization in Taiwan', The Developing Economies, VII, No. 1, March, 1969, p.65.

31. Figures on agriculture for Korea come from Sung-Jo Park et al. (eds), Economic Development and Social Change in Korea (Campus Verlag, 1980) pp.69,58,56 and Harold Sunoo, 'Economic Development and Foreign Control in South Korea', Journal of Contemporary Asia, vol.8 no. 3, 1978, p.350 and B. Balassa, 'Industrial Policies in Taiwan and Korea', IBRD, Economics Department Working Paper No. 86, 1970; and for Taiwan from Bernard Gallin, Hsin Hsing, Taiwan: A Chinese Village in Change (University of California Press, 1966) pp.36, 50 and

Jacoby, ibid. pp.90, 280, 180, 207.

32. U.S. General Accounting Office, Disincentives to Agricultural Production in Developing Countries (Washington, 1975) p32.

33. Gallin, ibid. p.35. On p.109 Gallin writes, for 1958: 'Villagers who work outside Hsin Hsing have done more to raise the standard of living than has the decrease in tenancy. The increased use of cash has led to an apparent rise in living standards'. In Korea, farm income is said to have accounted for about 80% of total farm household income throughout the sixties (Sung-Jo Park, ibid. p.59).

34. Don Long, "Repression and Development in the Periphery: South Korea', Bulleting of Concerned Asian Scholars, vol. 9 no. 2, April-June 1972, p.33. The official figure in 1973 was 4.3%. Singapore's unemployment rate was 6% in 1970 and 4.5% in 1973 - see Kunio Yoshihara, Foreign Investment and Domestic Response: A Study of Singapore's Industrialization, Institute of Southeast Asian Studies (Eastern U.P., 1976) pl76. In Korea, non-farm unemployment stood at 7.4% in 1970 and 6.5% in 1976 (Hyung & Shin, ibid. p.95). More than this, throughout the region the incidence of part-time work and casual work is very high. In Hong Kong in 1969 only 60% of the economically active were regular full-time employees (Hopkins, ibid. p.234). In Korea in 1976 the proportion of the workforce employed on a temporary or daily basis was 43%, a rise from 41% in 1970 (Hyung & Shin, ibid. p.96). The insecurity attached to these forms of employment is itself a life-governing discipline.

35. For Hong Kong see England in Hopkins, ibid, p.235; for Singapore see Lee Soo Ann, 'The Singapore Economy and Its Development Problems', The Developing Economies, XI no.4, Dec. 1973, p.396; for Taiwan see Anton Galli, Taiwan: Economic Facts and Trends (Weltforum Verlag, 1980) p.89.

36. Together, grants, loans and military expenditure up to 1970 constituted an enormous $12.5 billion - see G. Breidenstein, in Frank Baldwin (ed), Without Parallel: The American-Korean Relationship Since 1945 (Pantheon, 1974) p.182.

37. W. Rosenberg, 'Economic Comparison of North and South Korea', Journal of Contemporary Asia, vol. 5 no. 2, 1975, p.182. According to official figures, foreign savings as a percentage of gross investment peaked at 83% in 1962 and fluctuated around 40-50% for the rest of the decade - see Bank of Korea, Economic Statistics Yearbook 1978, p.302.

38. All figures below from Jacoby, ibid.

39. Only about 6% of all aid funds went to strictly private enterprises but about 27% went to mixed public and private projects.

40. Karl Marx, Capital (Penguin, 1976), vol. 1, p.777.

41. Ibid.

42. One must distinguish, however, between big capitals and big factories; a big capitamay divide its output between many production processes or invest in a big process which uses technologies which do not exhibit substantial scale economies.

43. GATT, International Trade 1978/79 (Geneva, 1979) p.2. Total world exports grew at an annual average rate of 8.9% over 1960-70 compared to 6.2% over 1950-60 - UNCTAD, Handbook of International Trade and Development Statistics (UN, 1979) p.25.

44. Wideman in Baldwin, ibid. p273 and China council on Sino-American Co-operation in the Humanities and Social Sciences, 'Sino-American Conference on Manpower in Taiwan', 1972, pp.271-2.

45. Chen, ibid. Table 1.2. In this section figures for Korea are from S. Cohen ibid. p.4 and Breidenstein, ibid. p.255; for Taiwan from Galli ibid. Table 4; for Hong Kong from Chen ibid. p.15; and for Singapore from Lee Soo Ann ibid. p.320 and Cheah Hock Beng, 'Export Oriented Industrialization and Dependent Development: the Experience of Singapore', IDS Bulletin, vol. 12 no. 1, December, 1980, p.37.

46. B.I. Cohen, Multinational Firms and Asian Exports, Yale U. Economic Growth Centre (Yale U.P., 1975), Table 3.2. Total exports from Hong Kong grew at an annal average rate of 13.6% in the sixties rising to 19.4% in the seventies - UNCTAD, ibid. Table 1.5.

47. In this section figures for Korea are from Suk Tai Suh, 'Import Substitution and Economic Development in Korea', Korea Development Institute, Working Paper 7519, December 1979, Table 5.3.2 and S. Cohen, ibid. p.425 and Korea Development Bank, Industry in Korea 1980, ppll, 13 and UN, Economic Survey of Asia and the Far East 1972, p.61; for Taiwan from Mo-Huan Hsing, ibid. p.164; for Hong Kong from Podmore in Hopkins, ibid. Table 2.2; and for Singapore from Yoshihara, ibid. p.178. Also Balassa, ibid., pp.5, 13, Table 1 on Taiwan and Korea.

48. The government does not compile figures on the internal economy. In 1968 GDP was estimated at HK$15.8 billion while total exports and re-exports stood at HK$10.6 billion. Re-exports were 89% of total exports in 1950, a figure closer to 20% in recent years although rising with the reopening of China.

49. Balassa ibid. Table 1. Note that in 1960 the share of exports in GDP in Korea was only 1% compared with Taiwan's 11% - ibid. p.13.

50. UN, Economic Survey of Asia and the Far East 1972 p.61. Balassa also notes that in 1960 Korea and Taiwan each ad total markets for manufactures of less than US$1 billion compared with India's $23 billion, Brazil's $14 billion and Argentina's $10 billion.

51. Korea Development Bank, ibid. 1980 p.13. Note also that the ratio of overseas trade to GNP stood at 71% in 1979.

52. References for this section are Galli, ibid. Table 40. S. Cohen, ibid. Table VII: Chen, ibid. Table 1.18; Lee Soo Ann, ibid. p.394 and Yoshihara,;ibid. Tables 2.5 & 2.6.

53. In this section figures for Korea are from Bank of Korea, ibid. 1981 Table 123 and Korea Exchange Bank, Monthly

Review, no. 11, 1980 pp.6-8 and Breidenstein, ibid. p.237 and Sunoo, ibid. Table 1; for Taiwan from Mo-Huan Hsing, ibid. p159; for Hong Kong from Phelps-Brown in Hopkins, ibid. p12 and Hung in Lethbridge, ibid. pp.205, 214 and Table 6.1; for Singapore from Yoshihara, ibid. p16 & Tables 2.7, 2.9, 2.10, 4.3, 5.4, 6.3, 8.1 and 8.2 and Cheah Hock Beng, ibid. p.37; for both Korea and Taiwan from Economist Intelligence Unit, The New Industrial Countries and Their Impact on Western Manufacturing by Anthony Edwards, EIU Special Report No. 73 (London, 1979) Table 1.2 and for the Four from Yoshihara Table 4.18.

54. Of the rest, by the end of 1970 foreign capital was made up of 29% public loans and 64% commercial loans.

55. At the end of 1973, 39% of approved Japanese direct investments in Taiwan were in electronic and electrical products (29% in Korea), 22% in chemicals (15% in Korea), and 13% in textiles (Korea 18%).

56. At the end of 1971 it totalled HK$759 million, rising 2 1/2 times by end 1976 to HK$1952 million. Of total foreign investment in manufacturing at the end of 1976, 53% was from the USA and of this more than 60% went into electronics.

57. Domestic investment is not well represented by paid-up capital so these figures should be treated with caution.

58. In 1971, 97% of Korean manufacturing establishments employed fewer than 200 workers (98% in 1966) - Korea Development Bank, ibid. 1976 Table 8. Small-scale industry also remains very strong in Japan.

59. Ranadev Banerji, 'Small-Scale Production Units in Manufacturing: An International Cross-Section Overview', Weltwirtschaftliches Archiv, 114, 1, 1978.

60. EIU, ibid. (p.41) reports that of 268 significant foreign manufacturing enterprises in Singapore in 1978, 65% had gross fixed assets of under US$2.2 million and 11% had assets in excess of US$9.3 million.

61. England in Hopkins, ibid. p.212. England also wrote: 'Oligopolistic industries dominated by large corporations do not exist in Hong Kong'.

62. Yoshihara, ibid. p.101.

63. Hyung & Shin, ibid. chapter 3.

64. Liu, ibid. p.76.

65. Earnings in manufacturing: selected countries - monthly earnings in US$, 1975

USA	812	Singapore	141
Australia	737	Taiwan	115
W. Germany	641	South Korea	79
Japan	537	Sri Lanka	57
U.K.	407	Philippines	45
Hong Kong	149		

Source: Chen, ibid. Table 1.14.

66. Korea Development Rank, ibid. 1980, pp.11, 87, 100.

67. See Far Eastern Economic Review, September 4, 1981.

Chapter 11

OUT OF THE DEPENDENCY PERSPECTIVE

John Browett

INTRODUCTION

Over the last three decades there have been a number of profound changes in the approaches adopted to the analysis of the processes leading to patterns of unequal development within and between nations. In brief, what can be recognised is that in the 1950s the demise of neo-classical economic theory was accompanied by the rise of modernisation theory and what has been termed the diffusionist paradigm (see Browett, 1980). Subsequently, from the mid 1960s onwards, these approaches were challenged and then eclipsed by new and more radical perspectives - those within the dependency paradigm (see Browett, 1981) - which sought to establish necessary and causative inter-relationships not only between underdevelopment and dependency (underdevelopment is a process induced and constantly reinforced by dependency) but also between underdevelopment and development (they are opposite sides of the same coin). These perspectives, in turn, have recently come under attack both from the right, which seeks to reformulate and refurbish the diffusionist paradigm in the light of the critiques which have been made against it, and from the left, which now regards the dependency paradigm as constituting an inadequate basis for the analysis of world capitalism. As a result, the dependency paradigm approaches, although not yet dead, appear to be under a mounting threat of being transcended, to be replaced on centre stage either by Reformist or Marxist approaches. It is the purpose of this paper to evaluate the extent to which the latter approaches provide a way out of the cul-de-sac of the dependency paradigm and to assess their contribution in terms of the derivation of policy options for overcoming unequal development.

OUT OF THE DEPENDENCY PERSPECTIVES

The earliest, most prominent and mainstream of the dependency perspectives which pertain to the underdevelopment of dependent peripheral nations is taken to be the positions espoused by Frank, Wallerstein and Amin. From the world systems perspective of these theorists it is maintained that, as a result of dependency, capitalist development in the core continuously creates and perpetuates underdevelopment in the periphery. Early critiques of this position focussed upon (a) the maintenance of the colonial structure - relations of transfer of value across space - in a position of pre-eminence over class structure (Arrighi, 1971: pp 1-2; Roxborough, 1976: p 121; Brenner, 1977: pp 27 and 53-67), and (b) the domination and definition of relations of production by exchange relations and the consideration of distribution as somehow independent of the mode of production (Arrighi, 1971: p 3; Laclau, 1971; Brenner, 1977: pp 31-33). More recently it has been emphasised that this dependency paradigm reflects, and is constrained by, its origins as a critique of orthodox (diffusionist) development theory. Its perspectives are plagued by the mirror-image trap of attempting to create a new paradigm through direct, polemical opposition to the old one whilst remaining in the same problematic (Bernstein, 1976: pp 9-11; Skocpol, 1977: p 1089; Leys, 1977: p 98; Villamil; 1979: p 4).

For the purposes of this paper, however, the most significant limitation of the dependency perspectives is their failure to formulate alternative prescriptions for social change. This is indeed a strange outcome for a perspective which rose to prominence largely because of dissatisfaction with the failure of diffusionist economic growth strategies to alleviate poverty and suffering in the world. Certainly one must agree with Barrington Moore (1977: p 508) that "...if the men of the future are ever to break the chains of the present, they will have to understand the forces that forged them". Nevertheless, what we are left with is a barren analytic approach which can explain what has happened in the past, retrospectively (as Rostow claimed to do), but which, as yet, offers few, if any, insights as to how changes can be implemented in the structures it has interpreted. In brief, it provides some understanding of the basic structural causes of the contradictions within capitalism but does little to generate proposals for their elimination.

In its prescriptions it would appear that socialism is to be advocated as the strategy to achieve development. This is seen to be a desirable outcome for two reasons. On the one hand, a socialist revolution in dependent peripheral nations is favoured in its own right as the only short/medium term mechanism by which development - defined as "... an increase in the capacity for controlled transformation of the social structure" (Roxborough, 1979: p 39) - can be achieved. Thus, the only choice is between continued dependency and underdevelopment or a socialist revolution because (a) development cannot be attained in dependent peripheral economies without a fundamental restructuring of the mode of articulation of the economy with the world economy (Roxborough, 1979: p 69), and (b) socialism is a necessary condition for development (Roxborough, 1979: p 140). On the other hand, a socialist revolution in dependent peripheral nations is favoured because it may hasten the crisis for capitalism in core nations by closing markets, denying access to raw materials and restricting the ability of core nations to accumulate capital through transnational investment. Thus, whilst the impetus for a world revolution which leads to the institution of a world system based upon (utopian?) socialist principles must be located in the hegemonic centre of world capitalism, socialist revolution in the periphery will assist in its onset. As Rosa Luxemburg (quoted in Dunn, 1979: p 81) noted, the choice is between socialism and barbarism for,

> ... we stand today, as Friedrick Engels prophesied more than a generation ago, before the awful proposition: either the triumph of imperialism and the destruction of all culture, and, as in ancient Rome, depopulation, desolation, degeneration, a vast cemetery; or, the victory of socialism, that is, the conscious struggle of the international proletariat against imperialism. Against its methods, against war.

Four reservations are expressed against these propositions. Firstly, as Phillips (1977: p 20) has noted, there is the danger that if existing governments of peripheral dependent nations put into practice a series of enlightened interventionist policies which make possible a more rational and equitable employment of resources (for example, the move towards self-reliance), then development (as defined by dependency) can be said to be occurring, in part at least, and hence the case for socialism falls away. Secondly, the advocacy of 'socialism in the one country' not only raises problems for those nations with small resource bases (autarky is not possible) but also is likely to invoke nationalist ideologies which may, in the long term, prove counter-productive in the movement towards a world socialist system. Thirdly, as a development strategy, the socialist revolution would appear to be misconstrued for revolution is a process, not a single event - it is not sufficient merely to overthrow the status quo (Roxborough, 1979: p 148). Moreover, not only is the transformation process one that is likely to span a considerable period of time (witness that from feudalism to capitalism in Western Europe) during which the socialist revolution may fail, be deflected or be co-opted, but also there is little evidence to suggest that the oppressed of the world would thereby be emancipated. Gouldner (1978: p 386) writes that,

The Communist Manifesto had held that the history of all hitherto existing society was the history of class struggles: freeman and slave, patrician and plebeian, lord and serf, guildmaster and journeyman, and, then, bourgeoisie and proletariat. In this series, however, there was one unspoken regularity: the slaves did not succeed the masters, the plebeians did not vanquish the patricians, the serfs did not overthrow the lords, and the journeymen did not triumph over the guildmasters. The lowliest class never came to power. Nor does it seem likely now.

Fourthly, and most critically, there appears to be confusion in dependency perspectives as to the nature of the revolution which is required in dependent peripheral nations. Roxborough (1979: p 159) maintains that there are two sets of contradictions and two sets of struggles: the struggle against dependency and for national liberation - the historic task of the bourgeoisie - and the class stuggle against the local ruling class - the historic task of the proletariat. Since the bourgeoisie have not completed their historic task in peripheral nations there has not yet been created a viable nation state or a process of autonomous capital accumulation (Roxborough, 1979: p 142). This would suggest that a bourgeois-democratic revolution is a necessary pre-condition for the socialist revolution - a position which dependency perspectives, by maintaining either that the peasants are part of the proletariat or that class divisions are to be made at the international level, explicitly reject. Yet, as Roxborough (1979: pp 134-137 and 154) argues, in order for there to be a socialist revolution it is first necessary for there to be socialists.

The failure of the dependency perspectives to move towards praxis (action informed by theory) is seen as their fundamental weakness. By concentrating research effort in the past and by remaining within a macro-level economic structuralist framework, the dependency perspectives offer virtually no guidance as to the means by which (a) the overthrow of capitalism in the hegemonic centre may be achieved, or (b) the peripheral nations can escape from dependency, underdevelopment and oppression. In its revolutionary rhetoric it would not advocate short-run, low-order policies and strategies to assist the poor and hungry of the world because this would serve only to support and maintain the status quo (Hayter, 1971) - "the aim of aid is to perpetuate the system that makes aid necessary" (Robinson, quoted in Foster-Carter, 1973: p 20); "the doctor is the disease" (Foster-Carter, 1973: p 23); development assistance is necessary "... to mitigate the most calamitous results of capitalism in order to justify the very system that necessarily produces and reproduces these calamitous results" (Baran and Sweezy, 1966: p 127). Yet after more than a decade its only positive contribution is to write, in specialist books and journals in a language and terminology that few can, or care to understand (or have access to) on the necessity for a socialist revolution - and even in terms of this it is not clear how, and by whom, it is to be achived or what is the desired (superior) range of political, economic and social relations of production to be implemented in post-capitalist social formations after the revolution. The suspicion clearly remains that the changes of fortune and fashion in development theory are largely geared to meeting the internal needs of the development studies profession (van Arkadie, 1977: p 409).

The escape from the sterile theoretical cul-de-sac in which the dependency perspectives are trapped can only be achieved by the adoption of other formulations. This is not to suggest, however, that all of the insights provided from the dependency perspectives are to be disregarded or discarded. Rather, it is argued that there is not a great deal to be gained by the pursuit of further macro-level dependency analyses, either of the present or of the past. The formulation of the dependency perspectives should be viewed, and situated, as occurring at a specific historical conjuncture of capitalist development. At the present time, though, it is being suggested that one way forward, out of the dependency perspectives, is to transcend (rather than reconstitute) its distinctive neo-diffusionist underlying assumptions and concepts and so move towards praxis. Two competing candidates are the Reformist and Marxist perspectives.

REFORMIST PERSPECTIVES

Diffusionist and dependency perspectives were castigated for their macro-level abstract theorising, for the relegation of people to a subordinate or insignificant status, and for their lack of attention to, or their inability to resolve, contemporary 'real world' problems (see Brookfield, 1975: Ch. 7). Not only were the pre-eminence of economics, general systems theory and spatial organisation denied but also the fundamental message to emerge from the dependency writings - that solutions to the problems of poverty are not to be found within the confines of the poor areas themselves because poverty and exploitation are inherent and necessary features of capitalism - was also ignored. Instead, ideographic, micro-level studies were to be resurrected. These placed central emphasis upon ecology, anthropology, people/environment relations, the management of the biosphere and a belief by McGee's (1978: p 98) 'dirty boots begets wisdom brigade' that theory must be built from the ground up (from the grass roots or the asphalt pavements) - that "long before the macro-theory must come the micro-empiricism"

(Connell, 1971: p 262).

Whereas dependency perspectives offered alternative explanations for the failure of dependent peripheral nations to achieve development, Reformists offered alternative policies to bring this about. Changes in policy involved support for calls for a New International Economic Order which favoured poor nations (and their élites) in their external trade, monetary and aid relations and a proliferation of Reformist strategies which offered what were considered to be logical, rigorous, ameliorative, incrementalist prescriptions for the ills (symptoms rather than causes) of the dependent and underdeveloped nations of the world. In these latter, notions of Triage, Lifeboat philosophies and the trickle down effects of economic growth have given way to 'worst-first' approaches which emphasise basic needs, employment generation and national or collective self-reliance (ILO, 1976; Streeten, 1977; Friedmann, 1978; Connell, 1980), the redistribution with growth policies sponsored by the World Bank (Chenery et al., 1974), and rural sector expansion and development (Lefeber, 1974; Mabogunje, 1975; Lipton, 1977).

Advocates of all approaches believe that there is scope for outside assistance to expedite or to implement bold policy initiatives without fundamentally altering the existing order (Lipton, 1977: Chapter 14; Connell, 1980: p 104) and that dependent peripheral nations have control over their own destiny to the extent that they are able to make a deliberate, conscious and voluntary, informed choice from among a range of strategies. Autonomous states, acting in pursuit of the general national interest, should exert greater determination, urgently pursue more effective, meaningful policies of sound domestic economic management (rather than short term, ill-advised palliatives designed to achieve ephemeral gains), and launch their own comprehensive, balanced attack on poverty and so bring about a more morally justifiable and tolerable capitalist order. Given sufficient co-operation, some self-sacrifice and the goodwill of all concerned, rational and technical solutions can be devised by visiting experts to institute such harmonious adjustment and orderly change.

Such a re-orientation towards optimistic visions of necessary reform derives, in part, from a reaction against the despondency and despair experienced when the impossibility, short of a world revolution, or bringing about changes in a world dominated by capitalism came to be realised. The re-orientation, then, is a retreat (diversion of attention) from a position of having to continuously confront directly the most brutal consequences of capitalism (Eliot Hurst, 1980: p 7) and a movement towards realms where it is felt that 'something' can be done to improve the standards of material well-being of impoverished people; that some academic contribution can be made to science and society through a sympathetic and compassionate analysis of some of the problems faced by poor people in peripheral nations (Lipton, 1977: p 352). It has, therefore, retained its positivist origins of "... trust in the values and usefulness of modern technology, centralized authority, bureaucratic rationality and scientific control, and ultimately, confidence in the work of professionally trained experts" (Mercer, 1977: p 2). From their analyses would arise 'correct', 'well-conceived', 'sensible' and 'appropriate' (for the economy, society, polity and environment) panaceas (the intelligent application of intermediate technology, progressive land reform) which seek, through persuasion, to effect internal structural changes in a context which largely ignores not only institutional and external forces but also class structure and struggle. Unfortunatley, however, it is rarely made clear as to how the changes are to be achieved. Much of the literature focuses upon platitudinous statements of what must or should constitute the desired state - "existing rural systems must become more efficient producers of food and employment ... whilst simultaneously the extent of poverty and inequality within them must be reduced" (Connell, 1980: p 74). Whilst they admit that at least in some contexts "... attempted reform under capitalism is likely to be a particularly frustrating, even dangerous [for whom?], experience" (Connell, 1980: p 97), it is still believed that idealistic, utopian and paternalistic expert advice can produce a package of sound, well-designed development policies. Moreover, it is claimed that their implementation is more than the best hope, it is the only realistic and sensible alternative which is available.

Nevertheless, the dilemmas for the Reformists remain as always: integration or separation. If integration, then the destruction of indigenous society and the imposition of Euro-centric value systems. If separation, then the denial of access to most of the 'benefits of Western civilisation' and the permanent ossification, through imposition from above, of structures of inequity. As development strategies both are undesirable and unrealistic and yet, as processes, both are manifest today. For the former, the spread of 'Coca Cola imperialism' generates a revolution of rising expectations in the periphery and then opposes it with lifeboat philosophy prognoses as to the very rapid exhaustion of the world's physical resources if living standards for all are to be raised and made comparable with those of the average American. For the latter, ideologies of free will and nationalism generate calls for independence, self-determination, autarchy, self-reliance and a 'delinking' from the world economy which are confronted with the impossibility of reversing the impress of four centuries of integration and the creation and reproduction of inequity by international capitalism.

MARXIST PERSPECTIVES

The Marxist response was to argue that an alternative to dependency perspectives can only be derived by adopting a holistic, scientific theory of society (historical materialism) as the framework of analysis. As Harvey (1972: p 5) regarded Western Sociology, so it was believed that the marriage of development theory and Marxism, by employing Marxist language "... without conveying the essence of Marxist thinking, has effectively prevented the true flowering of Marxist thought". The dependency approaches were seen to be insufficiently Marxist in orientation (Kay, 1975) that this was the primary source of their confusion and weakness (Roxborough, 1976: p 116), especially in their lack of conceptual rigour and in their theoretical vagueness (Taylor, 1974). These inherent inadequacies can only be overcome by the re-establishment of class analysis and imperialism as central elements of an alternative political economy theoretical framework of historical materialism (Petras and Trachte, 1979).

One immediate response to the identification of contradictions within dependency perspectives was the recognition that the abstract and generalised macro-economic framework employed needed to be reconstituted - to be made more specific, concrete and diagnostic (Arrighi, 1971: p 506). What was required was the more detailed explication of why, how and under what conditions underdevelopment has been, and still remains, a necessary and inevitable consequence of capitalism. There was need to investigate

> ... changes in the capitalist system and its articulation on the world scale, the diversity of forms of production it encompasses, its mechanism of appropriation and accumulation, the class alliances engendered by the new forms and modes of operation of capital, and the class struggles against capital in its various manifestations (Bernstein, 1976: p 11).

In essence, however, the major focus has been upon the differences, and the reasons for their existence, between the internal relations of production (the economic base) of dependent and advanced capitalist nations. Four viewpoints have been predominant.

Warren (1973; 1979) argued that capitalist development is proceeding 'normally' in dependent peripheral nations. He would thus appear to be in agreement with Marx's statement, in his preface to Capital, that "the industrially more developed country shows to the less developed only the image of its own future" (quoted in Dore, 1977: p 14). By asserting that the slow pace of industrialisation can be attributed both to the profitability criteria of monopoly capitalism and to backward conditions within these nations

(Mortimer, n.d.: p 1), Warren implied that the economic structure of peripheral nations is at an earlier stage of capitalist development through which the advanced capitalist nations have already passed. In support of this Warren sought to empirically demonstrate that in recent times widespread and unprecedented increases in per capita income have benefited the great majority of the world's population and that a significant number of major peripheral nations have successfully promoted rapid capitalist development. Since 1945 titanic strides forward have been made, Warren (1979: p 166) maintains, in the establishment, consolidation and growth of capitalism in the Third World (the dependent peripheral nations) and that this has been accompanied by a corresponding and historically unprecedented advance in the material welfare of the mass of the population and in the growth of productive forces. In these instances, the possibilities of progressing along the path to national capitalist development, free of dependency, were judged to be good (but see Emmanuel, 1974; McMichael, Petras and Rhodes, 1974; Myer, 1975).

Kay (1975: p 95-107), and Amin at times (see Amin, 1976: Chapter 4), argued that the transition to capitalist development in dependent peripheral nations has been 'blocked' by virtue of the specific nature of the penetration, by capitalism, of pre-capitalist societies. Whilst such an approach can be regarded as being directly at odds with dependency perspectives - Kay (1975:) comments that the crucial issue is that "... capital created underdevelopment not because it exploited the underdeveloped world, but because it did not exploit it enough" - it can also be seen (Mortimer, n.d.: p 2) to be veering back to diffusionist approaches and to the tradition/modern dichotomy (as can Warren's arguments).

The third viewpoint suggests that a dependent capitalist mode of production is different from an advanced capitalist mode of production.
This is the approach taken by Banaji (1972), Alavi (1972, 1975) and Magubane (1976) in their delimitation of colonial and post-colonial modes of production (see Harriss, 1979). There is, however, little support for such a viewpoint and indeed, Banaji (1975) has subsequently rejected Alavi's formulation. In particular, it has been argued that dependency does not constitute a unique mode of production nor a particular phase of another mode of production and hence there is no theoretical space in which to locate a new theory of dependent capitalism (Cueva, 1976: 15).

The fourth, final and most predominant viewpoint proposes that, whilst the dependent nations exhibit a capitalist mode of production, the articulation of this capitalist mode of production with other modes of production within the dependent social formation and with the world capitalist economy produces a distinctive and different dependent capitalist mode of production (Roxborough, 1976: p 129) - i.e., capitalist development. This is the approach taken by Cardoso (1973) and in the articulation of modes of production literature (Foster-Carter, 1978; Taylor, 1979). It finds its most detailed expression in the 'conservation-dissolution' arguments relating to the reciprocal inter-relationships between dominant capitalist and dominated pre-capitalist modes of production.

Three major, and inter-related, criticisms can be raised against these latter approaches. Firstly, the focus of attention has remained almost entirely upon structure and so insufficient consideration has been given to relations of exploitation between classes. Class formation, class domination and class struggle are not an intrinsic part of their analyses. Secondly, a substantial part of the research effort devoted to theoretical and methodological issues is based upon the transition from feudalism to capitalism in Western Europe from the sixteenth century onwards (Frank, 1978). Whilst it may be the case that, in order to transform the dependency perspectives, it is necessary to undertake such a task, it remains to be demonstrated how such research effort will contribute to facilitating desired changes in the existing social order of dependent peripheral nations - particularly since (a) their social structures, modes of production and internal contradictions are neither classically feudal nor capitalist and (b) models of endogenous social change derived from the Western Europe experience are likely, on their own admission, to be inapplicable (ahistorical) to peripheral nations incorporated, in a dependent position, in the world capitalist system (Roxborough, 1979: p 19) Such a retreat into the past, and this is the third criticism, is viewed as being symptomatic of the failure of these perspectives, as with those of the dependency paradigm, to formulate alternative prescriptions for social change.

This is surprising since it would appear that, for Marxists, there are a number of different attitudes that can be taken towards the derivation, from their analyses, of alternative prescriptions for the achievement of progressive change in the world. Two viewpoints are identified here. On the one hand, it can be argued in a deterministic, teleological manner, that

> No social order ever perishes before all the productive forces for which there is room in it have developed; and new, higher relations of production never appear before the material conditions for their existence have matured in the womb of the old society itself. (Marx in Marx and Engels, 1969: 504)

It is felt that this is both unsatisfactory and unconvincing: neither is it supported by the contemporary world experience of revolutionary change. It is necessary to go beyond such a passive, almost Rostovian, view as to the necessity and inevitability of the evolution of pre-conditions for social and economic change.

On the other hand, it can be argued that a Marxist perspective must involve much more that a return to, and a re-reading of, the 'sacred texts' in order to explain the past and present. It was, after all, Marx (Marx and Engels, 1969: p 15) who stated in the eleventh thesis on Feuerbach that "the philosophers have only interpreted the world, in various ways: the point, however, is to change it". Such an endeavour must comprise more than a moralistic/radical-liberal/humanitarian concern for the oppressed of the world. This will not, indeed cannot, produce revolutionary theory. Rather, many would argue, the unity of theory and practice must be re-established (see, for example, Bookchin, 1978). Folke (1972: p 17) has forcefully made the case that,

> the development of revolutionary theory is itself dependent on revolutionary practice. It is crucially important to understand that theory cannot be developed first and then put into practice. The revolutionary practice must be a dialectical one between theory and practice. Revolutionary theory without revolutionary practice is not only useless, it is inconceivable.

There are, however, at least two dangers associated with this approach. First, it is the height of arrogance to argue, from the safety and comfort of some pedestal in the ivory towers of academia, for others to overthrow the established order whilst not demonstrating a willingness or an ability to bear the costs associated with the attempt to bring about such a change. This is not to suggest that 'First World' academics should leave their native shores in order to ferment revolutionary activity in far-off lands. The lessons of such interventionism are to be found not only in the proselitising of christian religions but also on the battlefields of Spain. At least in this respect I agree with Lipton's (1977: p 329) comment that social scientists are not qualified to advise on revolutionary action and nor do they have the right to sacrifice human life to their ignorance [as development assistance experts have done in the past?]. Contra Debray (1967), in the national liberation struggles against colonialism, neo-colonialism and dependency there is no active role for a band of missionaries or international brigades to play. Their 'assistance' may not only be unwelcome but it may also involve a cost to the indigenous peoples greater than ever wrought by the development experts of the multi or bi-lateral aid and assistance bureaucracies. Change must, can only, emanate directly from the people themselves. Thus it can be suggested that if Marxists wish to be actively involved in praxis in order to bring about social change, to re-establish the unity of theory and practice, then the focus of attention should be upon the advanced capitalist nations (rather than the dependent peripheral nations). In this regard, though, it will not be sufficient merely to mimic the rhetoric of Lipton (1977: p 352) - "Our duty is to attempt to make the policies of our own countries more helpful to poor people in poor countries" - but to work with those forces actively seeking the overthrow of capitalism within its hegemonic centres. Banaji (1980: p 488), expressing similar sentiments writes that

> If a revolutionary Marxist theory of world capitalism is to make any progress at all in the 1980s, it must start by rejecting the entire framework of 'dependency theory' and shifting its focus radically to the working class and its real practice of self-emancipation from capital.

My concern with this approach, and this is the second danger, is that of the emergence of a new form of vanguardism among theorists who may delude themselves into believing that class relations can be manipulated or transformed from above. One recalls the constraints upon freedom of action recognised by Marx (Marx and Engels, 1969: p 398)

> Men make their own history, but they do not make it just as they please; they do not make it under circumstances chosen by themselves, but under circumstances directly encountered, given and transmitted from the past.

Of perhaps greater significance is the implicit assumption that strategies designed to achieve the self-emancipation of workers can be derived and prescribed from theory or by theorists. The experience of Eastern Europe, in which the intellectuals are on 'The Road to Class Power' as teleological redistributors and central planners (Konrad and Szelenyi, 1979) in a relatively autonomous socialist mode of production which still oppresses workers and which shows little evidence of its supposed transitory status between capitalism and communism, should serve as a sufficient warning to all those who wish to espouse élitist 'views from above'. It is along similar lines of argument that theorists like Fanon and Debray, writing in the aftermath of the Cuban revolution and the Algerian independence movement, sought"... the abandonment of revolutionary theory conceived of as an analysis of the dynamics of the social structure which could serve as a guide for revolutionary action" (Roxborough, 1979: p 134).

It appears to me, therefore, that the adoption of Marxist methods of social analysis necessitates (a) the end of the study of development as a distinct and separate area of academic enquiry, (b) the engagement by 'First World'

Marxists in praxis in advanced capitalist nations, (c) a diminution in the relative significance of theory (or at least the rejection of the notion that theory can be imposed upon practice), and (d) following Blaut (1974: pp 44-45), the abandonment by academic development theorists of their class-designated role. If strictly adhered to this would tend to imply and call for a departure from the halls of academia - something which is regarded as an unlikely outcome for self-sacrifice is not particularly attractive for many, and neither is martyrdom necessarily guaranteed for those who desire it. Yet, without a move towards the directions stated above, it is difficult to envisage how the Marxist project, on the basis of its own value criteria, can offer a range of strategies for social change which can, in the present be put into action. Thus, the inexorable conclusion from both the viewpoints considered is that Marxism cannot, should not, prescribe change from theory. The alternatives remain as barbarism or socialism.

CONCLUSION

The critiques of the diffusionist and dependency perspectives are so well established that a further concentration of research effort in this direction would not appear to be able to contribute all that much. There is need to move away from abstract grand theorising to more empirically-based and lower-order theory. This is what the Reformists are attempting, albeit in an ostrich-like manner, by 'dropping out' and seeking refuge in their investigations of 'current local area development problems' which are thought to be amenable to solution within the constraints of world capitalism. In contrast, Marxists appear to have retained a predilection for nomothetic approaches and for the investigation of time periods other than the present - emphases which, if maintained as their central focus, will have a diminishing marginal utility in the future. Yet the move away from this towards praxis, overt activism and the establishment of dialectical relationships between theory and practice may also be questioned in an advanced capitalist world that is inexorably, and rapidly in some instances, moving away from the political left. But if resigning oneself to wait for the inevitable in order to justify lack of action is seen as unacceptable, then the Marxist project must move beyond both 'technical solutions' to 'development problems' and the notion that it is their role to develop and expand upon theoretical knowledge which can then be applied to moves to achieve social change in the 'real world'. The journey out of the dependency perspectives will not be as easy as the road in (which was part of the attractiveness of these perspectives in the first place) but one thing is certain, neither utopian socialist dreams nor the technical competence of development experts will, by themselves, be sufficient.

REFERENCES

Alavi, H. 1972. "The State in Post-Colonial Societies: Pakistan and Bangladesh." New Left Review, 74.

Alavi, H. 1975. "India and the Colonial Mode of Production". in R. Miliband and J. Saville, eds., The Socialist Register 1975 London: Merlin Press.

Amin, S. 1976. Unequal Development Hassocks, Sussex: Harvester Press.

Arrighi, G. 1971. "The Relationship between the Colonial and the Class Structures: A Critique of A.G. Frank's Theory of the Development of Underdevelopment". Dakar: IDEP

Banaji, J. 1972. "For a Theory of Colonial Modes of Production". Economic and Political Weekly 7 (52).

Banaji, J. 1975. "Comment on India and the Colonial Mode of Production". Economic and Political Weekly 19 (49).

Banaji, J. 1980. "Gunder Frank in Retreat". Journal of Contemporary Asia 9, and this volume.

Baran, P.A. and Sweezy, P.M. 1966. Monopoly Capital New York: Monthly Review Press.

Bernstein, H., ed. 1976. Underdevelopment and Development Harmondsworth: Penguin.

Blaut, J.H. 1974. "Commentaries on 'Values in Geography". pp. 44-45 in A. Buttimer, Values in Geography Commission on College Geography Resource Paper No. 24. Washington, D.C.: Association of American Geographers.

Bookchin, M. 1978, "Beyond Neo-Marxism", Telos, 36.

Brenner, R. 1977. "The Orogins of Capitlist Development: A Critique of Neo-Smithian Marxism". New Left Review 104. 25-92

Brookfield, H.C. 1975. Interdependent Development London: Methuen

Browett, J.G. 1980. "Development, the Diffusionist Paradigm and Geography". Progress in Human Geography 4(1).

Browett, J.G. 1981. "Into the Cul de Sac of the Dependency Paradigm with A.G. Frank", Australia and New Zealand Journal of Sociology forthcoming

Cardoso, F.H. 1973. "Associated-Dependent Development: Theoretical and Practical Implications." Chapter 5 in A. Stepan, ed., Authoritarian Brazil: Origins, Policies and Future, New Haven, Conn.: Yale University Press.

Chenery, H. et al. 1974. Redistribution with Growth: Policies to improve Income Distribution in Developing Countries in the Context of Economic Growth. London: Oxford University Press.

Connell, J. 1971. "The Geography of Development". Area .

Connell, J. 1980. "Rural Development: Green, White, Red or Blue Revolutions?" in J. Friedmann, E.L. Wheelwright and

J. Connell, Development Strategies in the Eighties. Monograph No. 1. Sydney: Development Studies Colloquium, The University of Sydney.

Cueva, A. 1976. "A Summary of Problems and Perspectives of Dependency Theory: Latin American Persectives 3:

Debray, R. 1967. Revolution in the Revolution? Harmondsworth: Penguin.

Dore, R. 1977 "Underdevelopment in Theoretical Perspective." Discussion Paper 109.Brighton: Institute of Development Studies, University of Sussex.

Dunn, J. 1979. Western Political Theory in the Face of the Future, Cambridge: Cambridge University Press.

Eliot Hurst, M.E. 1980. "Geography, Social Science and Society: Towards a De-Definition". Australian Geographical Studies 18 (1):

Emmanuel, A. 1974. "Myths of Development versus Myths of Underdevelopment". New Left Review 85

Folke, S. 1972. "Why a Radical Geography must be Marxist". Antipode 4 (2)

Foster-Carter, A. 1973 "Neo-Marxist Approaches to Development and Underdevelopment". Journal of Contemporary Asia 3 (1)

Foster-Carter, A. 1978. "The Modes of Production Controversy". New Left Review 107

Frank, A.G. 1978. World Accumulation New York: Monthly Review Press.

Friedmann, J. 1978. "Basic Needs, Agropolitan Development and Planning from Below, Comparative Urbanization Studies." Los Angeles: School of Architecture and Urban Planning, University of California.

Gouldner, A.W. 1973. "The New Class Project, II: A Frame of References, Theses, Conjectures, Arguments, and an Historical Perspective on the Role of Intellectuals and Intelligentsia in the International Class Contest of the Modern Era". Theory and Society 6

Harriss, J. 1979. "The Mode of Production Controversy: Themes and Problems of the Debate". Discussion Paper No. 60 Norwich: Development Studies Centre, University of East Anglia.

Harver, D. 1972. "Revolutionary and Counter Revolutionary Theory in Geography and the Problem of Ghetto Formation". Antipode 4 (2) : 1-12.

Hayter, T. 1971 Aid as Imperialism Harmondsworth: Penguin.

International Labour Office. 1976. Employment, Growth and Basic Needs: A One-World Problem Geneva: I.L.O

Kay, G. 1975. Development and Underdevelopment: A Marxist Analysis. London: Macmillan.

Konrad, G and Szelenyi, I. 1978. Die Intelligenz auf dem Weg Zur Klassenmacht, Suhrkamp Verlag, Frankfurt am Main, translated by A. Araro and R.E. Allen (1979) as The Intellectuals on the Road to Class Power: A Sociological

Study of the Role of the Intelligentsia in Socialism. New York: Harcourt Brace Jovanovich.

Laclau, E. 1971. "Feudalism and Capitalism in Latin America." New Left Review 67

Lefeber, L. 1974. "On the Paradigm for Economic Development". World Development 2 (1)

Leys, C. 1977. "Underdevelopment and Dependency: Critical Notes". Journal of Contemporary Asia 7 (1) and this volume.

Lipton, M. 1977. Why Poor People Stay Poor London: Temple Smith.

McMichael, T., Petras, J. and Rhodes, R. 1974. "Imperialism and the Contradictions of Development". New Left Review 85

McGee, T. 1978. "Western Geography and the Third World". American Behavioural Scientist. 22 (1)

Mabogunje, A.L. 1975. "Geography and the Problems of the Third World". International Social Science Journal 27: 287-302.

Magubane, A. 1976. "The Evolution of Class Structure in Africa". Chapter 7 in P.C.W. Gutkind and I Wallerstein, eds., The Political Economy of Contemporary Africa Beverly Hills: Sage.

Marx K. and Engels, F. 1969. Selected Works volume 1. Moscow: Progress Publishers.

Mercer, D. 1977. "Conflict and Consensus in Human Geography". Monash Publications in Geography No. 17. Clayton, Victoria: Department of Geography, Monash University.

Moore, B. 1977. Social Origins of Dictatorship and Democracy Harmondsworth: Penguin (first published in 1966).

Mortimer, R. n.d. "Underdevelopment/Dependency Theory (UDT): A short Selected and Annotated Bibliography", Mimeo

Myer, J. 1975. "A Crown of Thorns: Cardoso and Counter-Revolution". Latin American Perspectives 2

Petras, J. and Trachte, K. 1979. "Liberal, Structural and Radical Approaches to Political Economy: An Assess,ent and an Alternative." Contemporary Crises. 3

Phillips, A. 1977. "The Concept of Development". Review of African Political Economy 8

Roxborough, I. 1976. "Dependency Theory in the Sociology of Development: Some Theoretical Problems." West African Journal of Sociology and Political Science 1 (2)

Roxborough, I. 1979. Theories of Underdevelopment London: Macmillan.

Skocpol, T. 1977. "Wallerstein's World Capitalist System: A Theoretical and Historical Critique". American Journal of Sociology 82 (5)

Slater, D. 1978. "Towards a Political Economy of Urbanization in Peripheral Capitalist Societies". Problems of Theory and Method with Illustrations from Latin America ". International Journal of Urban and Regional Research 2(1)

Streeten, P. 1977. "The Distinctive Features of a Basic Needs Approach to Development." International Development Review 19 (3)

Taylor, J. 1974. "Neo-Marxism and Underdevelopment - A Sociological Phantasy". Journal of Contemporary Asia. 4 (1).

Taylor, J. 1979. From Modernization to Modes of Production. London: Macmillan.

Van Arkadie, B. 1977. "Town Versus Country?" Development and Change 8

Villamil, J.J. 1979. "Introduction." in J.J. Villamil, ed., Transnational Capitalism and National Development: New Perspectives of Dependence. Hassocks, Sussex: Harvester Press.

Warren, W. 1973. "Imperialism and Capitalist Industrialisation". New Left Review 81

Warren, W. 1979. "The Postwar Economic Experience of the Third World", in Rothko Chapel Colloquium, Toward a New Strategy for Development. New York: Pergamon.

Chapter 12

NEW PERSPECTIVES ON IMPERIALISM AND SOCIAL CLASSES IN THE PERIPHERY

James F. Petras

INTRODUCTION

The issue which conventional development theorists and neo-Marxists like Baran and Frank focused upon from different perspectives was the issue of growth - "the political economy of growth", "capitalism and underdevelopment";[1] the central problem was stagnation, the incapacity of capitalism to achieve high growth rates in the colonial/semi-colonies/neo-colonies; the argument centered on the reasons for "economic stagnation" - the major focus being external surplus extraction/appropriation/drainage, a variety of mechanisms of external surplus appropriation were analyzed: trade relations, financial and investment controls, aid policies, etc. Socialism was conceived of largely in terms of its utility as an instrument of development: rapid growth and sustained economic expansion became the justification for socialism. This approach was significant in that it immediately engaged non-Marxist development economists, insofar as it shared many of the same concerns notwithstanding the different political and ideological orientations that informed each discussion. This convergence of neo-Marxism and conventional development writings contained latent within it a series of problems that would surface and elude the left in due time.

With the rise of formally independent regimes in the Third World, efforts were made to avoid the extreme economic fluctuations resulting from their dependence on export sales and the ensuing political instability. Efforts at economic diversification occurred (in many cases directed by traditional-conservative regimes): policies promoted various types of industrialization, in most cases externally financed and directed. Some of these efforts resulted in an increase in industrial output, though not necessarily of the productive forces - a substantial part of this "industry" is nothing more than assembly plants.

As this process of industrial expansion occurred in the Third World (varying in intensity with time and place), bourgeois social scientists, drawing on the "data" from the Third World, began to challenge the premises and conclusions of the neo-Marxists: growth rates in some of the neo-colonies matched those of revolutionary societies; externally induced and fragmentary industrialization led to exploitive but increasingly diversified class structures. Vague formulas, such as Frank's "development of underdevelopment", anchored in an historical analysis of agro-mineral societies acquired an elasticity that, while giving the appearance of explaining new developments, merely added to the confusion: probing questions surfaced concerning the utility of discussing the new industrial enterprises and emerging proletariat in the Third World in the context of "underdevelopment". And if the nexus of the struggle was shifting to class relations what did the notion of "development of underdevelopment" have to do with the emerging class consciousness and class struggles which were increasingly not over "development" but the conditions of imperial capitalist exploitation. The essential bankruptcy of "developmental Marxism" was evidenced in the multiplication of labels: the emergence in the Third World of a bourgeoisie became the "lumpen-bourgeoisie", the expansion of the productive forces bacame "lumpen-development".[2] In a word, the incapacity to move further within the stagnationist framework led to ad hoc explanations and attempts to mystify through categories which carried derogatory connotations - their analytical value was nil.

Given the growing untenability of this approach, it was inevitable that a reaction would set in. Expansion of the Third World, not stagnation, was the distinguishing characteristic of the new school (Cardoso, Warren, Emmanuel).[3] National capitalism, independent industrialization, sub-imperialism, favoured neo-colony all served to describe Third World economies in which growth was the crucial feature. In this debate, both the stagnationists and the expansionists shared a common narrow perspective in which the quantity of units produced was the point of departure for organizing their analysis. The efforts to anchor this discussion in the class structure led to discursive exercises in which labels and prescriptions were substituted for historical analysis: comprador bourgeoisies and landlords and lumpen-bourgeoisie were ascribed responsibility for stagnation by the neo-Marxists; the critics differ widely as to who is responsible for expansion: the "development" agencies range from the petty-bourgeois class to "development states", the military, external powers - or some combination of the above.

Expansion on a world scale has been characteristic of our epoch - though the process has not been as smooth as some commentators would have us believe. In fact, recurring "crises" - recessions, depressions and fluctuations, are indeed the very mechanisms through which the economic system has sought to recover its dynamic. [4] The problem then is not one of absolute stagnation but of examining the conditions under which the process of capital accumulation takes place and its impact on the class structure. The issue in debate has been over "underdevelopment" and the focus has been on which social system is more conducive to growth and "development" to overcome "underdevelopment". While of late some attention has been paid to income distribution and inequalities[5] - the sources of those inequalities, their roots in social relations and state control, have been passed over. The issue of exploitation rooted in capitalist social relations or in bureaucratic collectivistic forms of statism, has hardly been analyzed; even less so have the class relations served as a point of departure within which to locate the problem of capital accumulation and expansion.

The conditions under which accumulation takes place include: (a) the nature of the State (and state policy); (b) class relations (process of surplus extraction, intensity of exploitation, level of class struggle, concentration of work force).

The impact of capital accumulation on class structure includes: (a) class formation/conversion (small proprietors to proletarians or kulaks, rural proletarians to urban sub-proletarian, landlord to merchant, merchant to industrialist, national indurtrialist to branch plant manager of a multi-national corporation - these are just some examples of the processes under this rubric; (b) income distribution (concentration, redistribution, reconcentration of income); (c) social relations: labour market relations ("free" wage, trade union bargaining), semi-coercive (market and political/social controls), coercive (slave, debt peonage).

Production expands, growth does occur in cyclical patterns, largely as a function of external decisions ("demand") and internal conditions (externally linked classes, alienated state, repressed social movements).

Accumulation is characterized by uneven development reflected in the particular product areas integrated to the external world and sharp income inequalities derived from the external class linkages, control over state revenues, and coercive controls over working class and peasantry.[6]

Unlike dependency studies which centered on the growth of productive forces and how the external ties "blocked" growth, the focus on conditions of accumulation and its impact on class relations allows us to focus more concretely on the nature of the state ultimately involved in both accumulation and class formation, as well as internal class relations as they emerge from, as well as shape capitalist development.

A discussion of imperialism which focuses on its expansionary/stagnationist tendencies overlooks the essential character of it as the international expression of capitalism's historical mission to develop the forces of production in accordance with the logic of capital accumulation, a process that is, by its nature, uneven, exploitative and contradictory.

Imperialism has passed through three distinct phases which reflect three different stages of capitalist development and which, in turn, correspond to three types of peripheral exploitation. During the early phase of capitalist development, a period that straddles both the period of mercantilism and industrialization, the periphery was subject to a type of plunder that most closely resembles the operations of pirates: the forcible extraction of goods and services through military and administrative controls, while the economic exchanges played a subordinate role. The process of exchange was largely between the European countries; Spain serving as a conduit for wealth from the colonies in exchange for finished goods from its northern European trading partners. The "piratical" form of exploitation was modified over time with the growth of settler colonies and through these settlements trade relations began to emerge, ultimately establishing the form of colonial trade relations which served as the basis of extractive colonialism. The importance of pirate colonialism is found in the fact that it occurs in the early period of European capital accumulation - a period during which the transfer of resources from the periphery is decisive in stoking the engines of the industrial revolution. Here it is not a question of unequal exchange; but rather given the low level of development of the productive forces in the West, its capacity to "exchange" with the periphery being thus constrained, it commands through military conquest the unilateral exaction of income. The earnings from slavery, gold, silver, the tribute exacted from the commerce and labour of the periphery did not contribute to the "underdevelopment" of the periphery - it simply decimated whole civilizations and populations, especially in Africa and Latin America, while it served to finance the expansion of manufacturers and technological innovation in the metropole. The creation of an internal market in the metropolis was made possible by the lack of market relations in the periphery: the purely extractive exploitative relation, allowed the metropole to expand inwardly, with growing cities and internal markets which provided further impetus to industrial expansion.

The exhaustion of this type of colonialism was inherent in its mode of operation: the end of easy exploitation of precious metals and of substantial segments of the labour force. More important, the growth of industry required new forms of exploitation in the periphery. Beginning the latter half of the 19th century, commercial ties between colony and metropole were modified by the growth of industries, whose production exceeded the bounds of the internal markets, which increasingly sought new markets abroad as well as profitable outlets for surplus capital and raw materials to fuel the increasingly complex and voracious appetite of diversified industrial operations. The early infusions of wealth from the colonies during the period of pirate colonialism contributed to the export of surplus capital in the period of early monopoly capital, in the form of investment, which in turn returned high rates of profit to the metropole. The outflow and inflow of capital from metropole to periphery varied with time and place but in the process accumulation became world wide. In the later stages of "early monopoly capitalism", the economic networks were extended to the interior of the periphery: moving away from simple labour intensive extraction, imperial expansion during this phase brought with it the latest technology, to increase profitability through higher productivity as well as to fulfil the growing demands of large-scale enterprises. Mineral extraction, especially those types most closely tied to the high growth areas of the imperial economies, became points of conflict in the growing competition between imperial empires. If the surplus extracted from the periphery served to facilitate the growth of industries within the metropole and the creation of an internal market initially, in the second period of capitalist development, the surplus was tied to industrial empires and served to accelerate world-wide expansion: it contributed to the growth of the multi-national corporations and the creation of a world capitalist market.

Intervening between the periods of early and late monopoly capitalism were a series of world historic events: the eruption of class/national/imperial struggles on a world-scale which delayed, modified and then accelerated the pattern of world capitalist exploitation. The world depression weakened the ties between centre and periphery; the inter-imperialistic war of the 1940s depleted the old empires and set in motion a whole series of events culminating in the rise of national revolts throughout the periphery. The socialist revolutions in Russia, China, Cuba further delimited the areas of imperial operations. The demise of the old colonial empires, however, gave rise to a new form of peripheral exploitation, initially centered in the US and later amongst competing imperial poles (US-Europe-Japan). Both in terms of the quantity of capital flows, the dimensions of the organization, the ease with which capital mobility was evidenced (the continuous circularity of the flow of the capital in and out of countries), the predominance of investment and bank loans as well as the diversification of investment, late monopoly capitalism defined a new period of capital accumulation. The emergence of non-revolutionary national regimes in the ex-colonies led to collaboration with the metropoles; the needs of the metropole for strategic raw materials and investments outlets as well as the constant search for new revenues to sustain the national state in the dependent neo-colony led to the diversification of economic activity within the periphery beyond administrative and economic enclaves to increasingly lock-in the entire network of local economies: commerce, banking, industry and services. The world-wide network and power of imperial capital resolved the latent (and overt) conflict with the newly emerging national state through a variety of forms of penetration: joint partnership, management contracts, exploitation rights, royalty and licensing agreements, etc. At one and the same time the extension of capitalist networks lends credence to the notion of greater stability to the empire, consolidation, and yet at the same time, poses an immediate threat: by increasing the decision-making capacity within the periphery, by drawing it closer to the webs of power and capital accumulation, it tends to allow it to observe the inner-workings of the system, laying the basis for new demands and redefinitions of relationships between the periphery and metropole.

<u>Capital Accumulation - Phases of Imperialism</u>

Phase of Capitalist Development	Type of Peripheral Exploitation
1. primitive accumulation (1500-1880)	a. pirate colonialism extraction from periphery of surplus (gold, spices, slavery, trade, agro-products,) build up of basic industry, expansion of manufacturing-technical innovation.
2. early monopoly capitalism (1880-1945)	b. extractive colonialism export of surplus capital, capturing of raw materials, search for markets for excess production, outflow of capital as well as inflow albeit proportions vary with time/place, process of accumulation became world-wide, extension of networks to interior of country, expansion of production/technology with focus on industrial-mineral

			resources, surplus and mineral extraction tied to industrial empires.
3.	'late' monopoly capitalism (1946-1975)	a.	"dependent neo-colonialism" circular flow of capital into and out of countries, investments and bank loans predominate, diversification of investment; imperial state and neo-colonial state create new opportunities for activity, markets for goods; need for strategic raw materials and investment outlets, leads to diversification of economic activity within periphery extension of activity beyond administrative and mineral centres, to increasingly lock-in with entire network of local economies: commerce banking, industry, services; a variety of forms of penetration: ownership, joint-partnership, management contracts, exploitation rights, royalty and licensing agreements, commercialization and transport agreements, etc.

THE OLD AND NEW CONTRADICTIONS

In the period prior to neo-colonial type of peripheral exploitation, the political and social forms of domination were largely extensions of metropolitan institutions. The exceptions were mostly colonial-settler regimes who in the first instance developed autonomist tendencies as wedges to open up political space and commercial opportunity; the existence of pre-imperial social formations and traditional political authorities (chieftancies, high caste functionaries) mostly served as surrogates of imperial authority largely delegated to tribute collecting functions. The process of surplus extraction was therefore relatively direct, the colonial official inside was the foreign officer outside. The essential contradiction was between imperial capitalism extracting surplus value from colonized classes; the national struggle was in large part unmediated by internal class and political conflicts.

In the neo-colonial phase, national independence and the formation of the national state led to the creation of social strata between imperial capitalism and the labour force. Drawn from a variety of sources including political movements, the university, the army, the civil service, etc., this social strata is drawn from the propertyless "intermediary" groups; rooted in the state bureaucracy it has access to powers of the state, including revenues and expenditires; the impulse to personal property ownership and affluence through derivative "ownership" via association with metropolitan enterprises or through directorships in state enterprises created the basis for "negotiated conflict" between imperial/nationalist social strata on the one hand and on the other hand by enlarging the scope of class relationship heightening tension within the periphery between these intermediary strata and the labour force. Imperial capital exploitation mediated by internal class forces creates and multiplies contradictions and disguises them. Imperial policy is oriented toward manipulating national "intermediaries" as a protective covering while on the other hand the dominant national strata struggle to increase their social preponderence viz a viz their own labour force.

CLASS ALLIANCES AND CAPITAL ACCUMULATION IN THE PERIPHERY.

A number of strategies emerge for the national intermediaries dominant in the peripheral countries. But before discussing the principal options open to the dominant national strata, it is worthwhile to briefly survey three inter-related issues: the social basis of nationalist predominance over socialism during the independence struggle and subsequently in the post-independence period as well as the political, social and economic possibilities opened by independence to nationalistic regimes.

Nationalism emerged largely as a result of the low degree of social differentiation within the colonies leading to the amalgamation of various class and pre-class forces. The existence of subsistence farmers and their general isolation from political life contributed to making the land question less pressing than the national question. As a result, political organization was confined to the urban petty bourgeoisie, products of commercial and administrative expansion. The predominance of the petty bourgeoisie, the small size of the proletariat and its relative isolation from the peasantry created circumstances in which the tradition of class struggle was much weaker than nationalist politics. The large concentrations of urban petty-capitalists and state employees over and against the industrial proletariat set the tone and direction of independence politics.

Nationalism sustained itself in the post-independence period in part because the slowness of industrial expansion did not favour the growth of social classes which might be more receptive to class politics. As a result of the relatively weak position of the industrial proletariat, the trade unions were in many cases absorbed in the state apparatus, further undermining the socialist option. In addition to these organizational measures, the "national" state has ironically resorted to communal mystifications and regional loyalties to sustain its power, thus at one and the same time disintegrating the source of its legitimacy as well as undermining class divisions. Parallel to national disaggregation, the "nationalists" have followed a policy of external integration - grafting on to the police and military apparatus the ideology and orientation of the metropole. These structural adaptations and policies have been reinforced by specific changes in the mode of political activity: demobilization of the population and bureaucratization of political life. "Legitimate" political action is largely confined to competition over employment in the expanded state sector. While nationalism in power has not led to the demystification of oppresive class relations, control over the <u>government</u> has led to a number of economic "openings" or possibilities: the national intermediaries can bargain over terms of dependency, diversify the sources of dependency, increase revenues, create a framework for the development of internal markets through social expenditures and (state) investments, promote diversification of production, create the basis for the expansion of the national bourgeoisie - anchored in either the state or private sector or both - and the petty bourgeoisie (mainly public employees), and open up opportunities for statist development policies. These possibilities are in large part contingent upon the type of international and national class alliances which are formed as well as the bargaining strength of the classes within the alliance

The post independence national regime can choose among at least three strategies or types of class alliances for capital accumulation. In the first instance it can join with imperial firms and regimes in intensifying surplus extraction from the labour force through a variety of post-independence working relationships outlined under the above-mentioned rubric of "dependent neo-colonialism". An alternative strategy for the national regime involves extracting the surplus from the labour force and limiting or eliminating the share going to the imperial firms, thus concentrating it in the hands of state and/or private national entrepreneurs. This approach, which can be referred to as national developmentalism without redistribution, leads to concentration of income at the top of the national class hierarchy.

A third alternative is for the national regime to ally itself with the labouring population, extend the areas of national control (through nationalization), reinvest the surplus of the national economy or promote a redistribution of income within the national class structure.

The type of class alliance on which the national regime rests and the strategy for capital accumulation directly affects the distribution of income. Capital accumulation from above and outside (what can be called the "neo-colonial" model) results in an income structure that resembles an inverted pyramid - with wealth and power concentrated in the hands of foreign capital. The national bourgeois developmental approach which "capitalizes" on the foreign elite and the national labour force concentrates income among the intermediary strata (in the form of the governing elite of the periphery), leading to income distribution along the shape of a diamond.

The alliance between national intermediaries and the labour force, what can be referred to as a "national-popular" strategy, leads to a broader based society in which income is more diversified, spreading downward and taking the shape of a pyramid.

Income Distribution and Class Alliance

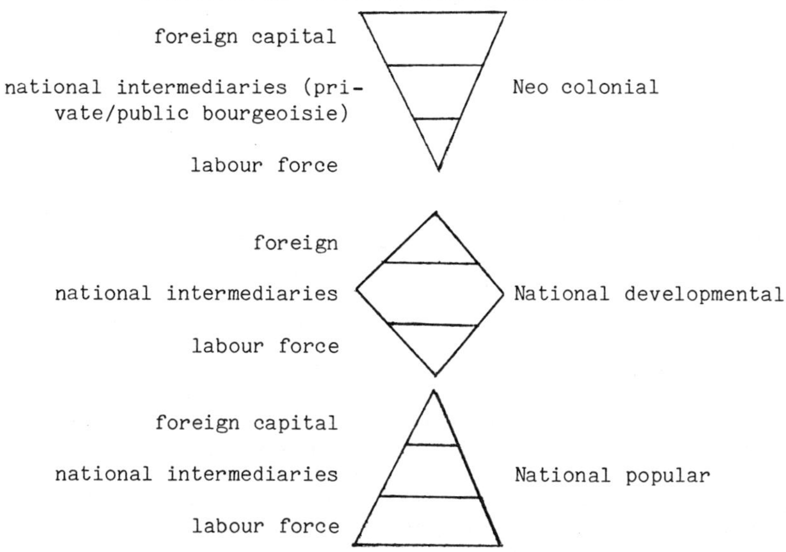

As the above indicates, the struggle against imperial domination is now mediated through a class structure which itself contains contradictions, i.e., is itself a source of exploitation. The pattern of exploitative relations varies from one development strategy to another. In the neo-colonial model the national bourgeoisie serves as a means of heightening imperial exploitation in order to extract a share of the surplus for itself; examples of this regime include Brazil, Chile, Indonesia, Iran, Taiwan, South Korea, South Vietnam. Coercion, and a demobilized population, open access to raw materials, tax and other "incentives" to foreign investors characterize policy. The forms of joint exploitation vary greatly, expressing the differences in bargaining power between the national and imperial bourgeoisie. Under conditions of total foreign control of the economy the national bourgeoisie obtains tax revenue. Under conditions of partnership in which majority ownership and management prerogatives are in foreign hands, the national bourgeoisie obtains a minority share of earnings plus tax revenues. Whatever the specifics, the foreign component is clearly dominant in internal as well as external relations.

In the development model, the bourgeoisie "dominates" foreign capital and exploits the national labour force. In this case, the national bourgeoisie serves as a means of "national capitalization" but at the expense of the labour force - reconcentrating capital in its own hands. This type of élite nationalism is difficult to identify as a "pure type" apart from the neo-colonial/populist models because the national bourgeoisie is generally numerically and socially in a weak position. The initiatives for this form of capital accumulation usually come from outside of the bourgeois class and its parties, usually from the military. Only under dictatorial conditions can this narrow and weak strata resist the pressures from below and from the outside and then not usually for any duration of time. Moreover, there is considerable overlap between national bourgeois developmentalism and the neo-colonial approach, in some cases and in other instances it approximates the national popular approach. Some possible examples of this type of regime would include: Mexico, (under Echevarria), Venezuela (under Perez), Peru (under Velasco), Argentina (the second Peron regime and the earlier Frondizi regime). The "developmental" model ostensibly gives the state the role of maximizing national bourgeois interests. In this context it has a double function, "anti-imperialist" and disciplining the labour force. In practical terms, the national developmental state attempts to redefine the terms of dependency to favour national capitalist strata and contain labour demands. The forms for capitalizing the national bourgeoisie include:

1. increasing tax revenues to include the majority of earnings;
2. extending ownership to majority shares including management rights;
3. limiting foreign capital activities to the external sector (commercialization), fragmenting their operations (exploitation rights, management contracts), limiting exploitations to specified time periods, limiting access to local capital,

directing foreign industry to export markets, etc.

4. selective nationalization: expropriation of particular enterprises by the state in many cases to provide cheap services to the private sector.

The developmental approach, however, while squeezing the foreign sector, also shares with the foreign sector an interest in maximizing exploitation of the labour force: maintaining production, labour discipline and popular demobilization. The success of this type of "establishment nationalism" depends on the avoidance of confrontations with foreign sectors and the labour force. Threats from either side may cause the national bourgeoisie to seek alliances: with populists if threatened by foreign interests or with imperial groups if threatened by the left. While the rise of establishment nationalism may have been influenced initially by radical nationalist pressures, the usual tendency has been for it to dissolve in a series of external agreements which erode the original national developmental project.

The national-populist alliance composed of bourgeoisie/petit-bourgeoisie, workers and/or peasants attempts to capitalize the economy on the basis of nationalist measures directed at foreign firms, state financing and stimulating national-populist regimes include Argentina (first Peron government, 1945-1955), Bolivia (MNR, 1953-1956), Brazil (under Goulart), Mexico (under Cardenas). The striking characteristic of this type of regime is the frequency with which they have appeared in the periphery, their short duration as "national-popular" regimes (usually they are overthrown or evolve into one of the two other variants) and the "special" conjectural conditions which favour the formation of this alliance (windfall earnings accruing to Argentina during World War II). One of the basic weaknesses of this type of regime as a vehicle for capital accumulation is found in its efforts to eliminate foreign exploitation without developing adequate substitutes: after the initial redistributive measures and after the initial euphoria over the reduction of the foreign presence, the issue arises as to which of the two national social classes will capitalize the economy: the national bourgeoisie or the workers/peasants. The national bourgeoisie without its external sources of finances must seek in and through the state means to promote the accumulation of capital, at the expense of the working class. On the other hand, the workers' participation in the populist alliance is not based on a change in the mode of production but on increases in consumption: to restrict consumption is by definition to terminate the populist aspect of the alliance. The continuation of populist measures beyond the initial period of the extension of nationalization beyond the foreign sector to encompass national bourgeois strata alienates the bourgeoisie and leads to an alternative non-capitalist model of capitalist accumulation.

The initial impetus to class formation, mainly externally directed capital accumulation based on simple surplus extraction, gave way to a more complex process where an internal ruling class with its own state apparatus emerged to "mediate" the process of exploitation and accumulation. Capital accumulation in the periphery has had a varied experience: the lest durable and expansive regimes have been the most popular and nationalist; the least popular have been the most expansive and least national; and the regimes which have been national but not popular have eventually evolved into one of the other two approaches.

Recent historical experience suggests that among capitalist countries in the periphery the most effective instrument of capital accumulation and growth is precisely the least national and most exploitative model, the neo-colonial or "from above and outside" approach. The historical conditions, more specifically the political pre-conditions, for this growth have in fact been non-popular, externally oriented regimes largely resting on alliances between military elites and property classes whose incapacity to accumulate capital leads them to rely on foreign capital. The imperial state plays a crucial role in changing the balance of forces favouring dominance by externally oriented developmental regime. The device has been the coup carried through by military and civilian officials in large part socialized, trained and/or financed by agencies of the state apparatus of the imperialist power dominant in its region. The property-based political-military regime functions to create conditions that permit externally induced industrial growth without danger of nationalization, wage demands, or autonomous trade unions.

DEVELOPMENT STRATEGIES SOCIAL REGIMES AND THE ROLE OF THE STATE.

The intensification of exploitative relations inherent in the neo-colonial and national (bourgeois) developmentalist approach accelerates the growth of economic inequality and social polarization. Where a modicum of political freedom exists, the bourgeois' drive to accumulate capital gives rise To new social forces which provided the base for national-popular or socialist movements and regimes with their commitment to redefining class relations and thus providing the basis for a new development strategy based on redistributive reforms, a reversal of previous approaches.

In this context of latent and overt class conflict within peripheral societies, imperialist relations are central in sustaining or destabilizing the two polar types of social regime. When a neo-colonial regime is replaced by a national-popular government which makes serious inroads on foreign corporate capital's exploitative capacity, the imperial response is to effectively collaborate with national political and social forces and end the national popular regime. The new orientation is based in a restructured state apparatus, whose initial function is to eliminate the obstacles to externally-based capital accumulation ("discipline labour", denationalize firms, demobilize populace, etc.).

The crucial instrumentality in this process of reversing regimes, reconcentrating income, and re-opening economic channels is the state.[7] The state is the critical unit in the process of converting class alliances into developmental strategies. The social and political nature of the state in the periphery is best understood through its relationship to the imperial state - whose role and activities in the formation of imperial networks, include shaping the state in the periphery. The imperial and the bourgeois state in the periphery can be studied from at least two dimensions:

1. the central role of the imperial state in creating conditions for neo-colonial capital-accumulation.
2. the role of the imperial state in state formation in the periphery:
    a. state-building in the neo-colonial context.
    b. disaggregating the state in the context of national-popular or even national developmental regimes.

The focus on private investment trade, the multi-national corporation in the study of imperialism is useful but not adequate. For these economic activities and organizations operate within a universe which is not explainable by the behaviour and activity of these units. To understand where, when, and how capital expanded into the periphery in a period of substantial political upheavals and class conflict one must look to the role of the imperial state. Three moments in the movement of capital are profoundly affected by imperial state activity:

1. initial entry
2. expansion
3. survival

At each point the imperial state plays a decisive role in creating the conditions for capital expansion and accumulation. In the initial period the imperial state is heavily involved in a number of activities:

1. "state-building", creating the formal machinery of government to secure the groundwork for effective exploitation; the creation of an imperially sound army and police force is crucial.
2. eliminating or containing internal dissidents.
3. minimizing external competition.
4. creating the economic infrastructure through loans and "aid".

While not always achieving maximum success, without these activities by the state it is quite doubtful that private enterprise, even on the scale of monopoly corporations, would have risked the financial resources and manpower which led to their becoming multi-national corporations.

The initial thrust of the state laid the basis for long-term, large-scale movements of capital. The relationship between the imperial state and the multinational corporation, however, was not confined to this initial effort but was continuous and comprehensive. The process of expansion and accumulation necessitated the elaboration of world-wide financial networks to finance a great diversity of activities in a variety of locales; alongside state-building, the imperial state assumed the much more complex task of fashioning a world monetary system, financial agreements, development banks, credit agreements, etc., which provided the multi-nationals with mobile capital to facilitate and accelerate the accumulation of capital and intensify the extraction of surplus. The decisions of corporate heads to extend their conglomerates was based on the financial networks organized and directed by the imperial state.

Yet the extension of imperial ties to the new states and the subsequent expansion of imperial capitalism throughout the periphery led to the simultaneous transformation of the class structure and polarization of society. Small proprietors and subsistence farmers became rural labourers, share croppers or urban migrants; urban masses were converted into day labourers or concentrated as unemployed/semi-employed slum dwellers. The neo-colonial state (product of imperial state-building), whose prime function was facilitating externally-induced capital accumulation isolated itself from a mass constituency. The petty bourgeoisie (including military officers) and other socially mobile or aspiring bourgeois classes, not having direct access either to imperial or state revenues became potential or actual detonators of a national-popular upheaval. It is out of this context then that the third function of the imperial state emerges, what might best be described as the "enforcer" role: the use of direct and indirect military and economic pressure to ensure the survival of the multi-national corporation and the conditions necessary for accumulation and reproduction. This imperial state enforcer function has manifested itself in a great variety of ways, from direct military intervention, financing of mercenary troops to economic blockades and credit squeezes. Imperial state power has been utilized against nationalist social movements out of power as well as governments in power. It has been used against populist as well as democratic socialist governments; against elected governments as well as non-elected governments. The critical issue for the imperial state is not the formal structure of government but access to the internally generated surplus and the creation of class relations which facilitate access.

The targets of imperial state intervention have been

those regimes and movements who attempt to alter substantially the conditions for imperial capital accumulation, limit the access points which the imperial state possesses within the periphery and create conditions for national capital accumulation. The isolation of the neo-colonial state, the vulnerability of the bourgeois developmental state and the porosity of the national-popular regime provides a great number of opportunities for imperial state activity: to buttress the former and to "destabilize" the latter.

THE IMPERIAL STATE AS STATE-BUILDER

In its broadest terms, imperialism in the periphery has been involved first and foremost in the creation of a new social order, one in which social relations are tied to the dynamic of externally induced expansion and accumulation. The foremost problem for the imperial state is to prevent political decay or disintegration through the creation of a durable political order, one in which social control over the labour force permits the continuous flow of capital and the reproduction of exploitative social relations. At the operational level, a number of imperial agencies, ranging from military missions to university advisory teams, have been involved in shaping the counterpart agencies, personnel recruitment programmes, as well as forging converging perspectives within the state bureaucracy as it evolves. The technical skills, such as budgeting, planning and project elaboration are imparted within an ideological framework which reinforces external bonds. Imperial "state-building", however, does not merely involve piecemeal administrative "block-building" (imperial agency insertion in distinct administrative areas), but the integration of the commanding heights of the peripheral state into the overall politico-economic project of the imperial state through long-term development agreements including trade, financial and technical assistance. The imperial strategy is largely directed toward influencing elites described euphemistically as "leadership training". The apex of the state pyramid is the central target; and within that pyramid the Army and police have a central position. The astronomical sums of military "aid" during the post World War Two period into the periphery are, in large part, efforts to create and later maintain the external allegiances of peripheral state apparatuses. Independently of social origins and within the context of technical preparations (professionalization), the military and police are pivotal groups in imperial state-building in the periphery. Out of these "foundations" of state-building a whole series of other administrative programmes have emerged linked to the imperial project. Tentative and isolated instances of neo-colonial parliamentary governments have been spawned, though the boundaries within which social and ideological competition takes places are sharply limited and transparent to those who aspire to participate.

The origins of the neo-colonial state are not always vested in élite transfers of power (from colonial to national). Moreover, national political leaderships meshed in neo-colonial networks are not always lacking a certain legitimacy derived from their role in the "national struggle". Nevertheless the process we are discussing concerns the formation and orientation of institutions of the post-independence national state, which does not preclude conflict in the period prior to national independence. In sum, the process of imperial state-building can be schematically considered in the following manner:

1. securing ties with the political leadership, including, at a minimum, the heads of the police and military, but not necessarily limited to these areas.
2. extending influence to budgeting, economy, planning, public works - administrative areas that directly affect specific economic opportunities for foreign enterprises, as well as general conditions for capital accumulation.
3. training programmes and technical missions to promote efficiency and ties with middle levels of the bureaucracy and research institutes which can provide inexpensive sources of information and effective implementation.
4. creation of new state power centres, including the development of special forces in the military, regional military alliances and economic authorities-international banking officials with project supervisory powers.

The whole point of imperial state-building is to provide a variety of access points to shape policy priorities and agendas in order to avoid the use of "external pressures", to avoid having to act "from the outside". Within the periphery the alienated state articulates the interest of imperial capital by promoting growth on the basis of the exploitation of national classes. Only sustained and continuous inflows of capital and elaborate political police/military apparatuses and surveillance provide this state with durability.

THE IMPERIAL STATE AS STATE DISAGGREGATOR

Social polarities and political mobilization have frequently accompanied the exploitative social relations characteristic of imperial capital expansions. Equally important, the socially exclusive and economically constricting effects of externally directed accumulation have set in opposition numerically and strategically important strata in the periphery. The process of imperial accumulation leads to concentration of wealth and opens opportunities to petty bourgeois strata for national capitalization through control over the state and its revenues. The emergence of national movemenns, and eventually governments, sets the stage for redefining relations with the imperial power. Yet in most instances controlling the government is not identical with controlling the state: the critical means of production, as well as important fractions of the Army/police/state bureaucracy, remain, at least initially, still tied to the metropolis and serve to countermand the orders of the national government. In this context, the imperial power may seek to renegotiate terms of dependency or disarticulate the national regime's development project through a variety of measures, and agencies located outside or inside the national state. The more decisively the national government challenges the process of external accumulation, the more likely efforts will be made by the imperial state to undermine the regime. Unlike the circumstance of a neo-colonial regime where "nation-building" is the key, with a national regime the imperial state operates disaggregate the state: the rhetoric speaks to destabilizing, not stabilizing society.[8] The "incomplete" transformation from a neo-colonial or national development regime to a national popular state provides several opportunities for reversing changes. The imperial state utilizes the financial networks and military-administrative apparatuses that were elaborated earlier to promote imperial-capital accumulation in order to coerce the national-popular state. Financial and credit constraints lead to disarticulating the economy and alienating the national bourgeoisie. External links with the military are reinforced in the process of disintegrating the state. Alienated from the national-popular project of the government, the pro-imperial segment of the military serves as the instrumentality for overthrowing the government, reversing changes and reconstituting a state to promote imperial capital accumulation.

State formation and disaggregation are then two crucial processes for imposing exploitative class relations located in imperially induced economic expansion. Without the intervention of the imperial state, the neo-colonial state would be difficult to sustain; without the neo-colonial state the conflicts generated by imperial-capital accumulation would become unmanageable. Without the "strong state" the polarization of class forces would be skewed toward the left; and the alternative of a petty bourgeois-led popular-national alliance would either limit the capacity of imperial capital to extract surplus from the labour force or lead to a more profound transformation of society.

BEYOND DEPENDENCY AND MODERNIZATION: CLASS POLITICS AND REVOLUTION IN THE PERIPHERY

Dependency theory describes the shifts in the locus of external control within the periphery from agriculture to industry, from industry to technology, in terms of the logic of metropolitan needs: the formulation which speaks of "new" forms of dependency assumes that changes in economic activities in the periphery are always or usually the result of external impositions; in this sense the class configurations, alliances and conflicts which underlie each type of peripheral relationship with the metropolis in discarded or in extreme cases is seen as also a product of high level manipulation from the "centre".

Shifts in peripheral economic activity and relationships with the metropolis are in many cases products of rising new class forces taking power. The displacement of the metropolis from agro-mineral sectors is in part the product of the rise to influence of national social forces (peasant movements, petty bourgeois or labour nationalists) and represents a significant increase in national control though not necessarily a lessening of class exploitation, i.e., surplus value may be appropriated by the national bourgeoisie or the bureaucratic state. Likewise, the growth of national control over industry cannot be viewed simply as a "new international division of labour between technologically advanced metropolitan industry and labour intensive peripheral industry" (though it could <u>become</u> that) but reflects the growth of power within the periphery of social forces (national bourgeoisie, petty bourgeoisie or working class) willing and capable of directing the industrialization process. The national appropriation of surplus value from these industries can function to develop higher forms of industrialization including technologically sophisticated enterprises. The incomplete nature of industrialization in the periphery should not obscure the nature of the process of change within the periphery: the emergence of new class forces and alliances that further circumscribe the areas of metropolitan dominance. For example, the emergence of a highly statist, agrarian reform regime in Peru is a product of the new class arrangements and reflects a new class configuration of power which is redefining its relations with the metropole, diversifying external dependence and constricting areas of imperial operation. It is absurd to extrapolate continuing links with the metropolis from these struggles and define them as the "new strategy" of imperialism; it is self defeating to describe the metropole's loss of concrete influence, resources, areas of operation as being supplanted by some vague notion of advantages from "future consolidation".[9]

By not examining the changes in class relationships within the periphery the dependency writers are at a loss to explain the changes in the nature and form of the external relationship as well as the possibilities for future changes implicit in the process of internal struggle.

Social revolution is not a product of the under-developed areas of the periphery but more likely initiated in those areas most penetrated by the metropolis, where capitalist social relations predominate and where productivity approximates that of the metropolis. Likewise, the growth of nationalism in the periphery is not a product of dependence per se but the result of a growing capacity among the petty-bourgeoisie to manage and control the productive forces under metropolitan domination. It is within this gap between capacity and control that petty-bourgeois nationalism emerges. The key issue in centre/periphery relations then is the growing social and political differentiation and autonomy of class forces within the metropolitan enclaves and their ability to limit the exploitative capacity of the metropole. The conflict is therefore not between undifferentiated dependent countries against metropoles; much less is the anti-imperialist vanguard located in the "traditional" poverty-stricken hinterland. The development of national and/or social revolutionary struggle in the periphery is less a product of "under-development" and more a response to the conditions of imperial capital accumulation which in the case of the wage labourers is exploitative and in the case of the petty bourgeoisie is "exclusionary", i.e., the imperial capitalists displace the local bourgeoisie as the locus of accumulation.

In this way, we demystify the notion of dependence which, as it has commonly been discussed, fails to take account of the different social formations within the periphery and the real sources of surplus appropriation located in the advanced sectors, i.e., enclaves. The initial formulation of the problem for the periphery is not "external dependency" but imperial exploitation located in the class structure of the periphery; and it is within this class structure and in the class struggles that ensue that this problem must be examined and eventually resolved.

If the principal contradiction between the periphery and metropolis is located in the technologically and economically advanced imperial enclave sectors of the periphery, the problematic is not "modernization" but socialization or nationalization, depending upon which class is hegemonic in the anti-imperialist struggle. It appears that in most of the socialist revolutions the original impetus, organization, leadership and ideology of the revolutionary struggle began precisely in the more "advanced" sectors of the peripheral economy: in Russia the Petrograd proletariat led by the Bolshevik Party; in China in the coastal cities; in Cuba in Havana. [10] In all cases, however, the success of the revolution which began in the advanced enclaves depended on joining efforts with the bulk of the social forces(peasants) located in the "backward" areas of the economy.[11] The process of transformation in the periphery combines two distinct but inter-related experiences: the socialization of production in the metropolitan enclaves and the modernization of the backward areas. Socialization of the economy is not based on the level of productive forces in the abstract (as Soviet ideologues, technocrats, managerialists, argue), nor is it a creation of individual will, of transforming individuals' social consciences (as some of the socialist voluntarists would have it) but of transforming social relations in the advanced sectors of the periphery and extending them outward to the hinterland in the process of the socialization of production.

Modernization of the periphery under imperialism was essentially uneven and imposed through class relations of domination. The introduction of technology and organization was essentially a means of heightening the level of exploitation, increasing the absolute and relative rates of extraction of surplus value. This form of modernization from above and outside created the social relations which led to the concentration, organization and politicization of the social forces which then became the source of nationalist and socialist movements. The latter grew, in part, as a response to the uneven and incomplete nature of modernization but more importantly as a response to the exploitative and exclusionary nature of the total social situation. To continue to discuss the periphery as if the principal issue continues to be one of "modernization" is to call for the continued and extended exploitative social relations that have already been established in the enclaves.

The modernization problematic is an imperial project: it proposes the introduction of new techniques and organizations to deepen and extend exploitative social relations from the enclave to the hinterland To enter into that problematic to redefine its methods is an effort at reformist politics: to ameliorate the conditions of capitalist accumulation without affecting the essential mechanisms.

The success of any nationalist or socialist development effort depends not upon gaining control over the numerically important but backward hinterland but of capturing the commanding heights of the economy oriented in the metropolitan enclaves - the modern and productive firms in the dynamic sectors of the economy: these are the enterprises that might serve as the principal source for financing national economic expansion. "Modernization theory" by locating the problematic in the hinterland, by focusing on the problems of economic backwardness in the periphery, by examining the peasant or poverty or food problem isolated from the periphery/metropolis, and the point of departure for national development.

In summary, the greatest source of imperial surplus

extraction is found in the advanced sectors of the peripheral economy. The imperial based organization of exploitation and the social relations of production have engendered antagonistic social classes - the urban petty bourgeois nationalist and/or the populist/socialist urban proletariat. The growth of productive forces in the advanced sectors of the periphery and their extension to the hinterland has increased the social weight of national forces in the political and social arena, increasing their capacity to contest imperial accumulation. The consummation of a successful national transformation, however, depends on forging links with the hinterland, a problematic not always envisioned in the initial national or socialist efforts. This is so in some cases because of structural links (between bourgeoisie and landlords) and in others because of structural discontinuities (workers and peasants are located in different social formations).

The central issue in the periphery then is not backwardness and the answer therefore is definitely not modernization. Nor is the central issue unequal exchange - an important but derivative problematic. The central issue is imperial exploitative social relations and domination of the dynamic sectors of the peripheral economy which limits modernization of the hinterland and determines the terms of exchange.

NOTES

1. Paul Baran, The Political Economy of Growth (New York: 1957) and Andre Gunder Frank, Capitalism and Underdevelopment in Latin America (New York: 1967).

2. Andre Gunder Frank, Lumpen-Bourgeoisie and Lumpen-Development (New York: 1972)

3. Fernando Cardoso, "Dependency and Development", New Left Review, No 74, July-August 1972, Bill Warren, "Myths of Underdevelopment", New Left Review, No 81, p. 3-46. Arghiri Emmanuel, "Current Muths of Development", New Left Review, No 85, pp. 61-82.

4. M.C. Tavares and Jose Serra, "Beyond Stagnation: A Discussion on the Nature of recent developments in Brazil" in J. Petras (ed.), Latin America: From Dependence to Revolution (New York: 1973).

5. Irma Adelman and Cynthia Taft Morris, Economic Growth and Social Equity in Developing Countries (Stanford: 1973); Jose Serra, "The Brazilian Economic Miracle" in J. Petras (ed.), Latin America: From Dependence to Revolution (New York: 1973).

6. For an informative discussion on accumulation see Samir Amin, Accumulation on a World Scale (New York: 1974)

7. For an interesting discussion of one agency of the imperial state see article Export-Import Bank in

September 1974, NACLA.

8. See James Petras and Morris Morley, U.S. Imperialism and the Overthrow of Allende: (New York: 1975).

9. See Anibal Quijano, Nationalism and Imperialism in Peru (New York: 1973)

10. On Russia see L.Trotsky, History of the Russian Revolution (New York: 1961) : on China, Harold Isaacs, The Tragedy of the Chinese Revolution (California: 1961); Lucien Bianco, Origins of the Chinese Revolution 1915-1949 (California: 1971); and Jean Chesneaux, The Chinese Labour Movement 1919-1927 (California: 1968), pp. 372-412: on Cuba see Ramon L. Bonachea and Marta San Martin, The Cuban Insurrection 1952-1959 (New Jersey: 1974).

11. In this sense we reject the thesis of Barrington Moore, Eric Wolfe and others who speak of "peasant" revolutions and identify the process of transformation in terms of "modernization" of the underdeveloped areas. See Barrington Moore Social Origins of Dictatorship and Democracy (Boston, 1966); Eric Wolfe, Peasant Wars of the Twentieth Century (New York: 1969).